Livingstone: Man of Africa
Memorial Essays 1873–1973

Livingstone: Man of Africa

Memorial Essays 1873 – 1973

Edited by Bridglal Pachai

Longman

LONGMAN GROUP LIMITED
London
Associated companies, branches and
representatives throughout the world

First published 1973

ISBN 0 582 64135 7 (Cased)

ISBN 0 582 64136 5 (Limp)

Printed in England by
THE BARLEYMAN PRESS
Bristol

Contents

List of Plates

Contributors

Sheila Brock, University of Edinburgh, doctoral candidate whose thesis title is 'James Stewart of Lovedale: a study of missionary influence on education, politics and society in the Eastern Cape, South Africa, 1870–1905'.

Paul A. Cole-King, Director of Antiquities, Malawi.

The Revd Philip Elston, Chaplain of Malosa Secondary School, where he teaches History, Bible Knowledge and Technical subjects; post-graduate research student, University of Malawi, History Department, Chancellor College

Professor Michael Gelfand, Head of the Department of Medicine, University of Rhodesia

Dr John McCracken, Lecturer in History, University of Stirling, Scotland. Formerly University of Dar-es-Salaam, Tanzania.

Professor Bridglal Pachai, Head of the Department of History, University of Malawi, Chancellor College.

Melvin E. Page, Fullbright Lecturer in History, University of Malawi, Chancellor College.

The Revd Dr Andrew C. Ross, Lecturer in Ecclesiastical History, University of Edinburgh, Scotland. Formerly Blantyre Mission, Malawi.

The Revd Dr Matthew Schoffeleers, Senior Lecturer in Social Anthropology, University of Malawi, Chancellor College.

Professor George Shepperson, Professor of Commonwealth and American History, University of Edinburgh, Scotland.

Acknowledgements

The editor and publisher wish to record their thanks to the following: Miss Maud Muntemba, Keeper of History, National Museums of Zambia, Livingstone Museum, for photograph of Livingstone in the Zanzibar slave market; National Archives of Rhodesia for various photographs acknowledged separately, and Professor Michael Gelfand for obtaining the photographs from the National Archives of Rhodesia; Mrs Chrissie Gonthako, Secretary to the History Department, Chancellor College, for cheerful and competent clerical assistance; the contributors for their speedy response and willing co-operation.

The publishers are grateful to the following for permission to reproduce photographs: T. and R. Annan and Sons for plate 1; Blantyre Museum, Scotland for plate 6; Blantyre Museum, Scotland and Dr D. A. W. Rittey for plates 3, 4 and 5; Lovedale Press for plate 11; National Archives of Rhodesia for plates 13 and 14; National Museums of Zambia for plate 12; The Royal Geographical Society for plate 2; the editor for plates 7, 8, 9, 10, 15, 16 and 17.

Introduction

On 1 May 1873, Dr David Livingstone was found dead, kneeling at his bedside, at Chitambo's village, Ilala, in northern Zambia. This was a dramatic ending to a life filled with drama. He was then sixty years of age, a fact not important in itself but significant in a special way when it is remembered that thirty of them were spent in Africa. It is not difficult, then, to understand why half of him belongs symbolically to Africa, where his heart was buried by those loyal few who took this step to pay their tribute, and the tribute of their continent, to a man whom they had come to admire even if, in many ways, he was difficult to understand. Outstanding people, as they would have learned the hard way, are difficult to understand partly because they are outstanding.

That was a hundred years ago. What kind of a tribute would be paid today? It is no longer a matter of the loyalty of the few who braved the African interior with him. Africa is now a different proposition; most of it is free, part of it is Christian, all of it is on the move. The entire face of Africa has changed since Livingstone died a hundred years ago. New priorities have replaced old commitments, new emotions have replaced the old. The past is taken for granted, while the physical and mental energies of the bulk of the continent are directed quite properly towards the challenges of the present. The age of emotional outpourings is behind us. As the twentieth century enters its last quarter hard practical judgements are the order of the day. Where would Livingstone feature in this order?

In modern Africa there are some of all colours and ranks who assert quite unashamedly that they are bored by explorers and explorations, missionaries and missions and that the slave trade and slavery should not be recalled to mind. For such critics there would be no room for David Livingstone because Livingstone was a bit of all three – explorer, missionary and anti-slaver. For the critics who would have it this way, History must serve as the purveyor of the desired nourishment for the mental frame of the moment.

There are others who take the more moderate view that man's march through the ages was a long, and often, tortuous one and that the halting places of the present – good roads, good schools, good churches and good food – are there largely because of those who travelled along the road before today. Such a view would find a place for Livingstone, the explorer, the missionary and the humanist.

Given his faults (and there were many, involving such questions as leadership, judgement, tact, consideration for his family and respect for international morality) he failed at crucial moments. His Zambezi expedition, for example, was beset with problems from start to end. Livingstone sacked three of the crew whom he had picked (Bedingfeld, Baines and Thornton) largely because of his disposition to listen to gossip which his brother Charles and the engineer Rae were prone to spread. His reports on the navigability of the Zambezi, the opportunities for mission work, the potential in agriculture were all disputed by members of his expedition as well as by his one-time admirer, the Revd James Stewart. But for all that, there was one quality in which he was not, and could not be, faulted. His father-in-law, the Revd Robert Moffat described him as 'the man of "one-thing" the temporal and eternal happiness of Africa's long trodden-down sons and daughters'.[1] This view was substantiated in the memoirs of a sailor who was in the H.M.S. *Gorgon* which reached the mouth of the Zambezi on 30 January 1862 carrying on board such notables as Mrs Livingstone, two female relatives of the first Anglican missionaries in Malawi, the Revd James Stewart and others. The memoirs were published fifty-one years later on the occasion of the centenary of Livingstone's birth and in them Livingstone was described as follows: 'He was so friendly with the natives, so much beloved by them, and so implicitly trusted that they came to him with information which we used to good purposes.'[2]

That he lived and died for Africa, believing that what he was doing and saying was in the broad, long-term interest of Africa cannot be denied even by his most outspoken critics. If, on the occasion of the centenary of his death, no monuments are erected to his memory in Africa, there are other ways in which he will be remembered, and

2

measured. The events of a hundred years ago are part of history and cannot be expunged from the records. Among them that poignant last march will stand as an everlasting memorial to Livingstone of Africa. Eight Africans carried his body over fifteen hundred miles from Ilala to the Indian Ocean coast: Susi and Chuma, the ex-slaves; Farigala, Jacob Wainwright, Amoda and Halima, who had served as Livingstone's cook; Gardner and Mabruki.[3] They were represented at the burial service at Westminster Abbey on 18 April 1874 by Susi, Chuma, and Jacob Wainwright, who was one of the pall-bearers in such distinguished company as William Cotton Oswell, W. F. Webb and T. Steele, who were associated with Livingstone in the days he was stationed in southern Africa; Dr Kirk, E. D. Young and H. M. Stanley, who were associated with the explorer during the Zambezi travels and later; and the Revd Horace Waller, one of the members of the pioneering Universities Mission to Central Africa.

There is another kind of monument not easily acknowledged or identified in independent Africa: the progress of the Christian faith which is manifest in so many ways both tangible and intangible. It is true that not all of it is due to the life, work and example of Dr Livingstone alone, but certainly some of the credit for it belongs to him.

In 1959 when the centenary of Livingstone's first visit to Lake Malawi was commemorated, his grandson, Dr Hubert F. Wilson, was asked to make a contribution by writing an article. This he dutifully did, but he made the following observation: 'Apart from note books and journals, it is now difficult to find anything to publish about David Livingstone that is new. Most of what he wrote has been ransacked by his various biographers.'[4]

What, then, is the justification for yet another volume? The most obvious one is the opportunity to take stock of Livingstone's place in the history of Africa in general and Central Africa in particular. There is room for a fresh look at the African side of the story. What did Africans themselves think of Livingstone? What was the effect on different communities of the white man's intrusion and presence at any one particular time? What may one say about Livingstone's African heritage?

Some aspects of these questions are looked at by the various contributors to this volume. It is significant that the contributors have had or have a very close involvement with Africa in general and Central Africa in particular. Their collective contribution in the form of the *Memorial Essays* represents team work by an interesting team. The editor was the founding historian and head of the history department of the University of Malawi, a university which was first mooted by those who were Livingstone's heirs in the missionary history of this country. Professor Shepperson has made a significant contribution to our understanding of the African response to European and African missionary factors, chiefly that of such mission products as John Chilembwe, Eliot Kamwana and Charles Domingo, and has helped to piece together various threads. Professor Michael Gelfand, with his medical and anthropological researches and writings, including a look at Livingstone the doctor, introduces an often neglected dimension. Two ministers of religion and scholars, one Catholic, the other Anglican, add to the variety of the team: Revd Dr Schoffeleers has for over a decade applied himself to a study of the various peoples of the country; Revd Father Elston has done the same over a shorter period in a more limited way. The team then includes three historians, two of whom have written doctoral dissertations on aspects of Malawi's mission history, while the third is presently engaged in a related exercise, and who are all, interestingly enough, from Scotland, Livingstone's country (as is Professor Shepperson): Dr MacCracken has done pioneer work on the Livingstonia Mission; Revd Dr Ross has done the same on the Blantyre Mission; Mrs Sheila Brock is now working on that important contemporary of Dr Livingstone, Dr James Stewart. Two other historians complete the team: Mr P. A. Cole-King, Director of Antiquities, has studied various aspects of Malawi's early mission history; Mr M. E. Page, for long interested in the slave trade, worked on this subject in the United States before coming out to Malawi in 1971 where his interest continues. One hopes, then, that a team so varied and so deeply committed to studies on Africa and its peoples will have something to offer in this volume.

Of all the places visited by Livingstone in Africa, few have felt the Christian impact more strongly than Malawi. The work of the pioneering missionaries and mission stations was started on a large scale only after the death of Livingstone, though he lived to witness personally the disappointments and the tragedies which surrounded the first attempt at mission work in the country. Malawians, both past and present, have been worthy recipients of the Livingstone heritage. In early June 1972, the grass-thatched house in Blantyre, Scotland, the birthplace of Livingstone, which is a model of the hut in Chitambo's village, Ilala, where Dr Livingstone died, was gutted. Students from Malawi now studying in Britain volunteered to reconstruct the hut.[5]

This may be a small gesture by a small number of Malawians but it symbolises the response of a grateful generation, the custodians of the future Africa. The old Africa which Dr Livingstone helped to shape and influence is no more; the new Africa, in the year of the centenary of his death, faces the future more surely and confidently only because the errors and the inadequacies of the past no longer exist.

B. Pachai
10 July 1972

Notes

1 George Seaver, *David Livingstone: His Life and Letters*, London, 1957, p. 317.

2 *Daily Telegraph*, 19 March 1913, quoted in Seaver, op. cit., p. 410.

3 B. W. Lloyd, *Men of Livingstone*, London, 1955.

4 Dr Hubert F. Wilson, 'David Livingstone. Some Reminiscences', *The Nyasaland Journal*, xii, 2, 1959, pp. 12–21.

5 Malawi *Times*, 8 June 1972.

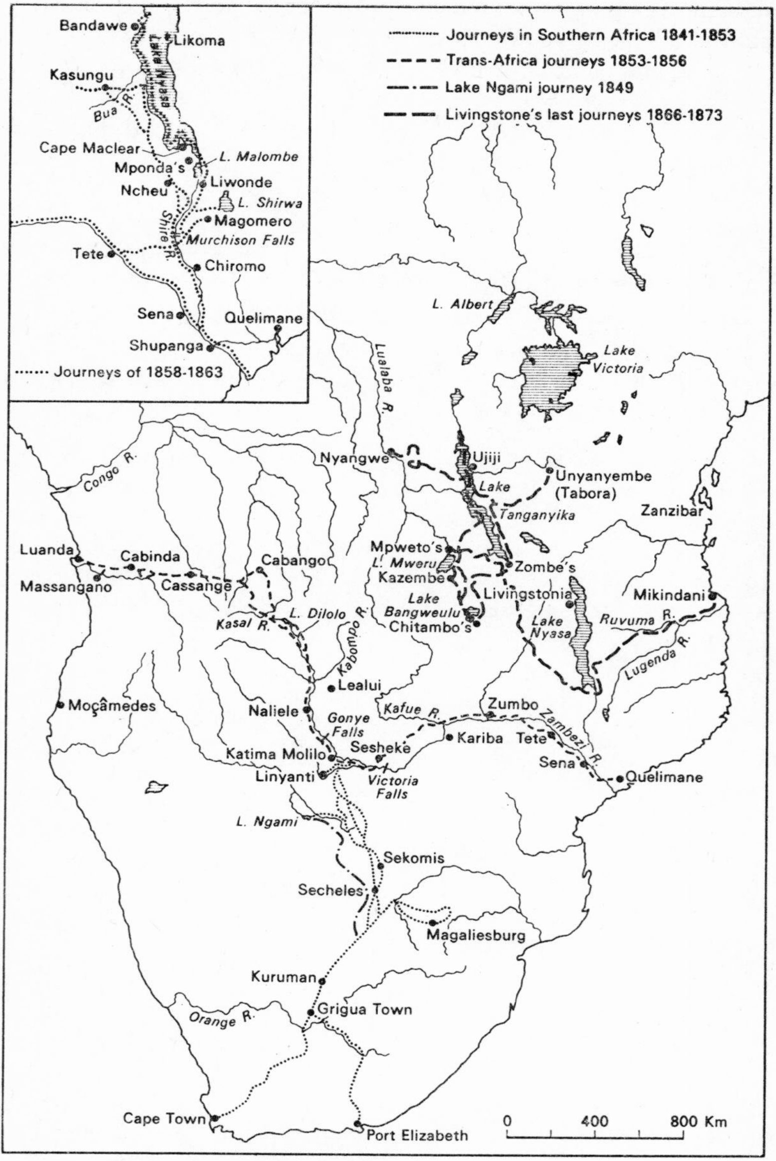

Journeys in Southern Africa 1841-1853
Trans-Africa journeys 1853-1856
Lake Ngami journey 1849
Livingstone's last journeys 1866-1873
Bandawe
Likoma
Kasungu
Bua R.
Cape Maclear
Mponda's
L. Malombe
Liwonde
Ncheu
L. Shirwa
Magomero
Shire R.
Murchison Falls
Tete
Chiromo
Sena
Quelimane
Shupanga
Journeys of 1858-1863
L. Albert
Lake Victoria
Lualaba R.
Nyangwe
Ujiji
Unyanyembe (Tabora)
Lake Tanganyika
Zanzibar
Congo R.
Luanda
Cabinda
Massangano
Cassange
Cabango
Mpweto's
L. Mweru
Kazembe
Zombe's
Livingstonia
Mikindani
Lake Bangweulu
Chitambo's
Lake Nyasa
Ruvuma R.
Kasai R.
L. Dilolo
Kabompo R.
Lugenda R.
Lealui
Moçâmedes
Naliele
Gonye Falls
Kafue R.
Zumbo
Zambezi R.
Kariba
Tete
Sesheke
Katima Molilo
Linyanti
Victoria Falls
Sena
Quelimane
L. Ngami
Sekomis
Secheles
Magaliesburg
Kuruman
Grigua Town
Orange R.
Cape Town
Port Elizabeth
0
400
800 Km

1 The four journeys of David Livingstone

1 Livingstone and the Years of Preparation 1813-1857

George Shepperson

To be asked to write on 'Livingstone and the years of preparation' is to be confronted with the question, 'Preparation for what?' Does the title indicate an examination of the course of Livingstone's life from his birth at Blantyre, Scotland, on 19 March 1813, in very humble circumstances, to his return from Africa to Britain on 12 December 1856, to find himself a national hero – a period which, twelve months later, after he had completed a bestseller on the sixteen years of his African travels and had made preparations for a government-sponsored expedition to eastern and central Africa with command and consular rank for himself, came to a climax at Cambridge when he delivered his famous lecture in the Senate House? 'The building was crowded to excess with all ranks of the University and their friends. The reception was so enthusiastic that literally there were volley after volley of cheers.'[1]

It could be argued that the first forty-four years of David Livingstone's life were a preparation for this triumphant moment: no further climax of this kind, it might seem, was possible. Indeed, never again was Livingstone to be so enthusiastically acclaimed. His Zambezi expedition and his last journey into Africa during the period from 1858 to 1873 did not take place in an atmosphere of universal acclamation. In spite of all the admiration for Livingstone's courage, persistence and undoubted achievements during these years, his African ventures were often coolly received by many who were suspicious of his intentions and sceptical about his abilities and knowledge.[2] And yet, a decade and a half after the first celebrated Cambridge climax to Livingstone's career, there occurred an even more famous second. This was the bringing back to Britain of his crudely embalmed and almost unrecognisable body, after his death, in an apparent attitude of

7

prayer, at Chitambo's village on 1 May 1873. The body was interred on 18 April 1874, in a prominent position in Westminster Abbey, London, amidst scenes of national mourning almost unparalleled since the death of the Duke of Wellington. It could be argued that 1813 to 1857 were years of preparation for this moment, too.

In this chapter, this period of Livingstone's life will be approached from the perspective of both of these climaxes. They are, to be sure, linked together by the concluding words of his Cambridge lecture of 4 December 1857, in which, with an implicit reference to his African achievements up to that time and with something of the spirit of a martyr, Livingstone seemed to envisage his end: 'I beg to direct your attention to Africa; – I know that in a few years I shall be cut off in that country; do not let it be shut again! I go back to Africa to make an open path for commerce and Christianity.'[3]

There are two famous understatements in Livingstone's life. The first was H. M. Stanley's 'Dr Livingstone, I presume?' in 1871. The second was Livingstone's own at Cambridge in 1857: 'I beg to draw your attention to Africa.' This was a massive understatement, if ever there was one, because from 14 March 1841, when he arrived at Cape Town in the service of the London Missionary Society, to 12 July 1856,

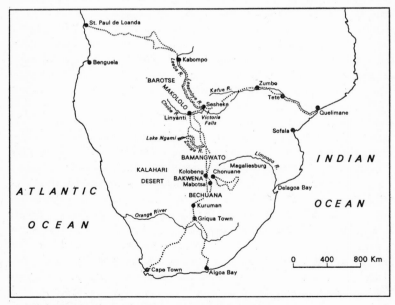

2 David Livingstone's journeys in Southern Africa

when he left Quelimane for England, Livingstone, through his letters, dispatches and the news of his explorations in the press, had never ceased to draw the attention of the world to Africa. During this decade and a half, Livingstone was constantly on the move into the African interior, creating for himself a growing reputation as a devoted Christian, a fearless explorer and a determined fighter in the anti-slavery cause. From Robert Moffat's mission station on the Cape frontier at Kuruman, at which Livingstone had arrived on 31 July 1841, he went northwards in search of converts to Christianity, attempting to spread the gospel through 'native agents' in places where the population was reputed to be greater. Marriage in 1845 to Moffat's daughter, Mary, did not stop him; and Livingstone's determination to achieve his purpose often over-rode family loyalties. His discovery of Lake Ngami on 1 August 1849, brought him the award of the Royal Geographical Society's gold medal and started a life-long association with this body which encouraged and spurred on Livingstone's ambitions as an explorer of Africa. In 1842 he sent his family back to Britain. In the following four years Livingstone's exploits in the interior drew the attention of a widening circle of peoples, of all colours and creeds, to Africa and its problems and possibilities.

'I shall open up a path into the interior or perish,' Livingstone declared. On 11 November 1853, with little equipment and only a small party of Africans to help him, he pushed northwards towards Linyanti. Livingstone was seeking a route to the Atlantic coast that would allow legitimate commerce to undercut the slave trade: a route which would be more suitable for reaching the Makololo people, whom he believed to be especially suitable for missionary work, than that which ran through hostile Boer territory. Livingstone reached Loanda on the west coast on 31 May 1854, after a journey of epic proportions. Another epic of travel, however, confronted him. Refusing an offer of a passage to Britain because he had promised to take his Makololo followers back home and because he wanted to explore the Zambezi further, Livingstone left for Linyanti again on 20 September 1854, reaching it nearly a year later. On 3 November 1855, he took up again his exploration of the Zambezi regions. A fortnight later he stood astounded before the thundering waters on the great river and bestowed upon them the Christian name of his sovereign. After six more months of stubborn travel, Livingstone arrived at Quelimane in Mozambique; and at the end of 1856 he was home again. He had roamed over territories which few, if any white men had visited, under arduous and often desperate conditions; he had made a complicated and competent series of scientific observations which gave him an immediate reputation amongst men of learning in Europe, America and Africa; and he had stirred the imagination of peoples in many countries, with his description of the dangers and the opportunities that the extension of the Christianity and commerce of the mid-Victorian era seemed to present in Africa.

Until the publication in the 1950s and the 1960s of Professor I. Schapera's important editions of David Livingstone's family letters, private diaries, missionary correspondence and African journal for the 1840s and 1850s[4] many details of the early period of Livingstone's life and of his career in Africa were not clear. And, of course, there are several aspects of his first forty-four years on which the student of Livingstone would like illumination. Although material about him is scattered around the world and, from time to time, comes to light in sale-room catalogues – often to be purchased by private buyers and then plunged back again into virtual oblivion – one substantial section of documentation for Livingstone's life has been lost forever: the dispatches, maps and journal of an important part of his first African expedition up to about May 1854. These went down with the mail-packet, *Forerunner*, which was taking them back to England for him from Loanda. (It says much for Livingstone's determined consciousness of the historic magnitude of his task in Africa that he immediately set to work to reproduce as many of these papers as he possibly could.) Nevertheless, if no other documentation were available for this period than Livingstone's book, *Missionary Travels and Researches in South Africa*[5] (first published in November 1857), and the digest of and commentary on this work which was published with his Cambridge lectures in 1858,[6] there would be adequate material available for appreciating the significance of the period from 1813 to 1857 in the story of David Livingstone.

Livingstone threw himself wholeheartedly into the composition of the *Missionary Travels*. In little more than six months he had written a book of over three hundred thousand words. His motives in tackling this herculean job, when his constitution was still ravaged by a long sequence of African fevers and maladies, were clear and commendable: to give an account to the world of his unique and extensive travels not only because of their intrinsic interest but also in order to further his aims of spreading Christianity and commerce in Africa by gaining public sympathy and support; and to provide for his family, particularly for his children's education and for the needs of his widowed mother. That this last reason lay close to his heart is apparent from a remark in the last chapter of the *Missionary Travels*: 'I have done something for the heathen, but for an aged mother, who still has more sacred claims than they, I have been able to do nothing.'[7]

The nine editions of the *Missionary Travels*, following each other in quick succession, were an outstanding example of the resilience of Victorian publishing; and they enhanced the excitement, at home and abroad, which was gathering around the figure of David Livingstone – perhaps raising expectations too high, so that the Zambezi expedition which followed could not but appear as something of an anti-climax. This has often been noticed. What, however, is frequently overlooked is the literary achievement of the *Missionary Travels*. As Professor Jack Simmons has said, 'It may be questioned whether the literary merit of the book has ever gained the recognition it deserves. . . . Altogether, the *Missionary Travels* may be claimed as one of the great books that we owe to unprofessional writers.'[8]

Perhaps much of the literary value of the work was due to Livingstone's sole authorship. Its successor, *Narrative of an Expedition to the Zambesi and its Tributaries* (1865), had been written in collaboration with his brother, Charles; and Livingstone's posthumously-published *Last Journals* (1874) were edited and over-abbreviated by an Anglican clergyman, Horace Waller, who had been a member of the 1861 Universities Mission to Central Africa. The *Missionary Travels*, in contrast, was all Livingstone's own. His first book, therefore, is unrivalled as an authentic source for the understanding of his 'years of preparation', from whatever perspective they may be approached. For this reason and because of the book's still largely unrecognised literary merit, this essay will pay particular attention to Livingstone's *Missionary Travels*, supplemented by the commentary on it in his published Cambridge lectures of 1857.

One statement in Professor Simmons' appreciation of the literary virtues of the *Missionary Travels* which may be questioned is his assertion that 'Even the occasional *longeurs* are in place, with unintended effect, serving to remind us of the tedium from which Livingstone himself suffered so much in travelling.'[9] Whilst recognising that what is a tedious and prolix passage to one person may not be so to another, it could be claimed that some of the undoubted *longeurs* of the *Missionary Travels* could have been excised by careful editing either by Livingstone himself or by a professional editor. But Livingstone and his publisher were anxious to rush into print and to cash in on the excitement, in Britain and overseas, which his return from Africa had aroused. This had also been the case with another Scottish explorer, Mungo Park, when he came back home in 1797. But Park had the assistance of a skilful writer, Bryan Edwards; and the resultant volume, Park's *Travels in the Interior Districts of Africa*, has a tautness and rapid sweep which is absent from Livingstone's first book. This may explain why Park's *Travels* is still in print,[10] in a popular series of books, whereas Livingstone's work, in spite of all its literary merits, is not readily available in bookshops.

Many of the complications of Livingstone's narrative – particularly the problem of exactly where Livingstone was at various times and places – may be ascribed to the loss of his dispatches, maps and journals in the sunken *Forerunner*. Although Livingstone had tried to re-create many of these documents in Angola in 1854, obviously he could not be completely successful. In spite of his remarkable memory, many places, dates and details of the first sixteen years of his African career are irretrievably lost; and confusion, from time to time, could not avoid creeping into the *Missionary Travels*.

When Professor Simmons speaks of the *longeurs* of the *Missionary Travels* reminding 'us of the tedium from which Livingstone suffered so much in travelling' one wonders whether the great explorer would have agreed with him. The multitude of Livingstone's surviving notebooks and the scraps of paper (even sometimes of newspaper) on which he scribbled his comments, notes and sketches of every aspect of life, animate and inanimate, in the countries in which he journeyed reveal a remarkable person for whom travel rarely resulted in tedium but was an unrivalled stimulant. As Livingstone wrote at the start of his last journey in 1866, 'The mere animal pleasure of travelling in a wild unexplored country is very great.'[11]

It is Livingstone's preoccupation with details of every kind – so typical of his native Scotland which had produced the first *Encyclopaedia Britannica* as early as 1768 – that gives to the *Missionary Travels* much of its fascination. In an age without television, radio, cinema and pre-digested, over-succinct publications of every sort, when people were prepared to sit down and read long books, there was something in the *Missionary Travels* for everybody: the vicarious thrill of travelling in regions barely recognised or totally unknown; adventures with lions, buffaloes, hippopotamuses, Boers, Portuguese and 'savages', noble and ignoble; the confident assertion of 'Progress' through scientific discovery and commercial advancement; appeals to the Christian conscience and humanitarianism, especially through the challenge of anti-slavery sentiments which had been a strong element in British life since the abolition of the slave trade in 1807; and a host of other details, many of which delighted Victorian readers as much, if not more, when they were in the form of digressions rather than as organic parts of the main narrative. To bind them all together there were Livingstone's genuine abilities as a writer of prose.

An example of the power of detail, digression and Livingstone's stylistic gifts is the section in the *Missionary Travels* at the start of Chapter XXVII for 2 November 1855. On his journey back from Loanda to the east coast and about a fortnight after he had visited the Victoria Falls, David Livingstone came to a group of villages under the chief, Marimba. 'Walking down to the forest,' he writes, 'after telling these poor people, for the first time in their lives, that the Son of God had so loved them as to come down from heaven to save them, I observed many regiments of black soldier-ants returning from their marauding expeditions.'[12] The ants of Africa fascinated Livingstone. As early as 1843 when he was in Botswana and at the start of his great journey northwards, he had written admiringly, 'In the midst of this dreary drought, it was wonderful to see these tiny creatures the ants running about with their accustomed vivacity.'[13] It was a fascination which never deserted him. At the beginning of 1855, for instance, he could not avoid this when he was attacked by red ants; and in May of that year, he noted the swarms of white ants ('. . . they appear like snow-flames floating about in the air.').[14] But at the beginning of November 1855, it was the black ants which caught his entomologist's eye, and he devoted nearly two thousand words to describing their activities. Livingstone's description is cogent and clear, interfused with striking but appropriate imagery:

> Without these black soldier-ants, the country would be over-run by the white ants; they are so extremely prolific and nothing can exceed the energy with which they work. They perform a most important part in the economy of nature, by burying vegetable matter so quickly beneath the soil, as the ferocious red ant does dead animal substances. The white ant generally keeps out of sight, and works under galleries constructed by night, to screen them from the observation of birds. At some given signal, however, I never could ascertain what, they rush out by hundreds, and the sound of their mandibles cutting grass into lengths, may be heard like a gentle wind murmuring through the leaves of the trees.[15]

Livingstone's miniature essay on African ants concludes with a theological reflection – not surprisingly, when one observes that in the middle of this section he refers to the late eighteenth-century British divine, William Paley. Livingstone's context is the work of the ants as scavengers, and he comments:

> When one looks at the wonderful adaptations throughout creation,

and the varied operations carried on with such wisdom and skill, the idea of second causes looks clumsy. We are viewing the direct handiworks of Him who is the one and only Power in the universe; wonderful in counsel; in whom we all live and move and have our being.[16]

Similarly, in his 1843 account, Livingstone saw religious implications in the ceaseless activities of the black ants:

... they never tire; their organs of motion seem endowed with the same power as is ascribed by physiologists to the insides of the human heart, by which that part of the frame never becomes fatigued, and which may be imparted to all our bodily organs in that higher sphere to which we fondly hope to rise.[17]

Passages of this sort in the *Missionary Travels*, with their mixture of scientific and theological thought and imagery, indicate Livingstone's interest in evolutionary ideas and their implications. Long before Charles Darwin published *The Origin of Species* in 1859, Livingstone had been fascinated by geology and zoology and the changing forms of matter.[18] For Darwin and his followers, the implications of evolutionary thought were often pessimistic. For Livingstone, they were optimistic; and there are times in the *Missionary Travels* when he seems to anticipate the attempted evolutionary synthesis of science and theology of the French Jesuit palaeontologist, Pierre Teilhard de Chardin.[19] Two further passages from the *Missionary Travels* may be used to illustrate this. The first comes towards the end of Livingstone's long trek to the east coast, on 14 February 1856, on his way to Tete:

In the quietest parts of the forest there is heard a faint but distinct hum, which tells of insect joy. One may see many whisking about in the clear sunshine in patches among the green glancing leaves; but there are invisible myriads working with never-tiring mandibles on leaves, and stalks, and beneath the soil. They are all brimful of enjoyment. Indeed the universality of organic life may be called a mantle of happy existence encircling the world, and imparts the idea of its being caused by the consciousness of our benignant Father's smile on all the works of His hands.[20]

The second passage is set in the period of April 1855, when David Livingstone was on his way to Loanda on the west coast. Discussing 'the great Quango valley', he writes:

We took a glance back to this valley, which equals that of the Mississippi in fertility, and thought of the vast mass of material which had been scooped out and carried away in its formation. This naturally led to reflection on the countless ages required for the previous formation and deposition of the same material (clay shale); then of the rocks, whose abrasion formed *that*, until the mind grew giddy in attempting to ascend the steps, which lead up through a portion of the eternity before man. The different epochs in geology are like landmarks in that otherwise shoreless sea. Our own epoch, or creation, is but another of that wonderful series which present a grand display of the mighty power of God; every stage of progress in the earth and its inhabitants, is such a display. So far from this science having any tendency to make men undervalue the power or love of God, it leads to the probability that the exhibition of mercy we have in the gift of his Son, may possibly not be the only manifestation of grace which has taken place in the countless ages, during which, works of creation have been going on.[21]

Livingstone's belief, clearly demonstrated at the end of this passage, in the complementary character of religion and science, is important for the understanding of his conception of Christian missionary work. The debate about the nature of Livingstone's work which arose at the time of the publication of the *Missionary Travels* and which continues to exercise the mind of anyone seriously interested in him, is best seen against this background. The question whether Livingstone was not so much a Christian missionary as an explorer, a geographer, a peripatetic scientist, is often answered by those who rightly see the predominance of the Christian vocation in his life by a reference to the famous remark which occurs towards the end of the *Missionary Travels*, 'I view the end of the geographical feat as the beginning of missionary enterprise.'[22] Taken out of its context this celebrated line can be misleading. But in its context it enables one to see the Teilhard de Chardin sweep of Livingstone's vision, and to begin to appreciate why it was not at all anomalous that a volume of missionary travels should be dedicated to a secular authority, the President of the Royal Geographical Society, Sir Roderick Murchison. The full passage reads:

I view the end of the geographical feat as the beginning of missionary enterprise. I take the latter term in its most extended signification, and include every effort made for the amelioration of our race; the promotion of all those means by which God in His providence is working, and bringing all His dealings with **man to a glorious** consummation. Each man in his sphere, either knowingly or unwittingly, is performing the will of our Father in heaven. Men of science, searching after hidden truths, which when discovered will, like the electric telegraph, bind men more closely together – soldiers battling for the right against tyranny – sailors rescuing the victims of oppression from the grasp of heartless men-stealers – merchants teaching the nations lessons of mutual dependence – and many others, as well as missionaries, all work in the same direction, and all efforts are overruled for one glorious end.[23]

Such ideas were germinating when Livingstone was a young man, working at the cotton mill in Blantyre, Lanarkshire, Scotland, and devouring books omnivorously. From this reading, Livingstone confirmed to his satisfaction 'that religion and science are not hostile but friendly to each other.'[24] These words are to be found in the autobiographical introduction to the *Missionary Travels*, a short but vital document in the Livingstone story which all his biographers have been compelled to use – but none of them, perhaps, with the degree of attention which it merits. For example, this autobiographical fragment reveals Livingstone's youthful interest in astrology. His first biographer, William Garden Blaikie, omits all reference to this.[25] The latest author of a substantial life of Livingstone, George Seaver, mentions Livingstone's reading of 'that extraordinary old work on astrological medicine, Culpeper's "Herbal"', but abbreviates what Livingstone has to say about its influence on him.[26] Livingstone's full remarks on the subject read:

Deep and anxious were my studies on the still deeper and more perplexing profundities of astrology, and I believe that I got as far into that abyss of fantasies as my author said he dared to lead me. It seemed perilous ground to tread on further, for the dark hint seemed to my youthful mind to loom towards 'selling soul and body to the devil' as the price of the unfathomable knowledge of the stars.[27]

What is one to make of this neglected passage? What is its relevance for David Livingstone's 'years of preparation'? It could be argued that it belongs to that darker side of the Scottish character, with its obsession with doom and the devil; to that schizophrenic world displayed in James Hogg's novel, *The Private Memoirs and Confessions of a Justified Sinner* (1824), with its fascinating and frightening picture of a young

Scot of the early nineteenth century tortured by the extremes of redemption and damnation. It was a world explored a century later by another Scottish writer, Lewis Grassic Gibbon, when he examined the Border heritage of Mungo Park: 'a little people on a dark little stage, an unhappy questing people, haunted by the unpleasant after-effects of death'.[28] George Seaver, in his valuable biography of Livingstone, speaks of 'the extreme simplicity of his faith',[29] drawing upon two passages in the *Missionary Travels* in which Livingstone sets out his belief in the atonement and concludes, 'In the glow of love which Christianity inspires I soon resolved to devote my life to the alleviation of human misery.'[30] Yet these passages are followed by Livingstone's note on his 'deep and anxious' youthful studies of astrology; and it is surely no disparagement of his motives and achievements to suggest that this implies that his faith was not one of 'extreme simplicity', and that there was a pessimistic as well as an optimistic side to his character. There was, indeed, an element of fanaticism in the make-up of Livingstone which, on the one hand, helped to drive him on to overcome obstacles that would have broken any ordinary man, and, on the other, occasionally beset him with obsessions (such, perhaps, as the Nile sources quest in his declining years[31]) which diverted him from essential tasks.

Another passage in the autobiographical fragment that prefaces the *Missionary Travels* and which biographers have neglected is a statement of Livingstone's social philosophy. His first biographer, Blaikie, was no doubt right to stress that Livingstone never regretted starting life as a cotton operative in one of the factories of the early industrial age in Scotland, and to claim that the 'fellow feeling he acquired for the children of labour was invaluable for enabling him to gain influence with the same class, whether in Scotland or in Africa.'[32] But to draw from this, as Blaikie does, the conclusion that Livingstone was essentially 'a man of the people'[33] is to raise the question, in what sense is this epithet to be interpreted? Livingstone, in the autobiographical passage mentioned above, reveals that he was by no means 'a man of the people' in the social revolutionary sense in which this phrase is often used. He begins by stating that the villagers of his native Blantyre, Lanarkshire, were interested in 'all public questions'; but then he goes on to say that 'the possession of the means of education [a reference to the relative ease with which literacy and other elements of education could be acquired in eighteenth- and nineteenth-century Scotland compared with England] did not render them an unsafe portion of the population.' And, to drive the point home, Livingstone emphasised that:

17

The masses of the working people of Scotland have read history and are no revolutionary levellers. They rejoice in the memories of 'Wallace and Bruce and a' the lave' [remainder] who are still much revered as the former champions of freedom. And while foreigners imagine that we want the spirit only to overturn capitalists and aristocracy, we are content to respect our laws till we can change them, and hate those stupid revolutions which might sweep away time-honoured institutions, dear alike to rich and poor.[34]

Livingstone, to be sure, was an outstanding example, both in theory and practice, of Scottish social mobility. It was not accidental that, two years after the publication of the *Missionary Travels*, another Scot, Samuel Smiles of Haddington, brought out the first edition of his influential *Self-Help*, a volume dedicated to social advancement through individual hard work and determination – or that its publisher (John Murray, another Scot who was climbing the social ladder through his earnest efforts in the coveted metropolis of London) was Livingstone's too. Indeed, in the eighth chapter of *Self-Help*, Samuel Smiles devoted a long paragraph to Livingstone's achievements in which the *Missionary Travels* is described as 'one of the most fascinating books of its kind that has ever been given to the public'.[35] In this chapter, Smiles was using Livingstone as an example of 'Energy and Courage'; but it is surely no exaggeration to claim that he became for many Victorians an example as much of social advancement from humble beginnings as of missionary and geographical endeavour and enterprise.

Just as the writings of the Unitarian minister, Horatio Alger, jun., taught young Americans in the nineteenth century that the 'struggle against poverty and temptation inevitably leads a boy to wealth and fame',[36] so the example of David Livingstone was used by other writers of this period as well as Samuel Smiles to encourage the young to advance up the social ladder. The Horatio Alger-ish title of the book by one of these writers (H. G. Adams' *David Livingstone. The Weaver Boy Who Became a Missionary*[37]) illustrates this – and also indicates the limitations of some Victorian conceptions of the Christian missionary vocation.

Half a century after the Union of the Scottish and English parliaments in 1707, Dr Samuel Johnson had declared that 'the noblest prospect a Scotchman ever sees is the high road that leads him to England.'[38] In David Livingstone's rise to fame, the cachet of English culture, the dominant partner in the Anglo-Scottish union, becomes clear. Early in his first great journey, in a letter to his children from

Sekeletu's settlement, Linyanti, on 2 October 1853, Livingstone had displayed this Anglophile tendency when he wrote, 'I am glad to hear that you go to the academy. I hope you are learning fast. Don't speak Scotch. It is not so pretty as English.'[39] Another example of Livingstone's leaning towards English standards was revealed in his Cambridge lecture of 4 December 1857, when he declared that 'Englishmen of education always command respect, without any adventitious aid.'[40] He then told a story of a Portuguese governor of Angola who conducted a dubious commercial transaction, and commented, 'Educated Englishmen seldom descend to that sort of thing.'[41]

Livingstone, of course, was every inch a Scot.[42] The autobiographical introduction to the *Missionary Travels* shows his deep affection for his 'ain folk'. To be sure, these few pages are a little classic of Scottish literature and deserve to be better known by students of Scottish as well as of African history. Throughout his first book and his other writings, published and unpublished, Livingstone makes frequent references to his native Scotland, especially to the Clydeside area in which he was born, as yet unpolluted by the Industrial Revolution. And yet, so often, Livingstone leaned towards English standards and expressions. The reasons for this, like much else in the life of this extraordinarily complex man, are probably concealed forever. Perhaps, however, one of them lay in the problem of Livingstone's loyalty to the crown. David Livingstone mentions at the beginning of the *Missionary Travels* that his great-grandfather fell at the battle of Culloden, 'fighting for the old line of kings'.[43] In this conflict, on 16 April 1746, the Duke of Cumberland's forces had massacred many of the Scottish Highlanders who supported Prince Charles Edward, the Jacobite Pretender to the throne. Like many Scottish families the Livingstones displayed divided loyalties. There are curious references to this problem of loyalty in Livingstone's letters home from Africa in the 1850s. From Kolobeng on 5 February 1850, he wrote to his sister, Agnes, 'I wonder you did not go to see the Queen. I was as disloyal as you when in England, for though I might have seen her in London I never went. I am more loyal now. Do you ever pray for her?'[44] Ten months later, after his discovery of Lake Ngami, Livingstone wrote to his family, with his characteristic combination of broad and pawky humour, 'The Royal Geographical Society have awarded twenty-five guineas for the discovery of the Lake. It is from the Queen. You must be very loyal, all of you, shout till you are hoarse. (Fear she forgot to put an o to the sum (250)). O you radicals, don't think it came out of your pockets. Long live Victoria.'[45] And, to cap it all, in a letter to his father-in-law, Robert Moffat, in 1856 Livingstone declared, 'I wish to name the Falls after our Queen, the "Smoke Sounding Falls of Victoria", as a proof of my loyalty.'[46]

Livingstone's great-grandfather from the Highlands of Scotland who was killed at Culloden was, presumably, a speaker of the Gaelic language. Certainly, Livingstone's grandmother used to sing Gaelic songs;[47] and he himself learned the language in order to read the Gaelic Bible to his mother.[48] Livingstone could move from standard English, the 'Queen's English', to the 'braid Scots' of his native Lanarkshire, and to the Gaelic tongue of his Highland ancestors. Furthermore, as he took pains to point out in his autobiographical fragment,[49] he spent his first week's wages from the factory at Blantyre on a Latin grammar, and studied this language two hours nightly for several years under a typically devoted dominie of early nineteenth-century Scotland with the misleading name – if the undoubted depth of Livingstone's learning is any evidence for this – of McSkimming.

It was this linguistic ability, acquired before he left for Africa, which probably enabled David Livingstone to cope with Tswana and other African languages, and to gain the rudiments of Portuguese and, perhaps, also of Afrikaans. He deliberately cut himself off from all European society for abour six months in 1842 in order to learn the Tswana language. In the acquisition of this language, Livingstone was fortunate to be at Kuruman when Robert Moffat was seeing his translation of the Bible into Tswana through the press at his mission station. The experience provided Livingstone with the opportunity to appraise the complexities of the language, and he set down a moving tribute to its qualities and potentialities in the sixth chapter of the *Missionary Travels.*[50] Indeed, during his residence at Kuruman in 1852, he wrote a short book entitled *An Analysis of the Language of the Bechuanas* of which twenty-five copies were printed in February 1858 for the members of the Zambezi expedition in order to acquaint them with the general structure of southern African languages.[51] Much of Livingstone's analysis has, of course, been outmoded by modern African linguistics. But in its day it was a notable piece of work. It indicates not only Livingstone's competence in foreign languages but also his determination to penetrate beneath the surface of African society.

Livingstone was never afraid to speculate about African languages if he thought this would serve his purpose of understanding Africa better. Such speculations illustrate how his interest in the life around him never flagged. For example, in his analysis of the Tswana language, he dabbled in speculations about its resemblance to some aspects of ancient Egyptian,[52] illustrating his wide reading by a reference to

20

Chevalier Bunsen's *Egypt's Place in Universal History.*

A further linguistic note of Livingstone's is worth quoting in full, in spite of its length, because it exemplifies the incessantly active quality of his mind, raising a multitude of details on a variety of subjects and comparing one with another in restless imagination: a quality which was to be invaluable to him in his later journeys when, alone and isolated, he needed all the resources of his intelligence and spirit to survive. There is, furthermore, in this linguistic note an apt Scottish analogy which is a good example of David Livingstone's frequent use of Caledonian comparisons.[53] The setting of the note is the concluding period of his long journey to the east coast. On 20 February 1856, Livingstone came to:

Monína's village (close to the sand-river Tangwe, lat. 16°13′38″ S., long. 32°32′ E.). This man is very popular among the tribes on account of his liberality. Boróma, Monína, Jira, Katolósa (Monomotápa), and Súsa, all acknowledge the supremacy of one called Nyatéwe, who is reported to decide all disputes respecting land. This confederation is exactly similar to that we observed in Londa and other parts of Africa. Katolósa is 'the Emperor Monomotapa' of history, but he is a chief of no great power, and acknowledges the supremacy of Nyatéwe. The Portuguese formerly honoured Monomotapa with a guard, to fire off numbers of guns on the occasion of any funeral, and he was also partially subsidized. The only evidence of greatness possessed by his successor, is his having about a hundred wives. When he dies, a disputed succession and much fighting are expected. In reference to the term Monomotapa, it is to be remembered that Mono, Moéne, Mona, Mana, or Moréna, mean simply *chief*, and considerable confusion has arisen from naming different people by making a plural of the chief's name. The names Monomoízes, spelt also Monemuíges[54] and Monomuízes, and Monomotápistas, when applied to these tribes are exactly the same as if we should call the Scotch the Lord Douglases. Motápe was the chief of the Bambíri, a tribe of the Banyai, and is now represented in the person of Katolósa. He is probably a man of greater energy than his successor, yet only an insignificant chief. Monomoízes was formed from Moiza or Muiza, the singular of the word Babísa or Aiza, the proper name of a large tribe to the north. In the transformation of this name the same error has been committed as in the others; and mistakes have occurred in many other names by inattention to the meaning, and predilection for the letter *r*. The river Loangwa, for instance, has been termed Arroangoa; and the

21

Luenya, the Ruanha. The Bazizúlu, or Mashóna, are spoken of as the Morurúrus.[55]

When he reached the east coast in mid-1856, Livingstone had been three and a half years without speaking English, with the exception of a short interval in Angola. For over a decade and a half, he had come increasingly into contact with a variety of African societies; and, in the final three and a half years, he had almost totally immersed himself in a succession of African ways of life. When one remembers this, it is strange to read, in a recent scholarly assessment of Livingstone's travels in Africa, that a 'principal lacuna in his writings is a lack of ethnographic information since, like many another talented missionary observer, he lacked real interest in customs so foreign and repugnant to his Christian norm.'[56] If Livingstone lacked real interest in many African customs, it is difficult to see why he devoted six pages early in the *Missionary Travels* to an account of the deep-rooted faith in the power of rain-making amongst the BaKwena;[57] or why he should say of such beliefs, which were profoundly at variance with his Christian ideas, that their practitioners, the rainmakers, 'carried the sympathies of the people along with them, and not without reason'. Their reasoning, to Livingstone, 'when the language is well understood', was 'remarkably acute'. 'Were we,' said Livingstone, 'as much harassed by droughts, the logic would be irresistible in England in 1857.' 'Ethnographic information', of course, will be defined in different ways by different students; but, from the present writer's point of view, the *Missionary Travels* is a valuable compendium of such information.

Livingstone, to be sure, was a man of his time and place, and he shared their limitations in looking at other societies, as did the Cambridge commentators in the published version of the two lectures which he delivered at their university. Nevertheless, they were not wrong to subtitle their edition of these lectures, 'a compendium of information on the central south African question'. Both of these lectures continue to warn men, in Livingstone's phrase from the *Missionary Travels*, against 'the stupid prejudice against colour',[58] and to provide them with material, acquired in unique conditions by Livingstone, by which both elements in the situation of prejudice, the observer and the observed, can combat it.

Of course, the reader who seeks such anti-racist material in Livingstone's early writings must be aware of his contemporary limitations.[59] Livingstone, for example, could subscribe from time to time to the 'noble savage' concept of the western world of his day. In his second

22

lecture at Cambridge on 5 December 1857, he could quote with approval:

> In those romantic regions men grow wild,
> There dwells the negro, Nature's outcast child.[60]

On the other hand, Livingstone expressed at times the view of the 'ignoble savage': that the blacks were a degraded people. This is apparent in his criticism of the Afrikaners who, as he put it, had 'been left by their own church for so many years to deteriorate and become as degraded as the blacks, whom the stupid prejudice against colour leads them to detest'.[61] But, in displaying such limitations, Livingstone was never, for reasons of race, antagonistic to African peoples; at his worst, he was paternalistic.

These limitations were usually overcome by Livingstone's firm belief that Black Africa must be brought into what he called 'the corporate body of nations'.[62] He did not, however, believe that even the most remote parts of Africa had ever been totally isolated from this: a perverted view which became a powerful weapon in the hands of nineteenth-century racists and their successors in the twentieth century. In 1849, for instance, Livingstone had written of the apparently barren Kalahari region, 'The so-called Desert, it may be observed, is by no means a useless tract of country . . . it sends something to the markets of the world'[63]: a reference to the manufacture of karosses, many of which found 'their way into China'.[64] (This reference, incidentally, serves to remind one that Livingstone had hoped originally to go out as a Christian missionary to China.)

But, in Livingstone's opinion, if Africa was to be saved spiritually and socially it must be opened up to much wider channels of commerce. 'The Boers,' he declared, writing of the time in 1852 when the frontier Afrikaners had plundered his home in retaliation for his support of the Tswana against them, 'resolved to shut up the interior, and I determined to open the country; and we shall see who have been the most successful – they or I.'[65] When Livingstone came out of Africa in 1856, it was clear that success was on his side. As a Scot, born in the tradition of economic thought of his fellow Scot, Adam Smith, with a conviction that an invisible hand of economic processes was pushing aside all fetters on trade and the bringing of the countries of the world into one unit, he could accept neither the restrictions of the Boers, nor of the Portuguese, the Arabs, petty and short-sighted African sovereignties nor, indeed, of the shackles on free trade amongst what he called, in his mid-Victorian language, 'the civilized nations' –

23

such impediments to the flowering of international commerce, he dubbed 'the remains of our own heathenism'.[66]

And yet, as David Livingstone left Africa in 1856, knowing that a hero's welcome awaited him at home, he was in no mood for complacent self-congratulation. 'As far as I am myself concerned,' he wrote, 'the opening of the new central country is a matter for congratulation only in so far as it opens up a prospect for the elevation of its inhabitants.'[67] These words at the end of the *Missionary Travels* were the leitmotiv of the rest of his life. In 1856, one apprenticeship in Africa had finished for him; two years later, when he went back, another was to begin. His concept of 'the elevation of its inhabitants' binds both together. As he himself had risen in the social scale, he was determined that others, black as well as white, should have the same opportunities; and, with a Victorian confidence in the inevitability of Progress, he did not doubt that this was possible.

A century later, many have lost this confidence. They question – and rightly – such assertions of Livingstone's as 'The universal effect of the more potent instruments of warfare in Africa is the same as among ourselves. Firearms render wars less frequent and less bloody.'[68] And they are cynical about some of his ideas such as his anticipation of Lugard's concept of the 'Dual Mandate'; 'by guiding our missionary labours so as to benefit our country, we shall thereby more effectually benefit the heathen.'[69]

But cynicism, although it may often perform the necessary task of putting a man like Livingstone back into the context of his times, can be taken too far. If many today, with a background of two world wars engendered by the nations of former Christendom, would cast a cold eye on Livingstone's reference to 'the glow of love which Christendom inspires', they do a grave disservice to the conclusion which he draws from this: the dedication of his life 'to the alleviation of human misery'. These words at the beginning of Livingstone's first book lead on, through the saga of his African adventures, to the noble aims set out at the end of the *Missionary Travels*. Whoever would appreciate the concatenation of the contemporary and the eternal in David Livingstone should turn to the *Missionary Travels*, his own and the best account of his years of preparation.[70]

Notes

1 William Monk (ed.), *Dr Livingstone's Cambridge Lectures*, Cambridge, 1858, p. 1.

2 See, for example, George Shepperson (ed.), *David Livingstone and the Rovuma*, Edinburgh, 1965, pp. 13–15.

3 *Cambridge Lectures*, p. 24.

4 I. Schapera (ed.):
David Livingstone. Family Letters 1841–1856, London, 1959, I (1841–1848), II (1849–1856);
Livingstone's Private Journals 1851–1853, London, 1960;
Livingstone's Missionary Correspondence 1841–1856, London, 1961;
Livingstone's African Journal 1853–1856, London, 1963, I (11 November 1853–30 April 1855), II (20 May, 1855–2 June, 1856).

5 The full title indicates well the scope and significance of Livingstone's career to 1857: *Missionary Travels and Researches in South Africa; including a Sketch of Sixteen Years' Residence in the Interior of Africa, and a Journey from the Cape of Good Hope to Loanda on the West Coast; thence across the Continent, down the River Zambesi, to the Eastern Ocean* By David Livingstone, LL.D., D.C.L., Fellow of the Faculty of Physicians and Surgeons, Glasgow; Corresponding Member of the Geographical and Statistical Society of New York; Gold Medallist and Corresponding Member of the Royal Geographical Societies of London and Paris, F.S.A., etc. (London, 1857).

6 *Cambridge Lectures*, op. cit.

7 *Missionary Travels*, p. 677.

8 Jack Simmons, *Livingstone and Africa*, London, 1955, pp. 73–4.

9 Ibid., p. 73.

10 Everyman's Library, London.

11 William Garden Blaikie, *The Personal Life of David Livingstone*, London, 1880, p. 370.

12 *Missionary Travels*, pp. 536–7.

13 Ibid., p. 21.

14 Ibid., p. 464.

15 Ibid., p. 539.

16 Ibid., p. 540.

17 Ibid., p. 21.

18 For a short description of the Scottish background of evolutionary thought, see George Shepperson, 'The Intellectual Background of Charles Darwin's Student Years at Edinburgh', in *Darwinism and the Study of Society*, edited by Michael Banton, London, 1961, pp. 17–35.

19 See, for example, Pierre Teilhard de Chardin, *The Phenomenon of Man; Le Milieu Divin; Letters from a Traveller; Hymn of the Universe* (available in various paperback editions).

20 *Missionary Travels*, p. 609.

21 Ibid., p. 377.

22 Ibid., p. 673.

23 Ibid., pp. 673–4.

24 Ibid., p. 4.

25 Blaikie, *Personal Life*, pp. 12–13.

26 George Seaver, *David Livingstone: His Life and Letters*, London, 1957, p. 19.

27 *Missionary Travels*, p. 5.

28 Lewis Grassic Gibbon, *Niger. The Life of Mungo Park*, Edinburgh, 1934, p. 18. Compare David Livingstone's remarks on an African grave which he found in 1868: 'This is the sort of grave I should prefer: to lie in the still, still forest, and

no hand ever to disturb my bones. The graves at home always seemed to me to be miserable, especially those in the cold damp clay, and without elbow room'. (*Last Journals of David Livingstone*, edited by Horace Waller, London, 1874, I, p. 307).

29 Seaver, op. cit., p. 20.
30 *Missionary Travels*, p. 5.
31 Cf. Blaikie, op. cit., p. 376.
32 Ibid., p. 15.
33 Ibid.
34 *Missionary Travels*, p. 7.
35 Samuel Smiles, *Self-Help*, London, 1968, p. 163.
36 James D. Hart (ed.), *The Oxford Companion to American Literature*, Oxford, 1956, p. 18.
37 A copy of this life of Livingstone belonged to John Chilembwe, leader of the 'Nyasaland Native Rising' of 1915: see B. Pachai (ed.), *The Early History of Malawi*, London, 1972, p. 426.
38 James Boswell, *Life of Johnson* (various editions), 6 July, 1763.
39 Schapera, *Family Letters*, vol. II, 230; cf. vol. II, 144: Livingstone on his children, 'I don't like them to speak broad Scotch . . .'.
40 *Cambridge Lectures*, p. 19.
41 Ibid.
42 For a commentary on Livingstone's Scottishness, see George Shepperson, 'David Livingstone The Scot', *The Scottish Historical Review* (Edinburgh), XXXIX, 2, 1960, pp. 113–21. Livingstone's interest in the country of his birth is revealed yet again towards the end of his life when he was carrying around with him William Forbes, *The Duties and Powers of Justice of the Peace in this part of Great Britain called Scotland* (Edinburgh, 1707). A copy of this old book was discovered in an Edinburgh second-hand bookseller's shop recently. It bears, in Livingstone's handwriting, the words on the inside front cover, 'Manyema country/ 180 miles Wg Ujiji / Nov. 1870/ The Scriptures of Truth'; and on the inside back cover, 'A cool and quiet/ evening/ friends longed in vain/ David Livingstone.'
43 *Missionary Travels*, p. 1.
44 Schapera, *Family Letters*, vol. II, 75.
45 Ibid., p. 116.
46 Ibid., p. 277.
47 *Missionary Travels*, p. 2.
48 Blaikie, op. cit., p. 6.
49 *Missionary Travels*, p. 3.
50 Ibid., pp. 114–15.
51 There is a summary of and a commentary on this book in *Cambridge Lectures*, pp. 106–25. A copy of this very rare book is in the possession of the Scottish National Memorial to David Livingstone, Blantyre, Lanarkshire.
52 Ibid., pp. 106–8. For the fascination of Egyptian parallels for Livingstone, see *Missionary Travels*, pp. 304, 399–400, 443, 449, 624, etc.
53 Further Scottish comparisons are used frequently in *Missionary Travels*; for example, pp. 18, 40 (Alexander Selkirk), 49 (James Bruce, the explorer of Ethiopia), 259 ('the back slums of great cities', probably a reference to Glasgow where Livingstone received his higher education), 303 ('*Scotticè* wersh', the old Scots word for 'unsavoury'), 311 (Mungo Park's *Travels*), 327 (one of several

comparisons of African rivers, etc., to Livingstone's native Clydeside: 360, the Clyde and Mary Queen of Scots; 522, 529, 655, Arthur's Seat, Edinburgh, also introduced, etc.), 361 ('keele', Scots for 'red clay shale'), 384 ('my Highland blood'), 526 (African and Scottish Highland cattle-thieving compared), 621–2 (the 'muavi', witchfinding, poison-ordeal, compared to 'the water-test for witches formerly used in Scotland'), etc.

54 This is the same as 'Monoe Mugi' ('Moenemugi', etc.) which appeared on many old maps of Africa (for example, the map for 28 December 1782, published by I. Fielding, London), some of which may have been known to Livingstone before he went out to Africa. This is the term which, it is reported, some African nationalists, seeing it on old maps in approximately the same place as modern Malawi, thought appropriate as a name for 'Nyasaland' when it became independent.

55 *Missionary Travels*, p. 617. Because of the linguistic knowledge and interest that Livingstone displayed in such passages, it seems odd that he permitted the tautological expression 'Lake Nyasa' to become current rather than the more appropriate 'Lake Maravi' or 'Lake Malawi'. *Missionary Travels* reveals that Livingstone was aware of the Maravi country and peoples before he visited that area during the Zambezi expedition: see *Missionary Travels*, pp. 379, 595 ('great numbers of tribes which pass under the general term Maravi'). That Livingstone was aware of the tautological nature of 'Lake Nyasa' (Nyanja, etc.) is revealed in *Missionary Travels*, p. 640: 'a lake 45 days to the N.N.W. of Tete, which is probably the Lake Maravi of the geographers . . . the lake Nyanja . . . which simply means a large water. . . .' Furthermore, in the two maps supplied in *Missionary Travels*, the lake appears as 'L. MARAVI or Nyanja' and 'Lake Marava or Nyanja.' What happened between 1854–6, when these observations were made, and 16 September 1859, when Livingstone 'discovered Lake Nyassa' (David and Charles Livingstone, *Narrative of an Expedition to the Zambesi*, London, 1865, p. 123), to make him drop the more appropriate 'Lake Maravi', particularly since, in the map in Livingstone's book about the Zambezi expedition, the 'Maravi' are shown as close to the Lake, is not clear.

56 Norman Robert Bennett, 'David Livingstone: Exploration for Christianity', in R. I. Rotberg (ed.), *Africa and Its Explorers*, Cambridge, Mass., 1970, p. 56.

57 *Missionary Travels*, pp. 20–5.

58 Ibid., pp. 30, 371. Livingstone was well aware of the infectious nature of colour prejudice. See, for example, his letter of 15 February 1861, to the Revd William King of Ontario Canada (Public Archives, Ottawa, William King Papers, M.G. 24, J 14), in which he replied to King's request for information about the possibility of settling Afro-Americans and Afro-Canadians in central Africa. Livingstone, writing with some knowledge of the settlement of New World Blacks in Sierra Leone and Liberia, told King that 'Some of them carry the prejudice against colour wherever they go and though many are superior to that silly nonsense it would prevent their cordial intercourse with their less enlightened brethren which is indispensable to successful settlement.'

59 For an interesting commentary on these, see Bennett, op. cit., pp. 53–7. Livingstone was often torn between an environmental and a Biblical explanation for the African characteristics which he observed on his journeys, as appears in the following passage whose last words illustrate his use of the legend of Ham in the Old Testament: 'Is the cowardice of the African the result of climate or flat country? The eastern tribes, living in a mountainous region are

generally fierce, those in the central plains effeminate and feeble. Perhaps the Divine prescience is chiefly exhibited in the words, "A servant of servants shall he be to his brethren."' (Schapera, *African Journal*, I, p. 13.)

60 *Cambridge Lectures*, p. 37.
61 *Missionary Travels*, p. 30.
62 Ibid., p. 28.
63 Ibid., p. 51.
64 Ibid., p. 50.
65 Ibid., p. 39.
66 Ibid., p. 28.
67 Ibid., p. 673.
68 Ibid., p. 200.
69 Ibid., p. 675.
70 Ibid., p. 5.

2 The Zambezi Expedition 1858-1864: New Highways for Old

Bridglal Pachai

The end of one dream

It is hard to say which of Livingstone's many exploits should take pride of place: his three-year journey across Africa from Loanda in the west to Quelimane in the east (1853–1856); his Zambezi expedition of almost six years' duration (1858–1864) when he sought to explore and exploit 'God's highway into the interior'; his forty-five day trip over a distance of two thousand five hundred miles from Zanzibar to Bombay (1864), when he braved the hazards of the Indian Ocean in a river steamer without the services of an engineer; his last, seven-year journey during which he was troubled by ill-health, disloyal and unwilling guides and carriers, and loss of supplies as well as his medical chest, (1866–1873). Any one of these exploits could stand out in its own right. All of them had features in common and unique features. If the Zambezi expedition stands out in a special way it is only because it has more unique features. No other trip was to test Livingstone's relations with fellow European travellers in quite the same way; no other was to lead to such a shift in the original plans and no other was to leave a more permanent bequest to the country which attracted the expedition's main attention. This chapter aims to analyse what the Zambezi expedition stood for; how much it achieved in its main object of opening up a highway and the reasons for this; and what impact it made on the African population.

The objectives of the Zambezi expedition must be seen firstly in relation to Livingstone's previous experience and secondly in relation to the country in which it was to operate. In his previous experience while crossing the African continent from west to east on or along the Zambezi river for most of the way, Livingstone had erroneously concluded that the Zambezi was navigable all the way with just one or two minor rapids. He had crossed over to the south bank of the Zambezi at a most crucial point and consequently missed the Cabora Bassa rapids, the most difficult impediment to navigation on that river,[1] by about fifty miles.[2] This erroneous conclusion was to influence most of Livingstone's thinking about the next steps on the Zambezi. Where he did not err, however, was in his observations on the extent of the slave trade all along the course of his previous travels, west, centre, and east; Mambari, Makololo, Arabs and Portuguese were all deeply involved in the traffic in human beings to the neglect of agriculture and other commercial activities. On 24 February 1856, just three months before he completed his coast-to-coast journey, Livingstone was sufficiently inspired by his new vision for Zambezia to address a letter to the king of Portugal in which he suggested that the Portuguese coloureds (mulattoes) could be more properly and profitably engaged in the production of cotton, sugar, coffee, oil and wheat. This was dependent, however, on a good road into the interior and for this he saw the Zambezi as an excellent highway. He also alluded to the lack of education and the lack of Portuguese women and free labourers.[3] A year later when his first book appeared and he had had more time to reflect, he was emphatic that what he had seen and done only marked the beginning: 'I view the end of the geographical feat as the beginning of the missionary enterprise. I take the latter term in its most extended signification, and include every effort made for the amelioration of our race.'[4] In spelling out what he meant by this Livingstone might well have substituted 'our race' with the 'human race', for this is what he saw in the roles assigned to scientists, soldiers, sailors, merchants and missionaries: 'Each man in his sphere, whether knowingly or unknowingly, is performing the will of our Father in heaven.'[5]

But he saw something else, too, which was nearer the restricted application of what he might have meant also by his reference to the 'amelioration of our race'. On his first journey home, Livingstone referred to this in a letter to Sir Roderick Murchison, President of the Royal Geographical Society: 'As I concieve (sic) that the future of the African Continent will be of great importance to England in the way of producing the raw materials of her manufactures as well as an extensive market for the articles of her industry, I feel anxious to give a few hints which your influential position may enable you to turn to good account in occasional intercourse with merchants and travellers.'[6] Here he sounded again what was to become one of his most repeated clarion calls of the future: the immense agricultural potential in this part of Africa for the production and export of cotton, coffee, sugar, indigo, oil, fibrous tissues and wood. He stated his position unambiguously in the book he was to write after his first Zambezian experience: 'I have a two-fold object in view and believe that, by guiding our missionary labours so as to benefit our country, we shall thereby more effectually and permanently benefit the heathen.'[7]

It is in the light of his first Zambezian experience that Livingstone's manifesto for the future must be seen. This he drew up at the request of the British government, in the form of instructions to the seven Britons,[8] including himself, who were to be the white members of the expedition, assisted as members of the ship's crew by the ten Sierra Leonean Kroomen to be recruited in that country. These instructions were no more than a restatement of what Livingstone had already communicated to the King of Portugal, to the British Secretary of State for Foreign Affairs and to the President of the Royal Geographical Society at various times between 1856 and 1857:

> The main object of the Zambezi Expedition, as our instructions from Her Majesty's Government explicitly stated, was to extend the knowledge already attained of the geography and mineral and agricultural resources of Eastern and Central Africa – to improve our acquaintance with the inhabitants, and to endeavour to engage them to apply themselves to industrial pursuits and to the cultivation of their lands, with a view to the production of raw material to be exported to England in return for British manufactures; and it was hoped that, by encouraging the natives to occupy themselves in the development of the resources of the country, a considerable advance might be made towards the extinction of the slave trade, as they would not be long in discovering that the former would eventually be a more certain source of profit than the latter.[9]

The geography of eastern and Central Africa, Livingstone understood to refer to the country he had traversed from west to east. Now the next expedition was being called upon to do it in reverse direction, mapping out the details he had missed on the earlier trip. Clearly its 'first object was to explore the Zambezi, its mouths and tributaries, with a view to their being used as highways for commerce and Christianity to pass into the vast interior of Africa.'[10] It was the Zambezian highway, then, that was to be explored and exploited. The access route passed through Portuguese territory and to that extent their goodwill and approval were necessary. He did in fact praise the liberality of the Portuguese in making Mozambique a free port. All that was necessary was a continuation of the liberal spirit by extending commercial facilities and by erecting a light house here and there. 'Their kindness to me personally', wrote Livingstone, 'makes me wish for a return of their ancient prosperity.'[11] Such expressions of rapport were soon to change on both sides. For the moment, as long as the interior was outside Portuguese control there was hope for the success of Livingstone's large design. The Portuguese, however, held the advantage of having been in possession of both the access route and certain settlements for hundreds of years before Livingstone came on the scene. As early as 1505 they had set up a coastal settlement at Sofala from which the western hinterland was tapped chiefly for gold. Twenty-five years later this was followed by the opening up of the Zambezi trading settlements at Sena, Tete and Quelimane. Within a hundred years, the port of Quelimane, served by the waters of the Indian Ocean, and the town of Zumbo, at the confluence of the Loangwa and Zambezi rivers, stood as the eastern and western extremities respectively of Portuguese territory. The Portuguese in these settlements from Quelimane to Zumbo, together with a few minor stations along the way like Mazaro and Shupanga, could by no means be said to be strongly settled. All that these places had were a few traders, a few more mulattoes and a handful of soldiers, if they were lucky. In 1875, that is over three hundred years later, there were just eighty-five soldiers at Quelimane, one hundred and eighteen at Tete and twenty-one at Zumbo. At Sena there was a military post. It had one soldier with four Portuguese residents.[12] If the position was so weak two years after Livingstone's death, it had been worse twenty years previously when Livingstone had passed through. There were few Portuguese persons around in Livingstone's day and many of those who were there, as will be shown later, were involved in the slave trade or in trying to put down rebellious Portuguese subjects. On 2 January 1859, in the midst of drought, slavery and rebellion, Livingstone noted in his journal: 'It is disgraceful to find a fine country like this so depopulated and ruined.'[13] Because of this he came to the conclusion that the Portuguese would not, and could not, obstruct a mission of the kind he had in mind. This was one of his miscalculations.

The Portuguese were not entirely to blame for their obstructive measures and their change of heart as the Zambezi expedition became a reality. They saw through the façade which Livingstone presented to them and to the outside world and feared above all that at bottom the plan was an imperial design to establish a British colony in the interior. In a confidential letter to his friend Professor Sedgwick of Cambridge Livingstone admitted as much: 'All this ostensible machinery has for

32

its ostensible object the development of African trade and the promotion of civilization, but I hope it may result in an English colony in the healthy highlands of Central Africa.' And to Admiral Sir Frederick Grey he wrote: 'We have to keep quiet about our plans to the Portuguese but a small steamer and a mission would in the course of time do incalculable good.'[14] This direct information on present and future intentions was not available to the Portuguese authorities. Their fears were aroused by circumstantial evidence. First, there was the British government memorandum drawing attention to the slave trade in Portuguese territory, to the need for both governments to lend their support for the development of free trade and to the call that the Zambezi river should be open for free trade to all nations. Secondly, there was the matter of the extent of Livingstone's forthcoming consular responsibilities. The British government, no doubt influenced by Livingstone's own preference, wanted the inland posts of Sena and Tete to be added to Quelimane. The Portuguese government, however, was not prepared to accept a British consular interest in the inland posts which were not yet open to foreign commerce. In the end, it was the Portuguese government which had its way, in spite of Livingstone's own wish that the doors be kept open by conferring on him accreditation 'to Sekeletu and other free tribes beyond the limits of Portuguese East Africa'. The Portuguese government drove home its diplomatic victory by issuing a proclamation on 4 February 1858 which gave the name Zambezia to all its territories from the mouths of the Zambezi in the east to the fortress of Zumbo in the west. Four days later Dr David Livingstone was officially appointed H.M. Consul at Quelimane and commander of the Zambezi expedition.[15]

What were the chances of the Zambezi expedition succeeding, given this new evidence of Portuguese resolution to protect and preserve Portuguese interests in Zambezia? Clearly, the initiative now passed to the Portuguese. They were not prepared to give the expedition a free hand to promote British interests, and, before the waters of the Zambezi could be navigated beyond the river mouth, the Portuguese government issued a number of rules to regulate trade and navigation in Zambezia: a military force was to be raised to subjugate unfriendly African tribes in Zambezia; Tete was to be a military colony; fortresses were to be built at Zumbo and other intermediate stations; a customs house was to be erected at the Zambezi mouth used by the new arrivals; and boats would only be allowed to navigate the river if they were in possession of permits and on condition that they flew the Portuguese flag. Some of these requirements were never carried

33

out,[16] nor were they intended to be enforced. They were introduced to show who was in command of the Zambezian waters. And since it was precisely this point of command and control that mattered for the success of the initial objectives of the Zambezi expedition, it is fair to comment with Martelli that 'the Expedition was doomed to failure even before its members landed in East Africa.'[17]

The final blow to the Zambezi enterprise was struck when Livingstone's optimism that the river would serve as a highway into the interior was proved wrong. It was a sad day for him when he made the admission in his journal on 20 November 1859:

> Things look dark for our enterprise. This Kebrabasa is what I never expected. No hint of its nature ever reached my ears. The only person who ever saw the river above where we did was Jose St Anna,[18] and he describes it as fearful when in flood. This I can very well believe from what I saw. A Government sent down two negroes in a canoe and neither they nor canoe was ever seen again. Then a canoe alone, and that was smashed to pieces! What we shall do if this is to be the end of the navigation I cannot now divine, but here I am, and I am trusting him who never made ashamed those who did so. I look back to all that has happened to me. The honours heaped on me were not of my seeking. They came unbidden. I could not even answer the letters I got from the great and noble, and I never expected the fame which followed me. It was thy hand that gave it all, O thou blessed and Holy One, and it was given for thy dear Son's sake. It will promote thy glory if Africa is made a land producing the articles now raised only or chiefly by slave labour.[19]

It was surely the extent of his disappointment that led to this emotional introspection. After all, much had been invested in the expedition in the form of money and expectations and this was the wrong time to reverse the course. For twelve difficult days he examined the Cabora Bassa prospects over the most rugged terrain he was ever to cross, in the company of Dr Kirk and four of the Makololo. On the day he took his decision to call it off – for the present – the explorers had reached the end of their tether, only Livingstone would not admit it. The stakes were far too high for him to arrive at the decision any more easily or quickly. His journal entry is revealing: 'The Makololo declared that they had always believed I had a heart till now, that I had become insane surely, for they shewed me the broken blisters on their feet in vain and, if they could only speak so as to be understood

34

by the other doctor, they would return with him and let me throw myself away.'[20]

Livingstone's decision was not to throw himself or his Zambezian dream away at this stage but to return when the river was in flood in the hope that at a high-water level, with some necessary channelling of the rocks, the rapids could be negotiated by river steamers, an optimism which Dr Kirk did not share.[21] Later events proved Dr Kirk right. Livingstone and his full entourage made the hazardous assault in canoes when on their way to deliver the Makololo to their homes in 1860. On 12 November, the rapids were encountered. All of them nearly drowned but none came closer to it than Kirk, who lost his eight volumes of notes, over one hundred drawings of plants, his surgical case and his clothes. Kirk's biographer has noted the impact this incident had on Kirk: 'For till the end of his life, when he was eighty-nine, he had never been so near death as that day in the Kebrabasa Rapids.'[22] Livingstone's recollections were not known, for the crucial twenty-nine pages of his diary which would have covered the period 12 June to 2 December 1860 are blank. This could not have been a deliberate omission whatever the disappointment he felt. There was no longer any doubt that the Cabora Bassa rapids stood between Livingstone and the realisation of his Zambezian dream. Is it fair to indict him on a charge of not being open enough to find out in the first place? It is argued that he would have found out in 1855-6 had he tried hard enough. This is an unfair suggestion, since the first intimation he ever had of the existence of the rapids was when he had already circumvented them by another route. When he did find out, he risked his life on more than one occasion to prove that he had not based his original plans on foundations of straw. Fortunately for Livingstone the closing of one highway into the interior marked the beginning of the opening of another.

The beginning of another dream

It was the Shire river which replaced the Zambezi as Livingstone's highway into the interior. This new lifeline turned out to be more than a poor substitute. Spilling its waters into the Zambezi a little to the east of Sena, about a hundred and fifty miles from the Indian Ocean, the Shire river is the only southern waterway providing access to its lowlands and to its highlands, serving as the southern gateway to Malawi. The gateway was inhabited, certainly by the sixteenth century and probably before this, by Maravi migrants under a powerful ruler

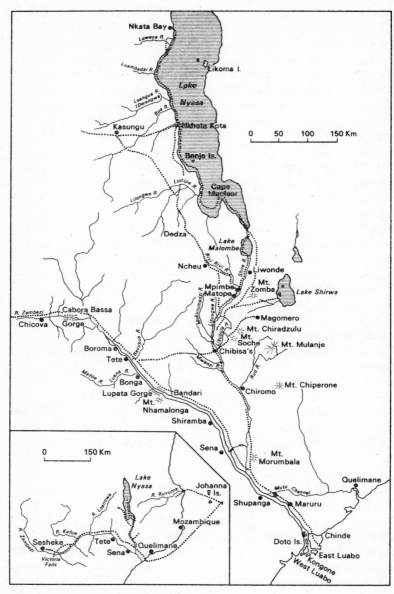

3 The Zambezi Expedition

named Lundu, an offshoot of that family of Maravi rulers headed by the senior king who held the title of *Kalonga* or *Karonga*. The Maravi peoples had migrated into the fertile lake and river regions in small clan groups over many centuries. Between the fourteenth and six-teenth centuries the Maravi farmers and ironmongers settled in almost two-thirds of modern Malawi and parts of Zambia and Mozambique, sometimes under centralised rulers, other times under clan leaders. In the country today known as Malawi, these migrants settled in various places under different names: north of the Dwangwa river they were known as the Tumbuka and the Tonga; south of it they were known as the Chewa, the Chipeta, the Nyanja, the Nyasa, the Nthumba, the Chikunda, the Mbo, the Zimba, and the Mang'anja. During Livingstone's day, and until more recent times, there was a mistaken belief that the different terms such as Mang'anja, Chewa, Maravi referred to different peoples. Livingstone himself noted in 1859: 'The whole region [i.e. the Shire] was well though not densely peopled with Manganja who inhabit both banks of the river Shire from Morambala up to Chibisa's place, but they occupy the eastern bank only and the adjacent mountains beyond that point. The western bank above Chibisa is peopled by Maravi. None of this tribe is to be met with near Shirwa, so it would appear to be improper to identify it with the Lake Maravi of the maps.'[23] Livingstone even called Chief Mwase of Kasungu a Mang'anja and the area to the west of him 'the Loangwa of the Maravi', and a little later added: 'We spent the first night, after leaving the slave route, at the village of Nkoma [site today of a famous mission run by Afrikaner missionaries from South Africa], among a section of the Mang'anja called Machewa, or Macheba, whose district extends to the Bua.'[24] All this was, of course, mistaken. The Portuguese before him, like Lacerda and Gamitto, put down incomplete references as to who the Maravi and the Chewa actually were. All this is understandable when one realises that their information was obtained in particular localities only and that they were not in a position to know how far the domains of tribes or chiefs extended. Generally, their area of the Maravi was associated with the Chewa kingdom of Undi, a younger brother of the original Kalonga, the main king of the Maravi people. Undi broke from Kalonga some time towards the late sixteenth century when the Kalonga's head-quarters were near the present railway station of Ntakataka, to the south of the lakeshore town of Salima. Undi moved westwards into present Mozambique territory. It was his area of influence which became synonymous with the Maravi. Again, the term Maravi was used variously; it referred to the *country* occupied by the Maravi migrants; it referred to the *rulers* of the people (who belonged to a particular clan, the Phiri); it also referred to the *subjects*. The various terminologies mentioned above could be taken to be references to geographical subsections of the same people under decentralised rulers like Lundu and Mwase.

Livingstone and his party came into contact with them all, but only a few of the more important chiefs were mentioned by name. The Tonga chiefs Marenga and Mankhambira in the north, the Chewa chief Mwase in the west and the Mang'anja chiefs Mankhokwe and Chibisa in the south were among the more notable of the chiefs whom he met and had any dealings with. These rulers and their followers may be described as the indigenous Bantu-speaking farmers. Had they been left to themselves, their lives might have gone on along age-old lines but when Livingstone's party became interested in this area from 1859 onwards, this foreign factor was one of five such nineteenth-century external influences which converged on to Malawi within twenty years of one another. Two of these came with the party: the Europeans and the Makololo. The other three were the Ngoni from southern Africa, referred to as the Mazitu and the Landeens in Livingstone's writings; the Yao, referred to as the Ajawa; and the Swahili Arabs under their ruler, the Jumbe, whom Livingstone met at Nkhota kota. These different groups were all opposed to one another in a way which made peaceful coexistence difficult. Among the conflicting aspects were the following: European versus African; Christianity versus Islam; legitimate trade versus slave trade; and peaceful persuasion versus military means.[25]

In addition to these five nineteenth-century external influences, there was one special factor which had many of the ingredients of conflict already listed: this was the Portuguese factor, both direct and indirect. The direct Portuguese interest in Malawi derived from the reaction of the Portuguese government in Lisbon and their representatives in Mozambique; the indirect interest came from unofficial sources but linked to the Portuguese presence in Africa. The main unofficial source met by Livingstone and his men along the southern gateway of Malawi came in the form of the descendants of a Portuguese Indian named Marianno. The first Marianno, whose full name was Paul Marianno Vas dos Anjos, arrived from Goa in 1824 and set up business in the Quelimane district, trading in gold dust and ivory and also running large plantations. As a trader of considerable means his influence was felt all along the Zambezi settlements and the surrounding regions like the Shire at its confluence with the Zambezi. The second Marianno carried this influence further by rising to the positions of colonel of the militia at Sena and commandant at Zimbabwe (in Rhodesia) and Zumbo. In addition, in 1854 while Livingstone was still at the early stages of his coast-to-coast trip, he led a military expedition in the area of the Shire gateway and captured considerable territory from the Mang'anja. He built a large stockade fifteen miles up the Shire river at a place called Shamo and, according to Richard Thornton, one of the members of the Zambezi expedition, his military strength at Shamo included some seven thousand muskets and four brass guns.[26] With his influence and his means, Marianno became one of the greatest slave traders on the Zambezi. With the support of his brother, Bonga, and thousands of African subjects, he used his position at Shamo to embarrass the Portuguese government at a time when they were concerned about the adverse publicity being received through reports by members of the Zambezi expedition.[27]

Had Livingstone decided that he would have no truck with a slave trader the Marianno control over the entry into the Shire region would have been as great a human impediment to the Shire expedition as the Cabora Bassa was a natural impediment to the Zambezi expedition. But Livingstone walked the diplomatic tightrope most adroitly. He first met Marianno at the Mazaro station towards the beginning of his Zambezi expedition, on 15 June 1858, and struck up a friendship immediately; two months later he met Bonga at Shamo and received rice, two sheep and some firewood from the rebel. The charge of double-dealing was once levelled against Livingstone in the context of his public and private utterances in connection with the Zambezi expedition. It could well be repeated in the context of the following statement written after he met Bonga: 'We managed, however, to keep on good terms with both rebels and Portuguese.'[28]

These were some of the factors and circumstances, then, which confronted Livingstone's party as it looked to the Shire to fulfill the hopes the Cabora Bassa rapids had frustrated – to find a highway into the interior for the promotion of civilization, commerce and Christianity. In this new venture the important factors would be the response of the people to the European presence and the agricultural and commercial potential of the country. A combination of these would show whether or not the Shire and Lake regions would be suitable for the promotion of the ideas inherent in Livingstone's three Cs.

First, there was the country to explore and the people to meet. With the exception of the few minor trips to the gateway, often ending up in the region of Marianno's Shamo, the notable short and long journeys were five in number: the first started on New Year's Day

1859 and it was intended to discover how far the *Ma-Robert* could navigate the Shire without being handicapped by duckweed or by unfriendly people. It succeeded in getting as far as modern Chikwawa (referred to as Chibisa's in contemporary reports) beyond which further progress was hampered by cataracts. The next journey would have to show whether a land route would offset the obstacle encountered. The second trip which was by land started from Chikwawa in late March 1859 and ended with the reaching of Lake Chilwa (written Shirwa in contemporary records but also referred to as Tamandua by Livingstone) on 18 April 1859. This was the largest party to date to explore the Malawi interior and it comprised Drs Livingstone and Kirk and sixteen Africans, all but two being Makololo. What Livingstone was enquiring about was, as he put it, the 'Nyanja Mukulu' (great lake) but he learned on reaching Lake Chilwa that the 'Nyanza Ninyessi' (lake of stars) was only a day's march northwards.[29] Reaching Lake Chilwa was the greatest success achieved so far by the Zambezi expedition and, besides learning of the ravages of the slave trade in the area, which strengthened his own resolution to do something about it, Livingstone did no more on this trip, leaving the next objective of reaching the 'Nyanza Ninyessi' to the third journey. The third was the largest party of all, a total of thirty-nine persons: four whites (the two Livingstones, Dr Kirk and the engineer Rae), thirty-three Makololo and two guides. The journey commenced at Chikwawa on 28 August 1859, passed east of present Blantyre and proceeded onwards to Zomba and beyond until the southern shores of Lake Nyasa were reached on 17 September 1859. The party covered 250 miles in forty days. It is amusing now to recall the explanation Livingstone himself gave for travelling with such a show of strength: 'We armed our men with muskets, which gave us influence, although it did not add much to our strength, as most of the men had never drawn a trigger.'[30] The fourth journey was intended to give Livingstone some idea of what the rest of the lake had to offer. This time the party was smaller: the two Livingstones, Dr Kirk and a sailor, John Neil, supported by about a score of attendants, hoped to do the water journey in a light four-oared boat. This trip, like the others before it, started from Chikwawa. Livingstone had just returned to it after settling the first mission party ever to come to Malawi, the Universities Mission to Central Africa, at Magomero mid-way between Blantyre and Zomba. The boat was carried by overland route along the sixty-mile distance from Chikwawa to Matope, that is from the last river port on the lower Shire to the first river port on the upper Shire, because of the cataracts which impeded navigation. This pattern was set for future travellers in Malawi: the river journey on the Zambezi, then on the Shire up to Chikwawa, then overland to Matope, then on the Shire again until the lake was reached at the most southerly point, and finally on the lake itself. The pattern survived unchanged from Livingstone's day until the opening of the Nyasaland railways to and from different points between 1908 and 1935 until the Indian Ocean became directly linked with Lake Malawi from Beira in Mozambique to Salima on Lake Malawi.

Livingstone's fourth journey which commenced on 6 August 1861 took him to the lake where his first experience of a severe storm drove him to consider the name 'Lake of Storms', which he did not settle for since the lake was only stormy in season. The actual lake trip lasted just under two months and among the ports of call the two northernmost ones of Nkhota kota and Bandawe featured prominently. The objects of the mission were many: first, there was the task of learning about navigation on the lake; secondly, the party wished to learn about the condition and activities of the people along the lake; thirdly, Livingstone was troubled by the threatened Portuguese interference with navigation on the Zambezi and wanted to have an alternative at hand. He thought of the Ruvuma river as providing a possible point of entry into Lake Malawi and for that reason took the U.M.C.A. missionaries to the Ruvuma before guiding them on the Zambezi route. On that occasion, he failed to make the complete Ruvuma journey from the Indian Ocean end and had a lingering hope that he might succeed in the reverse direction by looking for the connection through the Lake Malawi end.

The fifth and final Malawi journey undertaken in 1863, was in many ways the most remarkable in terms of actual physical endurance and achievement: Livingstone and his small party travelled 760 miles in fifty-five days, averaging about fourteen miles a day. Most of this was on foot. He had originally planned to place his new boat, the *Lady Nyasa*, on the lake to counteract the slave trade and had in fact arranged for its transportation as far as Chikwawa, where it was dismantled for the overland journey. It was at this point that he learned of the British government's decision to withdraw the expedition on the grounds that it was too costly and that Livingstone had spent far too long and far too much on his explorations. It was then August 1863 and the middle of the dry season. Before the return journey home could be undertaken, the summer rains had to fall so that the level of the Shire and Zambezi could rise to enable the *Pioneer* to be floated. A lesser man might have thrown up the enterprise in deep disappointment at this unhappy turn of fortune. Livingstone, however, decided to

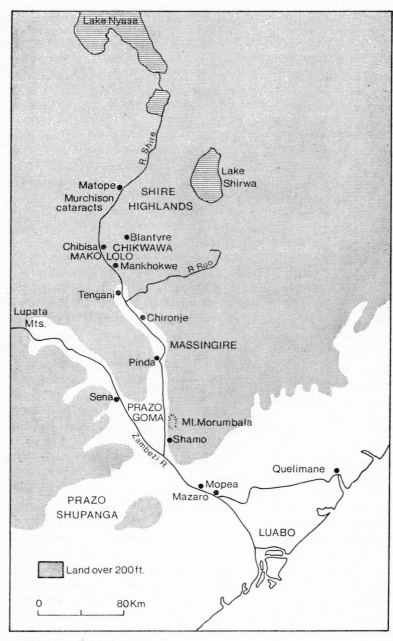

4 Livingstone's new highway

utilise this period of waiting by making one final excursion into the interior. This time he wanted to find out whether any large river flowed into the lake from the west; he also wanted to visit Lake Mweru and, above all, he wanted to collect information on the slave trade across the lake.[31] In short, he wished to complete his assignment by putting together a fuller picture of all that mattered for the promotion of his highway dream.

By now he knew something of the land and its peoples. He held the view that the land was generally very fertile and suitable for cotton cultivation in many places; he wrote of the opening of a cotton field from the Shire to the lake over a distance of some four hundred miles and reported that cotton was cultivated in every village in the valleys of the Shire. The expedition made a practice of buying cotton from the villagers as a first step towards inculcating in them pride in the economic value of their labours. From Dr Kirk's letter to his brother dated 26 June 1861 we learn that the first cotton gins were brought to Zambezia by the members of Livingstone's expedition; that the cotton they purchased was deemed to be superior to American cotton; and that the price paid for it was about 18d for 40 lb of raw or 10 lb of cleaned cotton. This investment realised the sum of 5s 10d in England,[32] or a profit of almost 400%.

Since Livingstone made so much of the prospects for cotton cultivation his views aroused considerable interest locally among his fellow travellers as well as overseas. Correspondents took up the matter through the columns of *The Times* in London, expressing fear that the growth of cotton and sugar plantations in Africa would lead to the need for slave labour. Livingstone was constrained to write to the Foreign Office that these were false assumptions: 'Enquiries among those best acquainted with the country as to what prospects there are of free people cultivating cotton for sale, the prompt answer was, "Certainly, if they find it (in) their interest to do so. They now work hard in raising provisions at a very cheap rate, and many of them cultivate cotton for their own use and, if they knew it would be purchased, would raise more." '[33]

Perhaps Livingstone honestly believed in what he wrote; perhaps a measure of it was intended to impress those who had doubts. The fact remains that some of his views and reports were contradicted by his fellow companions on the spot. Kirk contradicted his Zambezi river reports; the Revd James Stewart did the same to his reports on cotton. Though Stewart only arrived in 1862 he based his conclusions both on what he saw, which was limited, and on what he gathered from respondents such as Rowley of the U.M.C.A. From Rowley, Stewart learned that in the Shire valley, cotton was only cultivated by two to three persons in every village and that even this fluctuated considerably because of drought; that the acreage was small, not exceeding quarter of an acre in any field observed. As to Livingstone's claim that all the cotton grown was being purchased by the expedition, Stewart's information was that not a single bale of cotton had been collected by the *Pioneer* up till 5 August 1862. Since contrary reports were going out overseas, on the strength of which important decisions were being taken for the present and the future, Rowley maintained that the factual position should be laid bare.

Let the truth, the whole truth, and nothing but the truth, be known, and all will be well with us. But if a different policy be adopted I fear we must give up, for, without being more truthful than anyone else personally, I cannot, in an enterprise of such vital moment as a Christian Mission to the heathen of these lands, exist as a coadjutor in an enterprise that gains support through more or less fictitious representations. In ignorance many foolish things were no doubt said before we left England, but ignorance we can no longer plead, and I shall be very thankful if our Committee make a clean breast of it.[34]

On the strength of his own information, James Stewart sent a report to the Cotton Supply Association, Manchester, the gist of which was: 'That the amount of cotton grown is not large, I infer from the following facts. In the Shire valley, on the river itself, a considerable number of the people wear skins of goats and small wild animals; 10 miles and further from the river eastward they wear bark and skins. Fully one half of the people are thus clothed.'[35]

Livingstone's reports on cotton were based on his experiences and observations in Central Africa from 1854 onwards; those of Stewart and Rowley were based on observations made between 1861 and 1863. Much had happened in the Shire lowlands and highlands between 1859 and 1863 to alter the picture which Livingstone first painted before 1859. Drought, increase in slave traffic, activities of the Marianno rebels, the advent of the Yao, the role of the Makololo, all these factors separately or in collusion altered much of the complexion of the Shire area and consequently changed much of the original scene which Livingstone had beheld. Certainly his other associates, Dr Kirk and the Revd Horace Waller, did not agree that Livingstone had deliberately misrepresented the extent of the cotton industry. Waller, who was friendly with both Stewart and Livingstone, drew attention to the fact, in a letter to James Stewart on 5 July 1863: 'I have firmly stated, and stuck to it, that in as much as the country had undergone war, famine and drought and pestilence, sweeping pestilence, and that between the periods of the Dr's visit to spy it out and yours, there is nothing inconsistent in the two reports.' The Revd Lovell Procter, one of the members of the U.M.C.A., referred to the setting up of a cotton gin by Dr Kirk and Charles Livingstone, and observed that: 'The Doctor has bought a large quantity of cotton which the natives have brought along side in their canoes to sell, packed up in long bulging bales of palm leaves.'[36]

There were, however, other aspects of the industry of the Shire inhabitants on which both Livingstone and Stewart agreed. These were the excellence of their iron goods, basket making and pottery. From Livingstone we learn that every village had its own smelting house, its charcoal burners and blacksmiths making axes, spears, needles, arrow-heads, bracelets and anklets. Fishing was an important occupation: fishing nets were made from buaze fibre. All in all, most of the people kept themselves reasonably busy. 'A great deal of native trade,' he reported, 'is carried on between the villages, by means of barter in tobacco, salt, dried fish, skins and iron.' There was one fault he found with the Mang'anja generally: they consumed large quantities of beer. His actual words were: 'The worst feature we observed in the people was the consumption of large quantities of native beer and Indian Hemp. I saw more intoxication in the forty days of our march on foot than I have seen in other parts during sixteen years. It is a sort of silly drunkenness; only one man had reached the fighting stage.'[37] From Dr Kirk, we learn that iron hoes were manufactured in the Shire Highlands; a hoe weighing 2 to 3 lb could be purchased for 2d.[38]

So far Livingstone had accumulated sufficient evidence and information to establish that the prospects in the country along the four-hundred-mile course of the Shire were good for the setting up of mission stations. There was a further observation which supported this conclusion and that was the slave trade. There was plenty of it along the Zambezi; equally there was a lot of it in the Shire and the lake regions. On the party's third Malawi trip, a slave party was encountered in Chief Mbame's village, a few miles from Blantyre, on its way to Tete. With some misgiving on his part, chiefly arising from doubts concerning the Portuguese reaction, and possible retaliation against the expedition's possessions in Tete, Livingstone intervened and set free eighty-four slaves on that occasion, eight others immediately afterwards, one hundred in the Soche village of present Blantyre, six at Mongazi's village on the Zomba road and fifty others soon afterwards, giving a total of 248 persons liberated on a single trip. His strategy was based on the principle that the act was justified on grounds of self-defence only. On this point Livingstone differed with Bishop Mackenzie who, to his later disappointment, argued that the whites were perfectly right to take the offensive on this moral issue even if it did place them in an awkward position in their relations with African communities. This was tantamount to taking sides which Livingstone felt the whites should not and could not effectively do. This issue led to major disagreement between them.[39]

Higher up along the middle reaches of the lake, similar observations were made. Livingstone was struck by the picture of contrasts; some villages were well supplied with food; others in the same area were in obvious distress. It was not until his fifth and final trip that he was able to pinpoint the extent and organisation of the interior slave trade. In his earlier observations the signs were there: the presence of foreign cloth, beads, brassware and guns. What struck him more forcibly was the havoc wrought by the Ngoni, his 'Mazitu'. This menace extended as far north as Tongaland in Chief Mankhambira's area; in some instances whole villages were destroyed and people were wantonly killed. Livingstone found it hard to believe that the wholesale slaughter was part of the Ngoni politics of domination. It could not be since the Ngoni object in raiding was to conquer and assimilate rather than to destroy and alienate. Livingstone wondered whether such fate had not visited certain northern villages because they had dared to raid the cattle of the Ngoni.[40]

If Livingstone saw more of the Ngoni havoc, up to this stage he learned something of how the slave trade was progressing, and where and by whom it was carried on – enough to comment on how his interior plans would frustrate the trade: 'A small armed steamer on Lake Nyassa could easily, by exercising a control, and furnishing goods in exchange for ivory and other products, break the neck of this infamous traffic in that quarter; for nearly all must cross the Lake or the Upper Shire.'[41]

Besides the Arab slavers, Livingstone observed the conduct of the Yao slavers and made the interesting statement that the Yao entry into Malawi society was usually by starting the slave trade in a friendly way:

> Then, professing to wish to live as subjects, they have been welcomed as guests, and the Manganja, being great agriculturists, have been able to support considerable bodies of these visitors for a time. When the provisions became scarce, the guests began to steal

from the fields; quarrels arose in consequence, and, the Ajawa having firearms, their hosts got the worst of it, and were expelled from village after village, and out of their own country.[42]

This explanation may not account for the pattern of entry into Malawi of all the Yao groups, but as a contemporary report on a process of that time it deserves attention.

After his final visit in 1863 to the lake and its western hinterland, Livingstone was able to get the full picture of the slave trade and could then say that both local people and foreigners combined to create the opportunity for indulging in human traffic. The foreigners were the Arabs, the Swahili and the Yao; the locals were members of the Malawi communities in different regions. Of the foreign elements he observed, the situation of the Swahili ruler, Jumbe of Nkhota kota, struck him most forcibly: this ruler was settled in the most populous part of the lakeshore. When he had first visited the Jumbe's area in 1861 he noted that the Jumbe's following numbered some 1,500 persons; two years later the number had increased to 'tens of thousands'. These followers were mainly those who sought protection from a ruler who had guns and gunpowder. If the local people would rush to become subjects of a foreigner, especially one who carried the banner of Islam, Livingstone reasoned that a Christian mission in that same area would gain equal success if it could provide the security that was desired.[42]

The response of the local people to the influence of the foreign slaver, the Jumbe of Nkhota kota, leads us to a consideration of the response of the same people to the influence and presence of the foreign whites then in the country under Livingstone's leadership. On the first leg of the journey along the southern gateway into Malawi, from the confluence of the Shire and Zambezi rivers up to Chikwawa (Chibisa's), the Livingstone party encountered three important chiefs in the following order of contact: Tengani, Mankhokwe and Chibisa along the two-hundred-mile journey. All three were Mang'anja chiefs though the status of Chibisa was questioned at the time. He was stated variously to be of slave descent and linked to a Tete chieftainship by origin as well as by a common interest in the slave trade. Yet it was with this chief that the most amicable relations were forged. There was, of course, the dependence on the goodwill of this chief, for ten miles beyond him the first cataracts appeared and the overland route commenced. His area was thus the first stopping place, storage place and lower headquarters of the travellers. Livingstone described the Chibisa of the time as a 'remarkably shrewd man, the very image, save his dark hue, of one of our most celebrated London actors, and the most

47

intelligent Chief, by far, in this quarter'.[44] Livingstone could not say the same for the other two. Tengani had had for years the problem of guarding against the mischief created by the Portuguese slaving interests in the lower sections of his area: the slave raids, the fights between the Marianno rebels and the Portuguese. The seat of Marianno at Shamo was not far from Tengani's own headquarters. Hence it is understandable why Livingstone's party received a hostile reception at Tengani's: the people were armed with barbed arrows, and the chief only gave permission for the party to pass after receiving an assurance from Livingstone that his only interest was in purchasing cotton and other crops. It was here that the first cotton fields were observed in the lower Shire. Livingstone described him as an 'elderly, well-made man, grey-headed, and over six feet high'.[45] There was some doubt about his seniority in their extended area, especially in relation to the status of the third chief, Mankhokwe. It was with Mankhokwe that the party had the greatest difficulty. He was recognised as a paramount chief and was referred to as the 'Rundo' which is clearly a misreporting of the term 'Lundu'. On the first occasion, he refused to see the party and Livingstone made the following entry: '. . . he owns a number of fertile islands, and is said to be the Rundo, or paramount Chief, of a large district. Being of an unhappy suspicious disposition, he would not see us; so we thought it best to move on.'[46] About a month later, on the party's way back, Mankhokwe received them and blamed his young subjects for dissuading him from meeting them the first time.[47]

Why did Mankhokwe behave as he did? To begin with, he was a ruler of considerable status. The white travellers did not know just what his status was. Rowley, usually a careful observer, divided the honours between Tengani and Mankhokwe: 'The people in the Shire Valley were nominally under the rule of two great chiefs, Tengani and Mankhokwe. These chiefs were called Rundos. Mankhokwe's government extended to the highlands up as far as Lake Shirwa, and Tengani was, I believe, paramount lord over that portion of the highlands below the Ruo.'[48] But Rowley admitted, too, that 'his exalted position in the country had not been known; for he had avoided the English during their previous visits, and was not supposed to be the great man he was.' In 1861, when Livingstone was escorting Bishop Mackenzie's U.M.C.A. party to its first station in Malawi, the party met Mankhokwe and was dramatically reminded, according to Rowley's account, of his status:

Mankhokwe expressed himself glad to see the Doctor and the

Bishop, but upon our purpose in coming to his country he said nothing. On mentioning the chiefs it was intended to visit, he replied, 'You are going to Chinsunzi? he is a child of the Rundo.' 'We are going to Chibisa,' said Dr Livingstone. 'He is also the Rundo's child.' 'And we also want to see the Rundo.' 'You see him before you – I am he,' was the calm reply.[49]

In this situation, Mankhokwe's behaviour becomes explicable: the foreigners had by-passed him on earlier occasions and this was wrong according to traditional practice; they had called on his subordinates first and this was wrong, too. Further, whereas the subordinates were in an easier position to accept the foreigners, Mankhokwe was not. He was guardian over his people, the living and the dead, a temporal as well as religious leader. What *he* did mattered for the present and future of his people. In this context it is easy to understand why Mankhokwe approached Chibisa for support in keeping the white men out; why he returned the white man's presents, instructing his messengers to say on that occasion that the presents were being returned because the foreigners had assumed that by having given them in the first instance they were now entitled to consider the land as their own – and to occupy it permanently.[50] Mankhokwe's objection was to the party being officially connected with him. Rowley's account supports this: 'He afterwards said that, though Rundo, he had very little power over the other chiefs, and if they saw the English with him, they might not like it, they might be angry with him, for introducing strangers into the land.'[51] In addition to Mankhokwe's other difficulties, one should also consider that the times were not propitious for him to support the white men more openly: famine had reduced his people to extreme penury and as paramount chief it was his duty to protect his subjects from natural disasters of that kind. Two years later he was more amenable to receiving the strangers as friends because the unfriendly Yao had begun to use his domain as a raiding ground; but by then the Mankhokwe might was fast declining: 'Mankokwe professed himself glad to see us, but he could help us to no corn – he, the Rundo of the whole land, was barely able to supply us with enough meal for our dinner and breakfast.'[52]

The relationship between the Livingstone and the U.M.C.A. parties with Mankhokwe and his people draws attention to the intricate and often delicate nature of the contact between alien groups. Livingstone was not called upon to face a more complex situation elsewhere in the country. The three most important parts of the country in his scheme were the southern gateway (river access), the interior gateway (lake access) and the interior itself. The first has already been described; the second did not provide any obstacles and was not as much in ferment through the Yao and Ngoni raids as it was to become around the time Livingstone died, and later. Towards the north, Livingstone stopped at Nkhota kota (where he met Chief Malenga in the north and the followers of the Islamic ruler, the Jumbe to the south), and Bandawe (where he met Chief Mankhambira) and at Kasungu (where he met Chief Mwase). His observations and those of the local inhabitants and rulers in these places will now be considered.

Livingstone first visited Nkhota kota in 1861, when he travelled further north towards Bandawe and possibly touched again at Nkhota kota on his way back. The last time he visited this well-populated coastal area was on 10 September 1863 when he 'sat under a magnificent wild fig-tree with leaves ten inches long, by five broad, about a quarter of a mile from the village of Juma bin Saide, and Yakobe ben Arame, whom we had met on the River Kaombe, a little north of this, in our first exploration of the Lake.' Livingstone stated that Juma arrived to meet the travellers with a following of about fifty persons and invited the party to take up residence in his village. It is being assumed here that Juma and the Jumbe were one and the same person but this may be wrong. Livingstone described the hut set aside for them as dirty and the party preferred to sleep in the open. The Jumbe apologised for this inconvenience and presented the visitors with rice, mealie meal, sugar cane and a piece of malachite. The following day the party observed that the Jumbe was busy supervising the building of a dhow fifty feet long, twelve feet wide and five feet deep. It was in dhows such as this that the Jumbe carried on trade across the lake, including that in slaves. The Jumbe was friendly enough to provide Livingstone with a guide for the rest of his journey westwards into the hinterland where slaves, ivory and malachite were obtained.[53] It was in the Nkhota kota area, slightly to the north, that Livingstone hoped that his own mission house would one day be built and in the meantime encouraged the Revd James Stewart to consider it a suitable area for Stewart's own future mission.

On the 1861 journey Livingstone had moved on further northwards towards Chiefs Malenga (or Marenga) and Mankhambira. How the locals received the visitors on that occasion was recounted in 1913 by eye-witness reports at a meeting arranged by the Livingstonia missionaries to commemorate the hundredth anniversary of the birth of Livingstone. The meeting was held at Bandawe and the written account was preserved by the Livingstonia missionary, the

50

Revd A. G. MacAlpine. The gathering took place in Chief Marenga's area and four old men shared their memories after which Chief Marenga Phiri, the second successor of Livingstone's Chief Marenga Mzoma, also spoke. They referred to Livingstone as 'Chiswa-msangu', the pioneer; recalled how they had seen Dr Livingstone arrive at Chief Kanyenda's village on the Dwangwa river, shake hands with Chief Kanyenda, and after a friendly chat, depart. One of the speakers, an old man named Chimgwabada, said:

> The travellers were not taken for human beings but for 'spirits of the lake', visitors from another world who had arrived by a wonderful boat – (during) the season of bush-fires – (when the) villagers were busy at their *usipa* (anchovy) fishing – Chiefs and Headmen had gathered around, and Dr Livingstone asked for the *Karonga* or King. 'These are all Chiefs,' he was told, but Livingstone would not be put off – 'Where is the Karonga? Where is Marenga?' repeated the explorer, giving the name he got at Kotakota or at Kanyenda's further south – Though not the Head Chief of the Bandawe Tonga, Marenga Mzoma was at that time the Chief of most influence – Then the Chief appeared, decked out in all his insignia and ivory armlets and leglets. The *Mzungu* gave him hearty greeting: '*chuku, chuku, chuku*,' handshaking and more handshaking all around with the three white men. Then Dr Livingstone, taking Marenga by his arm, led him to his boat and shewed him its build and gear. This was all closely observed with such concern and some doubts by the people, who remarked, 'Viwanda vyambaya Fumu ya weni': Are the spirits going to kill other people's Chief? But no; there was only hearty friendship, and the Chief presented gifts, the strangers making return presents, and fears were dissipated.[54]

The speakers also recalled that Livingstone enquired about the Ruvuma river which many understood to be the same as Ruvu, a river which flows into Lake Malawi on its eastern shore, opposite the present Livingstonia Mission in northern Malawi. But the Tonga knew of another Ruvu, six miles to the south of where Livingstone then was and said that the explorer had just passed it, to which Livingstone shook his head in despair. Finally, they remembered that Livingstone left some of his goods with Chief Marenga as he proceeded northwards, promising that he would collect them on the return journey, a gesture of trust which was heartily appreciated.

Testimonies of this kind, unhappily, no longer exist. They throw light on Livingstone's friendly approach to African communities; his concern to locate the important chief (perhaps he was aware of the omissions in the party's dealings with Mankhokwe of the Mang'anja); the African response to the weird-looking light-skinned strangers. Other testimonies based on village traditions remain, but they are not as effective as the eye-witness accounts and these will be considered later for a few areas connected with Livingstone's travels. For the moment the last important chief on his northern trip of 1863 needs to be considered: Chief Mwase of Kasungu whom Livingstone visited on 21 September 1863. He found Mwase's village surrounded by a stockade, a necessary precaution since the area was much troubled by Ngoni raids; the many villages scattered widely were also stockaded and all of them owed allegiance to this chief whose headquarters was about two miles south-west of a hill named Kasungu. Of his meeting with this famous Chewa chief who, more than any other similar chief in that area, was able to resist the Ngoni attacks effectively because he had accumulated a good stock of guns and gunpowder, Livingstone noted the following:

> He was as frank and straightforward as could reasonably be expected. He did not wish us to go to the N.N.W., because he carries on a considerable trade in ivory there. We were anxious to get off the slave route, to people not visited before by traders; but Muazi naturally feared, that if we went to what is said to be a well-watered country, abounding in elephants, we might relieve him of the ivory which he now obtains at a cheap rate and sells to the slave traders as they pass Kasungu to the east; but at least he consented, warning us that 'great difficulty would be experienced in obtaining food'.[55]

The Livingstone party stayed at Kasungu for two days. They learned about the slave route and the slave trade goods to the west, saw cattle in large numbers but were surprised that the cows were not milked. For a further week Livingstone marched westwards hoping to learn more about the areas not blessed with legitimate trade, but time was running out on him and his mission. The deadline date set by the British government for the recall of the Zambezi expedition was 31 December 1863, just about four months away, and here he was in Bemba country to the west of Kasungu, hundreds of miles away from the *Pioneer* at Chikwawa. On 2 October 1863 he commenced his return journey from Kasungu. By the end of that month, the 760-mile journey was over.

So far we have considered the accounts given by the travellers themselves as well as eye-witness African reports of some of the events. How do Africans in modern Malawi, of an older generation, view Livingstone and his travels in their country?

In the Chikwawa area, so famous in contemporary accounts, Livingstone settled his Makololo. Of the sixteen whom Livingstone left behind nine became chiefs in subsequent years. One of the most famous of these chieftainships still in existence is that of Chief Massea. The present incumbent is Chief Massea II, seventy-five years old. His father had travelled with Livingstone and died in 1900. Chief Massea remembers a few of the highlights passed down the years. Livingstone was firm about observing the Sabbath, even forbidding his followers from hunting on Sunday. So severe was this injunction that in the Massea traditions it is stated that Livingstone left the Makololo behind because one of them dared to break the rule one day. The traditions also find room to justify the ascendancy of the Makololo. Livingstone gave them guns and gunpowder to protect themselves; with these they were able to restore order in a troubled area and thus assumed an ascendancy over the indigenous Mang'anja.[56]

The Mwase Kasungu traditions state that the person who held the position of Chief Mwase at the time of the Livingstone visit in 1863 was Chief Mwase Chiripadambo, a famous farmer and hunter. There were two things which Livingstone liked about the Mwase of that time, according to these traditions: the fact that he redeemed slaves from their Arab captivity as the slave caravans passed through his area (it was not stated how he did this) and the encouragement given to his people by the chief to worship god through the spirit of their ancestors or through the spirits of the chiefs' ancestors. On the matter of presents exchanged, these traditions are firm that the chief asked for, and received, needles (*Kasinje* or *Singano*), as well as cloth and that he gave Livingstone an ox.[57]

The more recent Nkhota kota traditions seem to be divided on a number of issues which still provide stimulus for lively debates in this lakeshore town. These are the number of visits Livingstone paid to the place, the number of fig trees he sat under and the number of chiefs he met and in what order. The opinions on the above were divided when eighteen persons were interviewed from 4 February to 8 February 1972. Three fig trees are in competition in the town for the honour of having provided shelter to the famous Christian doctor-missionary in that famous stronghold of Islam in Malawi: one is Chief Marenga's tree; another is the Jumbe's tree (Kombo Makalani); and a more recent third (and least supported) claimant stands in the premises of the

53

Anglican mission which opened in 1894. Most of them agree, however, that Livingstone met both Marenga and the Jumbe in 1863, and that Livingstone gave Chief Marenga a china plate and an umbrella, while the chief gave him a sheep, though opinion is divided between those who support two visits and those who favour three.[58] It might appear strange at first sight that these differences should exist, but when one remembers that this most densely populated rural area in Malawi has for long been a fertile ground for disputes between the original Chewa and the later Muslims, between the forces of Christianity, Islam and traditional African beliefs, one understands why and how local beliefs are nurtured along specific lines.

The two dreams evaluated

Dr Livingstone had set out to find a highway into the Central Africa interior. When the Cabora Bassa came between him and the realisation of his objectives he could have done one of two things: packed his bags or looked out for another highway. He did the latter, and creditably too.

But the Zambezi expedition must not be considered a total failure. There was much that Livingstone and his men, the British and the Portuguese governments, got out of it both positively and negatively: the shortcomings on the part of the Portuguese administration; the economic potential and problems; the information on river navigation; these were all very helpful then. They were helpful later and are even important today. The question of the navigability of the Zambezi, for example, is not a closed chapter. In a recent issue of the *Rhodesian Herald*[59] the following caption appeared: 'Barge traffic on Zambezi nearer with building of Cabora Bassa'. Once the modern dam is completed a 150-mile man-made reservoir extending westwards from the rapids to the town of Zumbo will be available to control the flow of the Zambezi. This would then make it possible for river boats to travel from Tete to the mouth of the Zambezi, a distance of about 380 miles. The hope is that barges would then operate on the Zambezi as they do on the Rhine and the St Lawrence. Rhodesia would then find it useful to have good road, rail or water links to the potential river port of Tete. Livingstone might not have visualised all this in the same grand design, but he saw the possibility of sappers making something of a channel and the flood waters providing the leverage to surmount the rapids. Men and means were not at the disposal of the

54

dreamers of that time.

The Zambezi disappointment could have broken the strongest of resolutions. This is what James Stewart, not the best of Livingstone fans, had to say about it:

It was the impression of one, perhaps of more than one of those who arrived at the mouth of the Zambezi on February 2nd, 1861, that Livingstone, Kirk and others were very thoroughly disgusted with the river, country, people, and Portuguese, and if they could have decently withdrawn from the region, they would have done so. The attempt to ascend the Ruvuma and that impression in Livingstone's letter to his wife that, if the Ruvuma were (not) practicable, they would then bid 'farewell to the Zambesi' and its abominable bars, this does not look very much like as if it were the highway into Central Africa, does it. . . .[60]

Of the whole enterprise it cannot be said that there was anything or the nature of either a decent or indecent withdrawal from the task at hand. When the notice of withdrawal came, the British government served it and Livingstone accepted it. But by then, the first stages towards the fuller realisation of his objectives had been reached and passed: he had undertaken a considerable number of trips within a short space of time, he had seen things for himself and he had made friends with African communities. The Makololo remembered him and his countrymen and were helpful in the promotion of British interest in Malawi.[61] E. D. Young, at the head of an expedition in 1867 to establish whether or not Livingstone was still alive, described how Chief Marenga, whom Livingstone had met in 1863, reacted to Young's presence: 'Marenga rushed towards me, and, seizing me by the hand, shook it heartily, saying "Where have you come from, and where is your brother that was here last year?"' The presents and the assistance which Young received were a further testimony to the goodwill which existed in African communities for Livingstone.

Livingstone preached the dignity of free labour and made a case for cotton cultivation. He had his critics, as we have seen, who felt that he was too optimistic on this score. Later events proved him right: the first recorded export of cotton was in 1893 when 400 lbs were exported. That was twenty years after Livingstone died. In 1902 the British Cotton Growing Association was formed and a year later cotton cultivation expanded in Malawi. In 1918, the cotton industry was the largest in the country. What was interesting about this industry was that it was mainly in the hands of African cultivators.[63] Though cotton has since 1953 given way to tea and tobacco, the existence of such projects as the Chikwawa Cotton Development Project and the Salima Cotton Development Scheme is continuing proof that Malawi is indeed, what Livingstone described it as, a cotton field.

The first attempt at promoting another of Livingstone's ideas, that of evangelisation, failed during his own life time when the U.M.C.A. moved away to Zanzibar in 1864. But, as Bishop Mackenzie's biographer has written, this was not the end of the road: 'To move to Zanzibar was to abandon the first of the terms in the doublet "commerce and Christianity". You could not from Zanzibar teach the natives how to grow cotton and coffee, you could not instruct them how to survive without selling men and women. Tozer and Steere reiterated again and again that they regarded Zanzibar only as a base, the starting point which must be secured before operations could be extended outwards towards the Nyasa country.'[64]

The doors remained open and the subsequent history of mission stations in the country ensured that they not only remained open but became wider with the passing of the years. If Livingstone was not himself directly responsible for all this, the indirect influences connected with his name and work cannot be ruled out.

What did Livingstone himself see in his labours in search for 'God's highway into the interior' before his Zambezi expedition finally assembled at the Zambezi mouth for departure on 13 February 1864? There was the discovery of a port of entry into the Zambezi; knowledge about the Zambezi, Shire and Nyasa waterways; the discovery of the potential for the cultivation of cotton, tobacco and sugar; the availability of good grazing lands for cattle; the absence of the tsetse fly in the highlands. These were considerations to be set aside for future exploitation. But he cautioned, too, that the future should take note of the negative aspects in the situation: the hazards of periodic droughts and the African and European involvement in the slave trade.[65] That was his balance sheet for the Zambezi expedition, 1858–1864.

He had found a new highway to replace the old: the Shire highway into the Malawi interior. That was his modest contribution to the future of a country. He could not predict that future. He could only express a hope for it:

'We are within sound of the waterfall. When will this fertile valley resound with the church-going bell? The Lord, the Good Lord, grant that our entrance may be the precursor to that happy time.'[66]

Notes

I am grateful to the following for assistance during the writing of this chapter: Mr Wilfred Plumbe, Librarian, Mr Melvin Page, Lecturer in History and Mr Steve Mwiyeriwa, Sub-Librarian, all of the University of Malawi, Chancellor College; Mr D. H. Simpson, Librarian, Royal Commonwealth Society, London; the Keeper of the Public Record Office, London; the District Commissioners of Chikwawa and Nkhota kota and Chief Mwase Kasungu.

1 The Cabora Bassa Rapids in 1972 constitute part of a great hydroelectric scheme which is aimed at the construction of the third or fourth largest dam in the world at a cost of $350 million. The Cabora-Bassa dam is expected to be completed by the international consortium called *Zamco* in 1975. The dam is situated 300 miles from the mouth of the Zambezi and about 86 miles from Tete. It hopes to generate 1200 megawatts of electric power, 75% of which is expected to be used by the Republic of South Africa. *Africa Digest*, 18–24 August 1968, 4058–9 and 1–7 October 1969, 4636–7.

2 George Seaver, *David Livingstone: His Life and Letters*, London, 1957, p. 260.

3 J. P. R. Wallis (ed.), *The Zambezi Expedition of David Livingstone 1858–1863*, vol. I, London, 1956 (Central African Archives, Oppenheimer Series Number nine), Introduction, pp. xv–xvi.

4 David Livingstone, *Missionary Travels and Researches in South Africa*, London, 1857, p. 575.

5 Ibid.

6 Wallis, *The Zambezi Expedition*, vol. I, Introduction, p. xviii.

7 *Missionary Travels*, p. 576.

8 David Livingstone was the leader; Commander Norman Bedingfield, R.N. was deputy leader; Dr John Kirk, botanist and medical officer was the third in rank; Charles Livingstone was general assistant and 'moral agent'; George Rae was the ship's engineer; Thomas Baines was artist and storekeeper and Richard Thornton was the geologist.

9 David and Charles Livingstone, *Narrative of an expedition to the Zambesi and its tributaries; and of the discovery of Lakes Shirwa and Nyassa, 1858–1864*, London, 1865, p. 9.

10 Ibid., p. 14.

11 *Missionary Travels*, p. 575.

12 B. Pachai, *Malawi: The History of the Nation*, London, 1973, Chapter 4.

13 Wallis, *The Zambezi Expedition*, vol. I, p. 144.

14 Seaver, op. cit., p. 308. On the strength of this letter Professor Debenham says: 'It is therefore clear that Nyasaland owes its establishment as a Crown Colony, even more definitely than most historians suppose, to the dreams of David Livingstone.' Also David Livingstone to Sir Frederick Grey, 20 October 1859, photocopy obtained through courtesy of the Librarian, Royal Commonwealth Society, London.

15 Seaver, op. cit., pp. 304–8.

16 We have Kirk's testimony on this: four Portuguese sailors were placed on duty at the Kongone mouth; a flag was hoisted but the task was beyond their limited resources and inclinations. He notes that the Governor of Quelimane admitted to Livingstone that the Portuguese were a miserable lot 'quite debased by debauchery, and with no enterprise whatever'. R. Coupland, *Kirk on the Zambesi. A Chapter of African History*, Oxford, 1928, p. 165.

17 George Martelli, *Livingstone's River. A history of the Zambezi expedition 1858–1864*. London, 1970, p. 53.

18 The Portuguese who accompanied them on this trip and who knew the country above.

19 Wallis, *The Zambezi Expedition*, vol. I, p. 63.

20 Ibid., pp. 69–70.

21 R. Foskett (ed.), *The Zambezi Journal and Letters of Dr John Kirk, 1858–1863*, vol. I, Edinburgh, 1965, p. 139.

22 Coupland, op. cit., p. 170. The adventure is narrated on pp. 177–9. In fairness to Dr Kirk, it must be said that he did not agree with a great deal that Dr Livingstone wrote about the Zambezi and its possibilities. 'The River Zambezi is not the river described by D.L.' is what he once wrote. Foskett, *The Zambesi Journal*, vol. 2, p. 544. In a private letter to Sir Frederick Grey dated 20 December 1858 Livingstone noted his first observations on the rapids: '. . . we have found the difficulty totally different from anything we could ascertain at Tette. Portuguese writers have known just as little as we did. . . .' Photocopy obtained through courtesy of the Librarian, Royal Commonwealth Society, London.

23 Wallis, *The Zambezi Expedition*, vol. II, p. 317.

24 D. and C. Livingstone, *Narrative*, pp. 528 and 548.

25 B. Pachai (ed.), *The Early History of Malawi*, London, 1972; see especially J. M. Schoffeleers, 'The meaning and use of the name *Malawi* in oral tradition and precolonial documents', pp. 91–103; H. W. Langworthy, 'Chewa or Malawi political organisation in the precolonial era', pp. 104–22; H. L. Vail, 'Suggestions towards a reinterpreted Tumbuka history', pp. 148–67; E. A. Alpers, 'The Yao in Malawi, 1860–1918; Some suggestions for future research', pp. 168–78; B. Pachai, 'Ngoni politics and diplomacy in Malawi, 1848–1904', pp. 179–215; K. J. McCracken, 'Religion and Politics in Northern Ngoniland, 1881–1904', pp. 215–36 and I. Linden, 'The Maseko Ngoni at Domwe, 1870–1900', pp. 237–51.

26 E. C. Tabler (ed.), *The Zambesi Papers of Richard Thornton*, vol. I, London, 1963, p. 70.

27 M. D. D. Newitt, 'The Massingire Rising of 1884' in *Journal of African History*, XI, 1, 1970, pp. 87–105 for both the early and the later history of the Marianno families. When the Livingstone party first visited Marianno's stockade at Shamo on 9 September 1858, it found a large stone-walled house surrounded by lesser sized houses; the stockade made up of branches fastened together was eight inches thick and fourteen feet high but a start had already been made to construct an outer stockade about five feet thick with sun-baked bricks. When the party returned to it on 4 October, they found everything in ruins and unrecognisable; Bonga was in hiding in the Morumbala hills, still friendly to the travellers but now acknowledging defeat at the hands of the Portuguese. This illustrates the rapid changing circumstances. Foskett, *The Zambezi Journal*, vol. I, pp. 72–4 and 97.

28 D. and C. Livingstone, *Narrative*, pp. 26 and 33–4.

29 Coupland, *Kirk on the Zambesi*, p. 141.

30 D. and C. Livingstone, *Narrative*, p. 104. Livingstone sent a lengthy despatch to Lord John Russell, the Secretary of State for Foreign Affairs, on 15 October 1859 on his trip to the lake. The opening paragraph reads: 'I have the honour to convey the information that we have traced the River Shire up to its point

of departure from the hitherto undiscovered Lake Nyinyesi or Nyassa, and found that there are only thirty-three miles of cataracts to be passed above this when the river becomes smooth again, and continues so right into the Lake. . . . We have opened a cotton and sugar producing country of unknown extent, and while it really seems to afford reasonable prospects of great commercial benefits to our own country, it presents facilities for commanding a large section of the slave market on the East coast and offers a fairer hope of its extirpation by lawful commerce than our previous knowledge of the country led us to anticipate.'
F.O. 63/87. Public Records Office photocopy.

31 D. and C. Livingstone, *Narrative*, p. 487.
32 Foskett, *Zambezi Journal of Dr John Kirk*, vol. I, p. 553.
33 Wallis, *Zambezi Expedition*, vol. II, p. 285.
34 H. Rowley to James Stewart, Mission Station, Chibisa's, 6 November 1862. J. P. R. Wallis (ed.), *The Zambesi Journal of James Stewart 1862–1863*, London, 1952, pp. 211–12.
35 Ibid., Appendix 3, p. 266.
36 Seaver, *David Livingstone*, p. 435; Norman Robert Bennett and Marguerite Ylvisaker (eds), *The Central African Journal of Lovell J. Procter, 1860–1864*, Boston, 1971, p. 60.
37 D. and C. Livingstone, *Narrative*, pp. 114 and 117. F.O. 63/87. Livingstone to Earl of Russell, 15 October 1859 on drunkenness.
38 Foskett, *The Zambezi Journal of Dr John Kirk*, vol. II, p. 553.
39 D. and C. Livingstone, *Narrative*, pp. 362–3. Three of the liberated slaves went on to play an important part in later developments: Susi, Sam Sambane and Tom Bokwito, the two last-named going on to Lovedale at the Cape in South Africa for their further education.
40 Ibid., p. 385.
41 Ibid., p. 392.
42 Ibid., p. 497.
43 D. and C. Livingstone, *Narrative*, abridged version, London, 1875, p. 365.
44 D. and C. Livingstone, *Narrative*, 1865 edition, p. 79.
45 Ibid., p. 76. The Revd Henry Rowley, who made copious notes as a member of the U.M.C.A. party to pass that way in 1861, gives the following account of his impressions at Tengani's: 'It was at this village that we first met with indications of the growth of cotton. Some – a small quantity, not more than a pound – was, on being asked for, brought to the ship for sale, and a yard of calico was given for it. Dr Kirk also purchased a large piece of native cloth for an equal length of unbleached calico. It seemed surprising that having the power to provide themselves with raiment so suited to their need as this cloth of their own make, they should desire our own manufacture so greatly.' The Revd Henry Rowley, *The Story of the Universities' Mission to Central Africa*, London, 1867, pp. 72–3.
46 D. and C. Livingstone, *Narrative* (1865), p. 102.
47 Ibid., p. 134.
48 Rowley, op. cit., p. 72.
49 Ibid., p. 85.
50 Foskett, *The Zambezi Journal of Dr John Kirk*, vol. I, p. 356. The presents were returned in July 1861. See entries for 1 July and 9 July, pp. 347–50.
51 Rowley, op. cit., p. 91.

52 Ibid., p. 348. Mankhokwe's difficulties reached the point of overflow according to the following testimony recorded by Rowley in 1863. 'Chimbeli, his ambassador, accompanied us to the canoe, and on his way said that all the trouble that came on the Manganja was owing to the Rundo not doing as Rundos did in days gone by. They went from village to village all over the land, every year, and at each place they prayed to Pambi to send rain, and to keep away enemies. Then they were a happy people; there was no war, no starvation, but now all things were against them, for the Rundo cared for nothing but his pombi and his wives, shut himself up with them, and got drunk every day, and would go nowhere.'

53 D. and C. Livingstone, *Narrative* (1875), pp. 364–9.

54 Gen. 766 2, MacAlpine Papers, Edinburgh University.

55 D. and C. Livingstone, *Narrative* (1875), pp. 376–8.

56 Chief Massea II testimony communicated in writing by the District Commissioner, Chikwawa, 22 March 1972. The Lundu paramount chieftainship of the lower Shire area was restored by the Malawi Government in 1970.

57 Written communication from Chief Mwase Kasungu, April 1972.

58 Written communication from the District Commissioner, Nkhota kota, 20 March 1972, based on interviews kindly carried out in his office.

59 9 June 1972, p. 25.

60 Wallis, *The Zambesi Journal of James Stewart*, p. 265.

61 See, for example, P. R. Warhurst, 'Portugal's Bid for Southern Malawi' in B. Pachai, G. W. Smith, R. K. Tangri (eds), *Malawi Past and Present*, Christian Literature Association of Malawi, Blantyre, 1971, pp. 20–36.

62 Proceedings of the Royal Geographical Society, XII, 1867–8, 'Livingstone's Search Expedition', pp. 76–91, at p. 84.

63 B. Pachai, *Malawi: The History of the Nation*, chapter 10.

64 Owen Chadwick, *Mackenzie's Grave*, London, 1959, p. 239.

65 D. and C. Livingstone, *Narrative* (1865), pp. 585–90.

66 Wallis, *The Zambezi Expedition*, vol. I, p. 80.

3 Livingstone and the Anglican Church

Philip Elston

The origin of this essay is to be found in a comment made by Professor George Shepperson during the 1970 University of Malawi conference on the early history of Malawi. He observed how remarkable it was that a Scotsman of such an independent outlook as David Livingstone should turn to the Church of England[1] for men to carry forward the work he had begun in Central Africa. What is no less remarkable is the connection that Livingstone established with this Church from the time of the Cambridge appeal in 1857 until his death sixteen years later. Those years are bounded by his relationship with four members of the Church of England, all of whom had an important part to play in shaping the events in which both they and Dr Livingstone were involved. To one of them he owed the introduction to Cambridge which enabled him to make his appeal; to the second the prospect of seeing his hopes for Central Africa fulfilled; the third member of this Anglican quartet was instrumental in destroying these hopes; while, as if to redress the balance, the last of the four became Livingstone's devoted friend and was later entrusted with the task of bringing his final testimony before an expectant public. The purpose of this chapter, then, is to look at the relationship between Livingstone and the Anglican Church through an examination of his relations with these men.

The Invitation

The invitation with which David Livingstone closed his address to the gathered academics, undergraduates and local worthies at the Senate House in Cambridge on the morning of 4 December 1857 was a clear

61

appeal to the Church of England. This by no means obvious fact deserves explanation.

A major cause of resentment and complaint amongst English Dissenters during the first half of the nineteenth century lay in the fact that they were excluded from the ancient universities of Oxford and Cambridge unless they were prepared to forswear their religious allegiance. At that time, entry to both institutions required subscription at matriculation and graduation to the Thirty-nine Articles of Religion contained in the Book of Common Prayer of the Church of England. Furthermore, compulsory attendance at college chapel was prescribed when the universities were in session. Cambridge went on to demand a declaration of membership of the Church of England. This was at a time when university life was at a low ebb, inviting Nonconformist attacks upon the 'walls of sloth, self-satisfaction and exclusiveness behind which the universities conducted their business and their pleasure'. This state of affairs was attributed by one contemporary critic to 'the canker of ecclesiasticism', a somewhat immoderate way of saying that the universities in question were part and parcel of the Established Church.

An early attempt to remedy the Dissenters' disability was made in 1834 when Lord Grey introduced a University Test Bill providing for the admission of all citizens to the universities and to their degrees, except those in divinity. The Bill passed the Commons by a comfortable majority but not surprisingly (with unsympathetic Anglican prelates voting) was thrown out by the House of Lords. A renewed bid twenty years later to loosen the grip of the Established Church upon higher education was more successful. By the interim settlement of 1854, the Oxford University Bill abolished subscription at matriculation and, save in divinity, at graduation. The Cambridge University Act of 1856 provided similar relief. Dire consequences were predicted by Dean Burgon, then a Fellow of Oriel College, Oxford: 'Oxford, I fear, has seen her best days. Her sun has set and for ever. She never more can be what she has been – the great nursery of the Church. She will become a cage of unclean beasts.'[2] The redoubtable Dr Pusey shared the same view, being convinced that 'Oxford is lost to the Church of England.' This was an overstatement, considering that Nonconformists were still debarred from the master's degree, from all degrees in divinity, from all headships, professorships and fellowships, and in consequence, from any real share in the teaching, administration or government of either university. In a word, while the walls had been breached, the universities remained for some time to come the embattled citadels of the Church of England. 'The reforms . . . had "opened the shutters", but more than twenty years were to pass before the doors were opened freely and widely, and even then a No Admittance notice hung over the entry to the best rooms.'[3]

Livingstone's entry to these privileged circles (he had visited Oxford in November) was as unexpected as it was providential. He had spent the first months after his seventeen years' absence from Britain writing an account of his missionary travels and researches which became the publishing event of the year. With the work completed, he made a royal progress through the country, being dined and fêted by the many learned bodies and ancient municipalities that were anxious to honour the man and his achievements. Towards the end of 1857 arrangements were made for him to visit Lisbon, but an outbreak of yellow fever there led to their cancellation, and made possible, at short notice, the Cambridge visit in circumstances oddly at variance with most popular accounts of the event. Dr Blaikie's *Life* makes no mention of how the visit was arranged, yet the official U.M.C.A. history, written forty years later, suggests that the initiative came from Livingstone: 'During his visit to England in 1857, the simple, large-hearted hero took England by storm, and when he announced his intention of inviting the Church of England, represented by her two oldest Universities, to plant a Mission in Central Africa, it is no wonder that Oxford and Cambridge responded to his call.'[4] By 1896 the Livingstone legend was well-established, and this comment is in character with the popular view of a great man, but it does less than justice to the evident truth of the matter.

Livingstone was introduced to the university by a missionary-minded curate, the Revd William Monk. The son of a Berkshire linen-draper, Monk was thirty-one years old, a member of St John's College and curate of Christ's Church, Cambridge. Because of the many conflicting accounts of the events connected with the visit, Monk felt obliged to give his own version:

I met Dr Livingstone in London, in May, 1857. On that occasion I asked him to come and lecture at Cambridge on Africa, promising to try and get the Senate-House, and hereby ensure him an audience of 2,000 persons, provided that he came during full term. In reply, he said that he could not come; that he had been to Oxford (which I did not before know) as well as other places, and that he should not lecture again before leaving the country. I represented to him the importance of influencing such an audience in behalf of Africa, especially when he considered the vast questions concomitant therewith. On these representations he consented to come, God willing, in November or December.

Early in the following November I revived the question by commencing a correspondence on the subject which extended to several letters on either side. In one letter Dr Livingstone's own words are; 'As it seems to be of great importance to get the young men of the Universities informed, and perhaps interested in Missions to the heathen, if I see my way clear, I shall try and come.' Hence results are not mere matters of accident or coincidence, but of design.[5]

If Monk's account, written three years after the events described, is accepted, then Livingstone's grudging acceptance of the invitation is at variance with the conventional portrait of the missionary. In view of the cordial relationship that existed between Monk and Livingstone there is no reason to suppose that Monk was trying to score points at the doctor's expense – but simply putting the record straight. Blaikie underlines the fact that by the autumn of 1857 Livingstone was heartily weary of all the 'public spouting' he had to undertake, and also testifies to the spurious accounts in circulation 'describing' Livingstone's African exploits.

The doctor arrived in Cambridge on Thursday 3 December and stayed the night with Monk and his wife at their Aubrey Villa home before addressing a large audience in the hastily-prepared Senate House the following morning. It is unlikely that Livingstone was intimidated either by his audience or his surroundings, beyond a natural diffidence about public speaking. He could boast as reputable an academic pedigree as anyone present, since Scotland had four 'ancient' universities of its own, the University of Glasgow where Livingstone had been a student having been granted its charter by a papal bull of Nicholas V in 1451.

The meeting, which was presided over by the vice-chancellor, Dr Philpott, was a resounding success; the welcome given to the missionary 'so enthusiastic that literally there were volley after volley of cheers'. Whatever his earlier feelings, Livingstone was delighted with his reception, confiding to a friend that it 'beat Oxford hollow', and it remained one of the happiest episodes of his life.

For Monk, too, the success of the visit was undoubted:

The cordial reception given by the University to such a man proves to the world at large that she is as ready as ever to recognize merit, advance science, encourage philanthropy, and promote religion. In this place of learning he has left a track behind him; and has sown seed which will, in the end, produce good fruits in Africa. He came here with the avowed purpose of striving to awaken a deeper interest in Christian Missions to the heathen; and spoke with the authority of the greatest of modern travellers, among men and in the place where a Missionary spirit ought pre-eminently to prevail.

The Senate-House scene was worthy of the most graphic painting which pen or pencil could portray. There was a solemn majesty about it which all present must have felt. It was an uncommon occasion. Cambridge elevation and culture came suddenly into contact with the mighty questions of African degradation and progress.'[6]

After the lecture, Monk's distinguished visitor was carried off to stay with more exalted company, dining that night in the Hall of Trinity College and sleeping at the Master's Lodge, before addressing a further meeting at the Town Hall the following day. He left Cambridge that same Saturday evening, 5 December.

In this commemorative volume it is both important and interesting to recall in its entirety what Dr Livingstone said in the concluding section of his Cambridge address:

A prospect is now before us of opening up Africa for commerce and the Gospel. Providence has been preparing the way, for even before I proceeded to the Central basin it had been conquered and rendered safe by a chief named Sebituane, and the language of the Bechuanas made the fashionable tongue, and that was one of the languages into which Mr Moffat had translated the Scriptures. Sebituane also discovered Lake Ngami some time previous to my explorations in that part. In going back to that country my object is to open up traffic along the banks of the Zambesi, and also to preach the Gospel. The natives of Central Africa are very desirous of trading, but their only traffic is at present in slaves, of which the poorer people have an unmitigated horror: it is therefore most desirable to encourage the former principle, and thus open a way for the consumption of free productions, and the introduction of Christianity and commerce. By encouraging the native propensity for trade, the advantages that might be derived in a commercial point of view are incalculable; nor should we lose sight of the in-estimable blessings it is in our power to bestow upon the

65

unenlightened African, by giving him the light of Christianity. Those two pioneers of civilization – Christianity and commerce – should ever be inseparable; and Englishmen should be warned by the fruits of neglecting that principle as exemplified in the result of the management of Indian affairs. By trading with Africa, also, we should at length be independent of slave-labour, and thus discountenance practices so obnoxious to every Englishman.

Though the natives are not absolutely anxious to receive the Gospel, they are open to Christian influences. Among the Bechuanas the Gospel was well received. These people think it a crime to shed a tear, but I have seen some of them weep at the recollection of their sins when God had opened their hearts to Christianity and repentance. It is true that missionaries have difficulties to encounter; but what great enterprise was ever accomplished without difficulty? It is deplorable to think that one of the noblest of our missionary societies, the Church Missionary Society, is compelled to send to Germany for missionaries, whilst other societies are amply supplied. Let this stain be wiped off. – The sort of men who are wanted for missionaries are such as I see before me; – men of education, standing, enterprise, zeal, and piety. It is a mistake to suppose that any one, as long as he is pious, will do for this office. Pioneers in every thing should be the ablest and best qualified men, not those of small ability and education. This remark especially applies to the first teachers of Christian truth in regions which may never have before been blest with the name and Gospel of Jesus Christ. In the early ages the monasteries were the schools of Europe, and the monks were not ashamed to hold the plough. The missionaries now take the place of those noble men, and we should not hesitate to give up the small luxuries of life in order to carry knowledge and truth to them that are in darkness. I hope that many of those whom I now address will embrace that honourable career. Education has been given us from above for the purpose of bringing to the benighted the knowledge of a Saviour. If you know the satisfaction of performing such a duty, as well as the gratitude to God which the missionary must always feel, in being chosen for so noble, so sacred a calling, you would have no hesitation in embracing it.

For my own part, I have never ceased to rejoice that God has appointed me to such an office. People talk of the sacrifice I have made in spending so much of my life in Africa. Can that be called a sacrifice which is simply paid back as a small part of a great debt owing to our God, which we can never repay? – Is that a sacrifice which brings its own blest reward in healthful activity, the consciousness of doing good, peace of mind, and a bright hope of a glorious destiny hereafter? – Away with the word in such a view, and with such a thought! It is emphatically no sacrifice.

Say rather it is a privilege. Anxiety, sickness, suffering, or danger, now and then, with a foregoing of the common conveniences and charities of this life, may make us pause, and cause the spirit to waver, and the soul to sink, but let this only be for a moment. All these are nothing when compared with the glory which shall hereafter be revealed in, and for, us. I never made a sacrifice. Of this we ought not to talk, when we remember the great sacrifice which He made who left His Father's throne on high to give Himself for us; – 'Who being the brightness of that Father's glory, and the express image of His person, and upholding all things by the word of His power, when He had by Himself purged our sins, sat down on the right hand of the majesty on high.'

English people are treated with respect; and the missionary can earn his living by his gun, – a course not open to a country curate. I would rather be a poor missionary than a poor curate.

Then there is the pleasant prospect of returning home and seeing the agreeable faces of his countrywomen again. I suppose I present a pretty contrast to you. At Cairo we met a party of young English people, whose faces were quite a contrast to the skinny, withered ones of those who had spent the latter years of their life in a tropical clime: they were the first rosy cheeks I had seen for sixteen years; you can hardly tell how pleasant it is to see the blooming cheeks of young ladies before me, after an absence of sixteen years from such delightful objects of contemplation. There is also the pleasure of the welcome home, and I heartily thank you for the welcome you have given me on the present occasion; but there is also the hope of the welcome words of our Lord, 'Well done, good and faithful servant.'

I beg to direct your attention to Africa; – I know that in a few years I shall be cut off in that country, which is now open; do not let it be shut again! I go back to Africa to try to make an open path for commerce and Christianity; do you carry out the work which I have begun. I *leave it with you*!

The visit was a great success, and the Senate House meeting an 'uncommon occasion', but what, apart from the general desire to awaken a deeper interest in Christian missions, prompted Livingstone to make this approach to the Church of England? There can be no single answer to that question, although in the mind of Miss Anderson-

Morshead, who compiled the first volume of the U.M.C.A. history, there was no doubt what it should be: 'That the working of our national Church should have so impressed this great man, who was not of her sons, was justly felt to be a testimony to the life and vigour of the Church of England.'

This view gains partial support from Professor Jack Simmons who has made the point that while the U.M.C.A. sprang from a denomination widely different than his own, Livingstone was the very opposite of a sectarian, and believed that the episcopal form of organisation was the most suitable for missionary work. Professor Simmons's comment is valid in regard to the 'working of our national Church', but it is doubtful whether Livingstone was particularly impressed by its 'life and vigour' at that time. Indeed, there is good reason to suppose that he felt that the Church of England was dragging its feet in the matter of missionary effort. This seems to be the force of his reluctant observation during the Senate House lecture in citing the Church Missionary Society's difficulty in recruiting Englishmen for work overseas. The same point was made by Monk who was in no doubt but 'that our national Church is much behind in missionary work'. Against this should be set the fact that in the twenty-five years 1832–57 so many new dioceses were created in various parts of the British Empire that the middle years of the nineteenth century were to be a time of considerable expansion.

But was this the only other consideration in the doctor's mind? By a strange paradox, Livingstone may have been attracted into the Anglican orbit through being too independent an Independent! In 1857 he was almost a Christian without a Church. The slight that Livingstone had suffered when it was hinted by the directors of the London Missionary Society that he was confusing the work of exploration with that of evangelism had led him to end the connection in order to save both the society and himself future embarrassment. As a Scotsman, he might have found a home in the Kirk, but for the fact that the Church of Scotland was only just recovering from a period of despondency and stagnation. This unhappy state of affairs was the result of the secession in 1843 of a considerable proportion of ministers and congregations to form the Free Church of Scotland. With them went much of the initiative and support for overseas mission work, and although no longer moribund, the disruption had left the 'Auld Kirk' largely preoccupied with domestic issues that were hardly likely to engage the interest of such a restless spirit as Livingstone.

A final factor may have been Livingstone's awareness that in creating interest amongst the academics of Oxford and Cambridge, he was stirring the Church of England and, in turn, wealthy and influential sectors of English society. He would have been astute enough to realise that support at Cambridge for his hopes for Central Africa would carry weight in the corridors of power. It remained to be seen what the response of these combined influences would be.

The Church of England has sometimes been described, unfairly, as 'the Tory Party at prayer'. Ignoring the jibe, the Church of England in the mid-nineteenth century could fairly be said to represent the wealth and influence of the Victorian establishment. Only a few years earlier the controversial test of religious opinions which had been conducted at the time of the 1851 General Census revealed that there were fifty-two Anglicans to forty-eight Christians of all other denominations in England and Wales. What the test did not reveal was from which sections of society the Church of England, credited with an attendance of 3,773,474 men, women and children, drew its support. Recent studies lend support to the view that, with the exception of rural areas, the established church was drawn mainly from the middle and upper classes. Bishop Tod Wickham is not the only Anglican to explode the myth of the national church being truly representative of the English people.[7]

The response

The response to Livingstone's invitation was not slow in making itself felt. Monk had taken advantage of the doctor's visit to introduce him to the activities of the Cambridge Church Missionary Union which had been formed among the junior members of the university, and was gratified to discover that Livingstone had belonged to a similar body during his student days at Glasgow. When the excitement of the visit had subsided, Monk set in hand the publication of the two Cambridge lectures, together with a considerable body of additional material of missionary interest, and a 'short' preface contributed by the Revd Professor Adam Sedgwick which accounted for ninety-three pages and effectively summarised *Missionary Travels and Researches*. With customary generosity Livingstone gave Monk the copyright of the lectures, and it was agreed between the two men that their publication should prepare the way for sending out a Cambridge Mission to Africa.

In March 1858 Monk took his leave of Dr and Mrs Livingstone, and they discussed ways and means of dispatching a mission to the Central African region. Monk's parting words to Livingstone were, 'Goodbye,

perhaps we – or you and other Cambridge men – may meet in Africa.'
Livingstone replied, 'God grant it.' And there the matter rested until
the following November.

The *Cambridge Lectures* did not achieve the success enjoyed by
Missionary Travels – in fact, a substantial loss was incurred – but the
book was favourably reviewed and quite widely read, and sustained
interest in Central Africa until some fresh stimulus should lead to more
definite support for the idea of a mission. The incentive came in the
person of a colonial bishop, Robert Gray of Cape Town, home on a
campaign of recruitment and support for the purpose of creating a
number of missions to the regions bordering the existing dioceses of
Cape Town, Grahamstown and Natal. In November 1858 Bishop
Gray visited Cambridge with this aim in mind, only to find support
for a mission further north in the area of Dr Livingstone's recent
travels and discoveries. With a generous gesture Gray gave the project
his backing and, after conferring with Monk, a Cambridge Committee
was formed. The Universities' Mission came into being with the first
meeting of the committee on 23 November 1858 when its promotion
was moved and an invitation issued to Oxford to share in the undertaking.

The cooperation of the sister university was readily promised, and
on Ash Wednesday 1859 the Oxford Committee was formed. In
May of that year at a public meeting held in the Sheldonian Theatre
presided over by Samuel Wilberforce, Bishop of Oxford, the two
committees adopted the name 'The Oxford and Cambridge Mission
to Central Africa', and it was agreed that a London committee, drawn
from members of both universities, be set up. So far as the actual field
of labour was concerned, the choice of a suitable area was to be left to
Dr Livingstone (subject to the sanction of the responsible metropolitan
authority).[8] The Home Committees were perhaps not readily mindful
of this early agreement when things started going awry.

The first year of activity was brought to a successful conclusion on
All Saints' Day, 1 November 1859, when, in the same place where
David Livingstone had stood two years before, and with the Vice-
Chancellor again in the chair, the 'Great Zambezi Meeting' received
the first year's report and made plans for the future. Prominent amongst
the speakers were Bishop Wilberforce, Sir George Grey (at that time
Governor of Cape Colony), and the Rt Hon. William Ewart Gladstone, M.P. During the meeting Adam Sedgwick took the opportunity
to pay a public tribute to William Monk's work:

The map now before you was constructed by Mr Monk, a

gentleman with whom rests the honour of having first introduced Dr Livingstone to this University – a gentleman, too, who has toiled as no other man has toiled, in the promotion of the objects of this meeting. Mr Monk's task may, in some respects, have been a humble one; but humble tasks must be performed, and without the performance of such tasks even the most powerful might fail.

One man, sitting in the gallery of the Senate House listening to the speeches and noting the rising tide of enthusiasm for the venture, turned to a companion and remarked, 'I am afraid of this: most great works of this kind have been carried on by one or two men in a quieter way, and have had a more humble beginning.' Whether this note of caution was no more than a comment on the fickleness of human nature which can so quickly turn from a mood of enthusiasm to one of disillusionment will never be known, but on the lips of Charles Frederick Mackenzie it has come to be interpreted as a premonition of misfortune and tragedy ahead.

At thirty-four years of age Mackenzie was back in Cambridge after an absence of nearly four and a half years as a missionary in South Africa. His presence in England at this time was difficult even for him to explain. Having been passed over for appointment as one of Robert Gray's missionary bishops he was at something of a loose end, and in Cambridge to fulfil a preaching engagement. Mackenzie had been given a copy of the *Cambridge Lectures* by a cousin six weeks earlier, but had no connection with the Senate House meeting which he attended as a spectator; a role that was soon terminated. After the meeting the committees met to discuss the critical question of who should lead the mission, and resolved: 'That the Ven. Charles Frederick Mackenzie, M.A., Fellow of Gonville and Caius College, Cambridge, Archdeacon of Pietermaritzburg (Natal), who is now in England, be invited to head the intended Mission.' The invitation was conveyed by Wilberforce and almost at once accepted by Mackenzie, who then assumed responsibility for finding the necessary money and men. As Charles Mackenzie took the centre of the stage, William Monk, like a latter-day John the Baptist, faded from the scene and after two further curacies, settled, in 1864, to life as a country parson in the Bedfordshire parish of Wymington where he remained for the next twenty years.

For such a crucial matter as the headship of the mission, it may be thought that the committees reached their decision with an almost indecent haste that was only matched by the readiness with which Mackenzie accepted. This becomes comprehensible when account is taken of the men who issued the invitation and the man who took it up. In the university circles to which Mackenzie had returned the attitude towards missions was ambivalent. A close interest in and ready support for the missionary work of the Church was balanced by some reluctance to work in the mission field itself. Before Mackenzie had gone out to Natal he had been approached by another Cambridge man about the possibility of founding a Cambridge mission in Delhi. After first agreeing to accompany him, Mackenzie withdrew, partly for family reasons and partly because he felt (and friends encouraged him in this belief) that he was needed in Cambridge. Only with the greatest difficulty could men of good education be found willing to offer for missionary work – a factor that doubtless exercised the minds of the promoters a good deal in that autumn of 1859. As for Mackenzie, his motive for offering to go, first to Delhi, then to Natal, and finally to Central Africa, was always the same: 'No one else will go, so I will.' It is a striking testimony to the nobility of Mackenzie's character; not that he minimised the risks that were involved by his acceptance. At the time of the invitation one of his friends, Dr Paget, gave it as his considered opinion that no insurance company would estimate his chance of life at more than two years. Mackenzie received this advice calmly, 'not treating it lightly, but as a subject which he had already well considered, and on which he had come to the same conclusion'. Such was the man chosen to lead the Universities' Mission.

Quite apart from the weighty problem of raising the necessary funds, which had been estimated at not less than £20,000 capital plus a guaranteed income of £2,000 for five years, there was the question of sending out a mission under a bishop to territory not subject to British control. It was a question which could not lightly be set aside in view of the special relationship between Church and State in England. With Gladstone committed to abolishing income tax which then stood at 9d in the £, the British government had no desire to become embroiled in a costly extra-colonial adventure in order to protect a handful of missionaries. There was also a further matter concerning the status that a missionary bishop would have in relation to his brother bishops and the Church at large. Under whose jurisdiction would he come? These constitutional problems were referred to the Convocation of Canterbury for decision, and occupied the first half of 1860. In the meantime, heartening news came from Livingstone of fresh discoveries and a promising area for the mission's work in the region of the Shire river and Lake Nyasa. Eventually, in June 1860 the way was cleared, and Bishop Wilberforce moved the motion in the Upper House: 'That the Bishop of Cape-town and his Comprovincials may be able to see fit to admit the head of this mission into the Episcopal order before he be sent forth to the heathen.'

Mackenzie sailed from Southampton on 4 October 1860 accompanied by his sister, Anne Mackenzie, the Revd Lovell Procter, the Revd Henry Scudamore, Horace Waller (the lay superintendent), and two artisans, Samuel Gamble and Alfred Adams. The party arrived at Cape Town in mid-November, and an enforced stay of several weeks became necessary while Mackenzie waited for the arrival of the South African bishops who were to take part in his consecration. There, on 1 January 1861 (despite government disapproval), the first missionary bishop of the Church of England in modern times was consecrated in St George's Cathedral, and made his oath of canonical obedience to Robert Gray in the following form: 'In the name of God, Amen. I, Charles Frederick Mackenzie, chosen Bishop of the Mission to the tribes dwelling in the neighbourhood of the Lake Nyassa and River Shire, do profess and promise all due reverence and obedience to the Metropolitan Bishop and Metropolitical Church of Cape Town, and to their successors. So help me God, through Jesus Christ.' A week later, Mackenzie and members of his party boarded the cruiser *Lyra* for the passage to the Zambezi mouth where they had arranged to meet Dr Livingstone, who had come down to take delivery of the new Admiralty steamer *Pioneer*. This vessel replaced the asthmatic *Ma-Robert* which had gone to its watery grave two months earlier. The first meeting was not encouraging.

Mackenzie intended to transfer to the *Pioneer* and proceed up the Zambezi and Shire with Livingstone until they reached the area where they were to prospect for a settlement, but when the two men met for the first time on 9 February he was disconcerted to learn that Livingstone had abandoned this plan and proposed, instead, to approach the lake by following the course of the Ruvuma river which flowed into the Indian Ocean, 450 miles further north. While Livingstone defended this change of plan on the grounds that the mission would be left without medical aid in an unhealthy area at an unhealthy time of year with no means of getting assistance, Dr Blaikie adds that he was also influenced by the 'many obstacles' placed in his way by the Portuguese which entry along the Ruvuma would remove. For two days the bishop begged the doctor to reconsider his decision, but in the end Mackenzie was obliged to give way, since Livingstone had the means and (it was supposed) the better judgement to enforce his decision. Such an unpromising start might have damaged permanently the relationship between the two men; in fact, the reverse was the case, and they came to have a very warm regard for each other. Even after this early setback to his plans Mackenzie could write of Livingstone 'He is an excellent fellow, and I have no fear of any difficulty at any time arising between us.' The same sentiments were put in more succinct form by Livingstone in a letter to his friend, Thomas Maclear, 'The Bishop is A I.'

The attempt to ascend the Ruvuma was fruitless and Livingstone was forced to revert to the original plan, having lost three months and, in consequence, the best part of the season. The passage up the Shire began on 16 May and was confidently expected to take no more than three weeks, but it was nearly two months before they reached Chibisa's where the mission planned to disembark. The journey was punctuated by frequent 'sticks' when the *Pioneer* ran aground and had to be hauled off. Yet if the delay was trying and laborious for the missionaries, it served to confirm Livingstone's liking for Mackenzie: 'On these occasions the Bishop, Mr Scudamore, and Mr Waller, the best and bravest of the Missionary party, were ever ready with their help in hauling.' He was sometimes scandalised to see the bishop toiling in the hot sun, while some of his subordinates were reading or writing in the cabin. At length, on 8 July, Chibisa's was reached, the mission disembarked, its stores were unloaded, and all eyes were turned towards the highlands where the mission was to settle.

The Outcome

The outcome was a disaster, compounded of misjudgement, circumstance and ill-luck, which revolved around four main issues: the militancy of the mission; the decision to settle at Magomero; the failure of the mission to impart any substantial Christian teaching; Mackenzie's ability as a leader.

On 15 July the missionaries, accompanied by Livingstone and his men, set off for the highlands. They soon encountered the slave trade, and during the course of the four-day march they released three parties of slaves after driving off their captors. Although the first encounter, at Mbami's village, was on Livingstone's orders (Mackenzie was bathing in a nearby stream at the time), it had the effect of reversing the policy of the mission respecting the use of force. The bishop had already established with his staff the principle of non-violence (even in self-defence), yet now found himself having to abandon their agreed policy. In their new situation self-defence was not the point at issue, but rather the oppression of the weak by the strong, and this was something they felt bound to resist. The other result of this early

74

hostility was the presentation of nearly one hundred liberated slaves to the bishop as his first flock.

Mackenzie seems to have been led by Livingstone again in the decision to settle at Magomero even though it was twice as far from Chibisa's as he thought prudent and located in a low-lying area that might prove to be unhealthy. In a letter to Mackenzie's friend, Harvey Goodwin, Horace Waller recalled the argument put by Livingstone to the bishop and himself, 'If you fall back to Mount Soche, all this densely populated country will go before the Ajawas: if you take your stand here it will be saved.' Strange advice for a consul to give a bishop, but as Waller concluded, 'Those who knew Bishop Mackenzie . . . can imagine what his decision would be.' Even so, if Mackenzie let his heart rule his head, he had the support of his staff.

Having settled the missionaries, Livingstone set off on his own business with a final word about their Mang'anja neighbours: 'You will be oppressed by their importunities, but do not interfere in native quarrels.' This was easier said than done, and in the ensuing months the missionaries found themselves sallying forth with the Mang'anja to repulse Yao raiding parties in a series of engagements which Mackenzie called 'The Ajawa Wars'. The attempts made later to shift the blame from one to the other are not convincing, and it is difficult to avoid the conclusion that Livingstone and Mackenzie were equally at fault, in so far as the bishop's position was compromised by the first hostilities, and yet he did not retreat from that position when he was responsible for the decision-making at a later stage. Lovell Procter admitted later that they 'had made a mistake in becoming the warriors instead of the teachers of the Mang'anja'.

Towards the end of 1861, with the onset of the rainy season and a growing scarcity of food, the perilous isolation of Magomero became clear, with sixty miles of hilly country between them and the river which was their contact with the outside world. Mackenzie, accompanied by a new recruit, Henry Burrup, now set out to make that journey in order to meet his sister who was to be brought up to Chibisa's by Livingstone. A fruitless attempt to find a more direct route to the lower Shire lost him valuable time, and he missed the *Pioneer* by a few days on its downward passage. The delay was to cost him his life, for he decided to sit it out and wait for the steamer to make its return trip. He and Burrup made their way to Malo island where the Ruo river flows into the Shire. Deprived of their medicines which had been lost overboard in a canoe upset, the two men succumbed rapidly to the effect of fever and dysentery, and after 'sitting it out' for three weeks Charles Frederick Mackenzie died on Friday

75

31 January 1862 at about five o'clock in the evening. At the time he was preparing to leave England for Natal, Mackenzie likened a man's going from home to 'a branch being cut from a tree to be planted somewhere else'. It was not clear that January evening whether the simile was more appropriate to the act of pruning than one of propagation.

When news of Mackenzie's death reached the Cape, Bishop Gray hurried to England to confer with the Home Committee about the appointment of a successor. From the names submitted they selected William George Tozer, the thirty-three-year-old rector of Burgh-cum-Winthorpe in Lincolnshire. After his consecration in Westminster Abbey in February 1863 the new bishop sailed for Africa with two neighbouring incumbents, Edward Steere and Charles Alington, and some artisans. In many ways Tozer was the complete opposite of Mackenzie, being forceful where Mackenzie was indecisive, and hard-headed where his predecessor was impulsive. It was perhaps inevitable that comparisons would be drawn between the two men – indeed, it had already begun before Tozer even reached the Shire! Arch-deacon Thomas of Rondebosch took it upon himself to acquaint Bishop Jackson of Lincoln shortly after Tozer's arrival at the Cape with the following intelligence:

> The general feeling I think here is that, with the exception of Mackenzie himself, this batch is far superior to the first party. There is more *head* and power of acting in emergencies; in *this* respect they are much beyond M. who seems to have leant on others too much to be in this way a leader. The differences of the three are most amusing. Tozer is the peace member, Steere the war-like, Alington does not say much.[9]

It is clear that the Victorian cleric enjoyed his piece of juicy gossip as well as the next man, and suggests that the characters devised by Anthony Trollope were not overdrawn.

It remained to be seen what Tozer and Livingstone would make of each other. Tozer's attitude was quite promising at the outset: on the way to the Zambezi he wrote, 'It is a comfort to think that we shall have Dr Livingstone to consult, and I shall be largely guided by his advice.' He qualified this by adding that should the need arise he would not hesitate to move the mission to a quieter and more healthy site. But when Tozer did arrive at Chibisa's his first thoughts were not of Livingstone. He was dismayed to find that the work of the mission had become 'merely a struggle to survive and nothing more'. This reaction was understandable. Further deaths amongst the missionaries had forced their withdrawal from Magomero in April the previous year in order to shorten their lines of communication. The remnant that greeted Bishop Tozer at Chibisa's confirmed his increasing conviction that the whole scheme had been too hastily planned, and the first settlement made with insufficient knowledge of the country. Tozer was also scandalised by how little active mission work had been undertaken, and showed little sympathy for Mackenzie's view that evangelism must wait upon mastery of the language. This episcopal disapproval could not long remain disguised from the survivors who in their exchanges with Tozer detected the half-hidden rebukes and veiled criticisms of what they had done or failed to do. As Tozer totted up the losses incurred by the mission and discovered their extent, his initial warmth towards Livingstone began to cool, and their relationship became even more strained when he announced his intention of withdrawing the mission to Mount Morambala, more than a hundred miles below Chibisa's, and well inside Portuguese territory.

The survivors pressed for a further attempt to be made at Mbami's, only twenty miles from Chibisa's on the way to Magomero, but Tozer was the bishop and marshalled his arguments with such force that it was difficult even for Livingstone to object to the move, much as he deplored it: 'It would have been no more than fair that Bishop Tozer, before winding up the affairs of the Mission should actually have examined the highlands of the Upper Shire; he would have thus gratified the associates of his predecessor, who believed that the highlands had never had a fair trial.'[10]

Tozer was confident that Morambala would prove to be the true 'door' to Central Africa; but even Tozer could be wrong, and finding that it was 'no place for a Church of England Mission', he decided to withdraw from the Shire altogether. That decision was the parting of the ways – not only for Tozer and Livingstone, but also for the survivors of the original mission, none of whom accompanied the bishop after he left the Shire. The reason is not difficult to apprehend. They had been recruited by Charles Mackenzie and found their new bishop out of sympathy with their point of view, and that of the man they had followed to Central Africa. Had they gone on with Tozer, Mackenzie's ghost would have gone with them as a disturbing and divisive influence.

Tozer took himself off to the Cape in the early part of 1864 to take stock of the situation and consider his next move. Various possibilities were open to the mission: Madagascar, Johanna Island (in the Comoro group), Zanzibar, Natal and South-West Africa. Of these, Zanzibar seemed the most promising for any future attempt to re-settle the mission in the Nyasa region. It was while Tozer was making this appraisal, and reviewing the reasons for the mission's failure, that he became openly critical of its 'indiscriminating reliance' upon Livingstone. In his anxiety to avoid making the same mistakes Tozer offered to accompany Burton or Speke on their next East African expedition to prospect for a new mission area, but any hope of embarking on such a trip was terminated by Speke's death a few months later on the eve of his 'Nile Duel' with Burton.

In the event, Tozer decided to re-establish the mission at Zanzibar which offered excellent communications with the Cape and India, and a reassuring 'British presence' in Lt Col. Playfair, the Consul. The Bishop and Edward Steere sailed from Cape Town on 28 July 1864 and stepped ashore at Zanzibar one month later. Three weeks after their arrival the Sultan presented them with five boys rescued from a slave dhow, and, just as Livingstone's action three years earlier had determined the character of the first settlement, so now, the Sultan's gesture had the effect of dictating the subsequent development of the mission in its new home. It also marked the final break with all that had gone before, committing the bishop and his much-reduced staff to a limited but definite objective: 'The work of this house will be the training of boys for the ministry and some girls as suitable wives for them (at least I hope to see our way to this, so as to make the scheme more complete).'[11]

Bishop Tozer's action left unanswered the question whether he was right to leave the Shire. The later history of the Universities' Mission would appear to vindicate Tozer, but Livingstone (understandably) did not:

> Though representing all that is brave and good and manly, in the chief seats of English learning, the Mission, in fleeing from Morambala to an island in the Indian Ocean, acted as St Augustine would have done, had he located himself on one of the Channel Islands, when sent to christianize the natives of Central England. This is, we believe, the first case of a Protestant Mission having been abandoned without being driven away.

Livingstone overlooked or ignored the fact that Augustine's courage failed him before he reached England, causing him to return to Rome where Gregory the Great exhorted him to continue with his mission. A further parallel with Augustine (although unintentioned) becomes interesting when it is remembered that Pope Gregory devoted part of

78

the papal revenue to buying up English slave-boys in order to give them a Christian education, before sending them as missionaries to their native land. Tozer had a similar purpose, and recorded in August 1865 the baptism of nine boys, four of whom were Yao, and one a Nyasa. In the following year he had his final contact with Livingstone who was at Zanzibar prior to setting out on his last journey, 'Livingstone is still here, but I see very little of him.' It was a matter of some embarrassment to both men when they were obliged to meet and appear civil on formal occasions.

Tozer remained at Zanzibar for a further six years, and his last days were, if anything, more terrible than those of Mackenzie as the following words written at the time of his death make plain:

> In 1872, the strain of the work, intensified by the cholera and a terrible hurricane, ended in . . . the breaking-up of Bishop Tozer's health. The Bishop became so ill that he could not even sign his name, and in 1873 he had to resign the see. He has been practically a broken-down man ever since. He attempted Bishop's work again at Jamaica and at Honduras, but in each case was hardly able to hold on for more than a year. Thus, after his final return to England, even the charge of a parish (South Ferriby, in Lincolnshire) proved too much for him.'[12]

For ten years after his final retirement Tozer battled with ill-health, living in various lodgings with his Bible and a few books for company. A number of seizures robbed him of speech and his remaining strength, until death came as a merciful release in 1899 in his seventieth year.

Any man who could command the affections of three such outstanding Victorians as David Livingstone, Charles Gordon, and Frederick Lugard deserves attention. Such a man was Horace Waller. He was born in London in 1833, the son of a stockbroker, and was educated privately under a Dr Wadham at Brook Green. He followed his father into business, and this experience qualified him for appointment as lay superintendent of the first Mission led by Bishop Mackenzie. Waller was not ordained until some years after he had returned from Central Africa, nevertheless, his education and business background marked him off as a gentleman rather than an artisan. He created a most favourable impression on Bishop Gray's household when the mission party were guests at Bishopscourt awaiting passage to the Zambezi, 'Mr Waller is here, going to town every day to make purchases. I can't describe him more truly or honourably than the Bishop does: "He is a Christian gentleman." You can't talk to him for a quarter of an hour without finding out what a noble fellow he is.'

Waller displays all the signs of having been more actively committed to the objects of the mission than any except Mackenzie himself, who found in his lay superintendent a staunch ally and friend. His immediate duties were to superintend the considerable quantity of stores and supplies that had been purchased by the mission in England and at the Cape, and supervise the artisans and the building programme at Magomero. Waller was much more adaptable to the strenuous conditions under which the mission lived, and, like Livingstone, sometimes found it difficult to sympathise with the outlook of those who found mission life irksome and laborious. This liking for the open-air life, added to his own temperament, won for Waller the early approval of Livingstone who observed that he and Scudamore had 'no nonsense about them'. If Livingstone conceived an early liking for Waller, he gained in Horace Waller a loyal and sometimes uncritical admirer and life-long friend. As one of the youngest of the party (though not a youngster) he was perhaps more impressionable and more ready to give himself to the cause for which he had been recruited. Yet if this was the case, it was a trait that remained with him for the rest of his life.

In all important matters Waller supported his bishop, and defended Mackenzie even when he questioned his judgement – as in a dispute over having ladies at Magomero. Like Mackenzie, he was inclined to be impulsive, and this may explain why the two men got on so well together.

While Mackenzie remained in relaxed control of the mission's affairs Waller went about his duties cheerfully, but Bishop Tozer's arrival came as a rude awakening and he soon found himself at odds with his superior. To begin with, there was the matter of his stewardship of the mission's stores which, in naval parlance, were 'on his slop-chit'. Any suggestion that he had been incompetent or irresponsible was hardly likely to make for a good relationship between them, yet reports were soon being sent to England which reflected upon his efficiency as a quartermaster: 'The account of their stores and their mode of distribution made one suspect a reckless wastefulness quite appalling.'[13] In fairness to Waller, he had to discharge his storekeeping and accounting duties in quite impossible circumstances, being responsible for mission goods that had been abandoned on Johanna Island, or left unattended at the Kongone entrance, without the means to secure their possession. Any failure, therefore, on the part of Waller in this respect must be judged part of the overall failure of the mission in logistics.

However, loss of stores and prodigality of store-keeping was not the issue that finally divided Waller and Tozer, even if the bishop had a poor opinion of the 'lay element' in the mission, regarding artisans (and, no doubt, lay superintendents) as an ill-advised and unnecessary encumbrance. The bitter feeling between them concerned the welfare of the liberated slaves who had come under the mission's protection during their sojourn at Magomero and Chibisa's. Waller was convinced that they had a continuing responsibility towards these people which any decision to withdraw downstream, or ultimately out of the area, could not change. Tozer was equally adamant that he was not bound by such a responsibility and refused to allow any of the mission's female dependants to accompany them to Morambala, taking only twenty-five boys who he believed were teachable. Horace Waller insisted on taking the women and young girls along, but in order to do so was obliged to resign from the mission since he was acting in defiance of Tozer's orders. For three months two separate parties camped on Mount Morambala, Tozer testing its suitability as a mission station, while Waller waited for Livingstone to escort his charges out of the country.

When Tozer decided to vacate Morambala his anxiety concerning the boys' future was solved by Livingstone who asked 'in rather peremptory terms' that they be handed back to him. Horace Waller made his way to the Cape on the *Pioneer* with the remnant of Mackenzie's flock and settled them there. This final act earned him the further praise of Livingstone who remarked, 'he continued his generous services to all connected with the Mission, whether white or black, till they were no longer needed; his conduct to them throughout was truly noble, and worthy of the highest praise.' Bishop Gray's estimate of Waller as a Christian gentleman was not misplaced.

Conclusion

This chapter has explored the relationship between David Livingstone and the Church of England by examining his contact with four of its accredited ministers. It is now time to assess the importance of that contact for the Anglican Church and for Livingstone himself.

William Monk has a strong claim to being prime mover in a process that stirred the Church of England to greater missionary effort through the creation of the Universities' Mission. If the acknowledgement that he was given in the official history of that mission could have been more generous, it is because he was overshadowed by men more prominent in the Church of his day. It was Monk's willingness to do the essential ground-work that gave meaning and purpose to their later patronage and support. In many ways, Monk personifies the churchman of the mid-nineteenth century – zealous and sincere in missionary interest, yet rather out of touch with the realities of the mission situation, and therefore over-optimistic about its results. 'In all probability about two years more will solve the grand Central African problem,' he wrote in 1860. How far this abundant optimism was the consequence of David Livingstone's writings and speeches is debatable.

Charles Frederick Mackenzie was chosen by the Home Committee because, at a time when the Church of England was hard-pressed to find men of the right quality, he seemed from his previous missionary experience to be the best-fitted for the work they had in mind. What neither they nor Mackenzie appreciated was that he would be exposed to situations and circumstances upon which the Church had formulated no clear policy. In New Zealand, Bishop Selwyn was working within the orbit of British influence, and in South Africa the same was true, though perhaps to a lesser extent. But in the unsettled conditions that prevailed in the central Africa of the 1860s there was no lawful authority that might be appealed to, and no colonial umbrella under which to shelter. Mackenzie was not asked to take up arms in defence of his own life (of which he was careless), but in order to protect the poor unfortunates who had stumbled into his care. Dr Pusey was right when he described this policy as 'a mistake', but to suggest that the bishop had used force in order to avoid suffering: 'The Gospel has always been planted, not by doing, but by suffering' was as unfair as it was inaccurate. The point at issue was not the safety of Mackenzie or his staff, but that of the people who appealed to him for help. We do not know what action the Good Samaritan would have taken if he had come upon the thieves while they were assaulting their victim. Of Mackenzie it can be said that with something of the romanticism that animated the Tractarian Movement he felt called upon to offer himself, going where others would not. In the end, he was found wanting – not in courage or self-sacrifice, but in caution and care. To those who remembered him as the Bishop of Magomero he was (in up-dated Chichewa) 'munthu wokoma mtima' – a man of a sweet heart.

William George Tozer's lot was not a happy one. He was sent out to pick up the pieces, to retrieve the mission from the predicament into which it had fallen. Furthermore, he had to follow a man who, whatever his shortcomings as a leader may have been, was already being revered as a martyr. Tozer was a man under pressure, with clear orders from England to keep the mission out of further trouble and reduce its crippling losses. None of those involved in the Central African enterprise had taken sufficient account of how much it would cost to plant the mission in a new area, and yet this was a recurrent feature of pioneer settlements from the time of Raleigh to the more recent experience in South Australia and New Zealand. In seeking reasons for the mission's failure it was left to Tozer to point out that by its close association with Livingstone's expedition it had confused the people it had been sent to evangelise, who assumed that it had some political purpose. The mission's militancy only confirmed this misunderstanding. Tozer was also quick to realise the fatal mistake in having such poor communications. When the remedy was applied it was already too late, and Tozer found himself obliged (in the face of popular opinion) to cut the mission's losses and make the move to Zanzibar in order to give it a second chance to achieve the original objective. Tozer was right.

Horace Waller returned to England in 1864, and was ordained three years later. After a curacy at Chatham, and four years as Vicar of Leytonstone in Essex, Waller moved to the rectory of Twywell in Northamptonshire in 1874 where he remained until his retirement in 1895.

Of the four Anglicans with whom Livingstone had direct contact in the early days of the mission, Waller is in many ways the most interesting and, after Monk, the least known. From the time he returned to England until his death in 1896 he devoted himself to championing those causes with which Livingstone was associated. The breach with the mission was healed and he became a valued member of the London Committee, but he made his most important contribution in the anti-slavery lobby. As a member of the British and Foreign Anti-Slavery Society he used his influence to secure the appointment of his Zambezi associate John Kirk as political agent at Zanzibar in 1871. Kirk's appointment paved the way for the agreement of 1873 between the Sultan and Great Britain which led to the prohibition of the trade and the closure of the Zanzibar slave market.

From his Twywell rectory Waller maintained an interest in all things African, and it was here that Charles Gordon would visit and pour out to his friend 'the abundance of his memory and thought'. In his later years, the retired missionary gave his friendship to the young Lugard, proof-reading *The Rise of Our East African Empire*. Beyond these personal attachments, Waller took a keen interest in the affairs of the Royal Geographical Society of which he was a Fellow, and wrote a number of books on African topics, remaining until the day of his death, 'a friend of Africa'.

Finally, what of Livingstone? Towards the end of *Missionary Travels* he wrote that the end of the geographical feat marked the beginning of the missionary enterprise. During his travels across the African continent he had repeatedly taken his life in his hands and had never been, prior to the Zambezi expedition, in a position to challenge the slave trade.

When the Universities' Mission entered upon its work this factor came into play, and led to the two mistakes that were to have fatal consequences. Livingstone was not prepared to admit that his prior use of force, and his strong recommendation that the mission settle at Magomero contributed to its eventual withdrawal from the Shire. He was never able to regard the continuing work at Zanzibar under Bishop Tozer (in his view a deserter) as part of the original enterprise which he had helped to launch.

To understand Livingstone's bitterness it is necessary to realise the keen disappointment he felt; in his darkest moments it must have seemed to him that the Church of England had wanted a success story, but had been unwilling to pay the price. That this was patently not the case was shown in the later history of the Universities' Mission – more than 150 of whose members died 'on active service'. To that mission he bequeathed what mattered most in the end – his own example, summed up by Adam Sedgwick: 'He taught . . . Africans to love him and to trust him, because he treated them with confidence and love. He visited them in their wants; he healed them in their sickness; he taught them the first simple lessons of Christian truth.'

Notes

In the preparation of this chapter I have made frequent use of the Malawi National Archives, and would like to record my appreciation of the unfailing assistance and courtesy of the Director and his staff.

Thanks are also due to the Revd Robert Hardy, Chaplain of Selwyn College, Cambridge who supplied information about William Monk, and to Mr Bernard Palmer, Editor of the *Church Times*, who provided copies of the obituary notices of Horace Waller and Bishop Tozer carried in that paper.

To Messrs Deighton, Bell and Company of Cambridge special thanks are due for permission to reproduce the final section of Dr Livingstone's Senate House lecture.

This essay has been written during odd moments in a busy life, and I have leaned heavily on printed sources. Anyone familiar with this period of U.M.C.A. history will recognise my indebtedness to Professor Owen Chadwick's lively study of the mission in *Mackenzie's Grave* (London, 1959). Anyone seeking a detailed account of that episode of missionary history cannot do better than consult Dr Chadwick's work.

1 The term 'Church of England' has been preferred to 'Anglican Church' which did not come into popular currency until later in the nineteenth century when, largely as a result of the first Lambeth Conference in 1867, the Church of England awoke to the fact that it had become part of a world-wide Anglican Communion. As this essay has shown, one of the central problems arising from the decision to send a mission to central Africa was its 'Englishness' which posed some diplomatic questions for the British government of the day.

2 E. M. Goulburn, *Life of Dean Burgon*, London, 1892, p. 283. Quoted by Dr A. R. Vidler in *The Church in an Age of Revolution*.

3 W. G. Addison, *Religious Equality in Modern England*, London, 1944, p. 141.

4 A. E. M. Anderson-Morshead, *The History of the Universities' Mission to Central Africa*, London, 1897, pp. 3–4.

5 William Monk, *Dr Livingstone's Cambridge Lectures*, Cambridge, first edition 1858, second edition 1860, pp. 326–7.

6 Ibid., p. 2.

7 'The class in our society which is dominant in industrial power, and overwhelmingly superior in numbers to any other, has so far shown itself to be quite untouched by anything which the Church has tried to do to win it.' Canon Roger Lloyd, *The Church and the Artisan Today*.

8 Morshead, op. cit., p. 5. 'The field for the Mission was left entirely to the choice of Livingstone.'

9 Gertrude Ward (ed.), *Letters of Bishop Tozer*, London, 1902, p. 295.

10 David and Charles Livingstone, *Narrative of an Expedition to the Zambesi and its Tributaries; and of the discovery of Lakes Shirwa and Nyassa, 1858–1864*, London, 1865, p. 573.

11 Ward, op. cit., p. 88.

12 The *Church Times*, 30 June 1899.

13 Ward, op. cit., p. 298. A letter of Edward Steere to Bishop Jackson.

4 James Stewart and David Livingstone

Sheila Brock

The random collection of Europeans on or near the Zambezi river in the years 1858–1863 displayed those characteristics normally considered the essential ingredients for any writer of fiction wishing to probe the psychological interplay of personalities uprooted from their accustomed surroundings and placed in an alien environment. The backcloth of the 'Dark Continent' threw into relief the characters of the protagonists, and exposed strengths and weaknesses no longer absorbed by cultural acceptability. H. A. C. Cairns in *Prelude to Imperialism* gives many telling examples of the way in which loneliness and isolation, fear and fever affected early explorers and missionaries in central Africa. Response varied according to the individual but none remained uninfluenced by these and other factors which sapped health and subjected integrity to severe strain.

Of all the men who made the journey to the interior at this time and who recorded their endeavours, experiences and emotions in private journals, James Stewart, it could be and has been claimed, responded most negatively and most neurotically to the challenge of the circumstances. In most books concerning Livingstone and the Zambezi expedition, especially those written after the publication in 1952 of Stewart's *Zambesi Journal*,[1] Stewart is portrayed as a 'humourless, introspective Scot', 'a moody, difficult, solitary morose young man', 'paranoiac', 'egocentric', 'a professional Presbyterian pessimist'.[2] These epithets derive, with some justice, from Stewart's self-portrait in his journal to which he confided all his loneliness and self-pity, his feelings of persecution, his disgust with the society in which he found himself (both white and black), his despair, his disappointment and, occasionally, in pathetic counterpoint, his determination to be more cheerful, his resolution to be more charitable. Even if it is emphasised, in his defence, that Stewart suffered more from intrigue, lies, calumny, hostility and, therefore, utter loneliness than any other man connected with Livingstone in this period it could still be maintained that he was out of place in Africa, that he could not stand the rigours of the psychological demands and thus it would scarcely have been surprising if he had succumbed to the pressures of friends to abandon thoughts of mission work and to devote himself to the parish ministry. Yet it is this same man who has been described, often by the same authors, as 'one of the great servants of Africa', as standing 'second only to Livingstone in his service to Africa', as 'one of the best friends and noblest workers for African regeneration . . . a strong man . . . with his whole heart in the cause of Africa'.[3] Whether or not these opinions are justified, any discussion of the relationship between David Livingstone and James Stewart inevitably raises the question of how it was that this man, so disillusioned with Livingstone, so physically and mentally sickened by his experiences on the Zambezi should, only a decade later, put all his energy, vigour and enthusiasm into promoting a scheme for a mission commemorating Livingstone, and should volunteer to head the advance party to Lake Nyasa. The answer to this lies not so much in a mellowing of Stewart's attitude to Livingstone, nor in a rebirth of resolve under the emotional impetus of Livingstone's death but in Stewart's enormous ambition which would not allow him to concede personal failure. He may have wished, in a histrionic moment, never to see Livingstone again but that did not mean that he had abandoned the idea of emulating Livingstone's achievements in central Africa nor, more significantly, of improving upon them.

The reading of Livingstone's book *Missionary Travels and Researches*, an exercise which 'not only modified my life but considerably influenced the lives of others', enabled Stewart to focus his previously vague desire to 'go abroad' upon Africa. He became convinced that 'if these recent discoveries were not utilised by missionary effort and the introduction of Christianity the opening of these regions would be productive of evil rather than of good to the unfortunate inhabitants.'[4] He was not, however, concerned merely with the establishment of evangelical forcing-grounds. Stewart was particularly impressed by Livingstone's description of the commercial possibilities of the area, by his assertion that the introduction of agriculture, cotton-growing and industry to Africa would divert the energy of Africans from the slave traffic and that as their material needs grew so would their desire for education and so on, in a never-ending spiral of increasing civilisation. The mission Stewart proposed, therefore, was intended to have evangelical, industrial and educational arms and to be staffed by trained missionary teachers and artisans.[5]

For the history of Scottish missionary activity in Africa, Stewart's efforts to organise his expedition were of greater significance than the journey itself. His overtures to the Foreign Mission Committee of the Free Church of Scotland met with a cool response. 'Good words in abundance but promises of assistance there were none.'[6] In October 1850, however, Stewart had a personal interview with Dr Candlish, Convener of the F.M.C., who was so far interested as to suggest that a letter should be sent to Livingstone seeking his opinion and advice. This letter would be sent out under Stewart's name so that the Committee, in agreeing to this, would be in no way committed, whatever the doctor's reply.[7]

The reluctant goodwill of the F.M.C. was scarcely sufficient for Stewart's purpose and without any financial backing he was faced with either the abandonment of the project or the necessity of looking elsewhere for funds and support. The result was the establishment of the New Central African Mission Committee, formed for the stated purpose of 'turning the discoveries of Dr Livingstone to practical account for the great ends of the gospel'[8] and comprising many important men, influential in commerce, church, education and local politics. For Stewart it was a critical venture bringing him into contact, for the first time, with men of means and of wide-ranging interests. He learned to talk their language and they in turn came to respect his judgement and were prepared to underwrite his enterprises. His fund-raising ability and his flair for organisation were to be used again and again, particularly with regard to Livingstonia and Lovedale.[9] The Free Church gave these missions her blessing, publicised their activities and took credit for their achievements but the financial power derived, not from Scottish congregations, but from the bank balances, business acumen and sensitive consciences of shrewd Protestant investors.

It was, therefore, largely due to his own initiative that Stewart had the means to go to Africa in 1861. In the end, he went without any official status and with inadequate resources, facts which were to weigh heavily with him in future months. Much has been made of Stewart's hero-worship of Livingstone as a motivating factor in this enterprise and yet there is scant mention of Livingstone in the copious correspondence preceding the establishment of the new Committee. Obviously Stewart admired Livingstone and was, at this stage, without having met him, impressed by what he had done, but he saw Livingstone as a means to an end. He even considered writing to Livingstone, recom-

David Livingstone and his daughter Anna Mary, 1864

H. M. Stanley

Livingstone's instrument case

mending that he should settle for a few years, 'to gain moral rather than geographical laurels', by watching over the two missions, examining the neighbouring country and rivers, doing all that could be done in the way of developing trade and arranging amicable relations with the neighbouring tribes.[10] His eventual disillusionment with Livingstone was based not on the breakdown of some sentimental daydream but on the realisation that Livingstone was too disorganised, too independent, too unrealistic for Stewart to be able to use him to further his own aims and ambitions. In a letter to a friend, encouraging him to join in this venture, Stewart gave an indication of his own purpose: 'I am going to Africa . . . my resolution is fixed. It can . . . but make us wellknown as fellows of missionary enterprise at least, as fellows of indomitable pluck and courage perhaps.'[11]

It is not known if Stewart regarded it as a stroke of good fortune that Mrs Livingstone should have asked to travel with him to the Zambezi. Given that even at this early date he was uncertain about his prospects and his standing with Livingstone *vis à vis* the Universities' Mission to Central Africa,[12] it must have occurred to him that should she find him a pleasant and discreet companion his chances of being acceptable to Livingstone were greatly increased. He must have had cause to consider later, however, that such benefits as accrued had been more than offset by the scandal and gossip that resulted from their having been so much in one another's company. The nature of the relationship between Stewart and Mary Livingstone has been the subject of much excited conjecture both by their contemporary observers and by modern writers. John Kirk's conclusion (arrived at only after he had been 'taken in' by the rumours) that, 'all the evil gossip which had passed regarding him [Stewart], had arisen out of a want of discretion,'[13] must still stand; there is no evidence that the travellers transgressed the strictly-fenced areas of Victorian propriety, despite an early coyness in their relationship. Stewart, according to Kirk, later maintained that he had discovered that Mary Livingstone drank too heavily and that he could not, from then on, absolve his own character without seriously injuring hers.[14] The extent of the affair is of less importance, however, than the effect which speculation and gossip had on Stewart, on the members of the expedition and on Stewart's relationship with David Livingstone.

It was with a genuine feeling of incredulity that Stewart heard in Cape Town of the interpretations that were being put upon his friendship with Mrs Livingstone.[15] The rumours which had been started in Scotland, presumably by 'maudlin ladies who insinuate, when a man leaves his family frequently . . . that he is not happy at home'[16] had been given an added flavour of possibility when Mary Livingstone elected to travel with the young and handsome Mr Stewart. Already in Cape Town when they arrived was George Rae, Livingstone's engineer, who in 1860 had been sent home to Scotland by Livingstone to supervise the construction of engines for a small river steamer, intended for use on Lake Nyasa. Rae's commission included a request to investigate Robert Livingstone (a source of anxiety to his father) and, because of this trust and Livingstone's favourable opinion of him, Rae had been brought into close contact with the family.[17] There can be little doubt that Rae, who had a reputation for scandal-mongering,[18] had carried the gossip about Stewart and Mrs Livingstone from Scotland to Cape Town and, for reasons of his own, now set out quite systematically to destroy Stewart's character and credentials. It is difficult to establish a motive for this victimisation. Rae and Stewart had met in Glasgow, amicably it would seem, yet Rae may have had genuine misgivings about Stewart's lack of official backing. (Rae accused Stewart of being a trader in disguise and even managed to persuade the Portuguese consul that Stewart was only a front-man.) More probably he felt that his own position with the Livingstone family was threatened by the arrival of this newcomer and therefore sought to undermine his honour and reputation. Initially Stewart was inclined to treat these rumours as 'too ludicrous to be noticed' but Mary Livingstone saw more clearly than he that this would mean trouble in the future, and that scandalous stories would accompany, if they did not precede, them to the Zambezi.

Rae was assisted in his attempt to prevent Stewart from going to the Zambezi by the Episcopalian establishment in Cape Town and by a small group, also of the Episcopalian persuasion, waiting to go on the *Hetty Ellen* with Rae to the Zambezi.[19] The ecclesiastical hostility to Stewart had the sanction of the highest authority, the Bishop of Cape Town, Robert Gray. It had been largely at Bishop Gray's insistence that the newly-formed Oxford and Cambridge Mission had directed its sights to the Zambezi and that their leader, Charles Mackenzie, had been consecrated a bishop. Livingstone had been enthusiastic about the mission, not least because he felt that the presence of a fully-fledged bishop would inspire confidence in his own expedition at a time when he sorely needed encouragement. Livingstone was well aware that he himself was a wayfinder, that he would never want to pause long enough to promote industries or agriculture, or to build up a church, but he believed that these things must be done. Nor did he care very much who did them, provided they were good and true brethren with energy and initiative. He was totally unsectarian and quite without the dogmatic, ecclesiastical narrowness of many of his contemporaries. Of the U.M.C.A. he wrote: 'I rejoiced when I heard that so many good and great men in the Universities had turned their thoughts towards Africa and . . . I welcomed the men they sent with a hearty unfeigned welcome.'[20] It was with similar enthusiasm that he heard of Stewart's projected journey and the reason for it.

Mission work, with its rigours and isolation, often minimised doctrinal differences and demolished denominational barriers. The same could not be said, however, of colonial towns, where European conventions of sectarianism were not only imported, but often intensified in white society. Stewart had already voiced his own apprehension about possible 'collision with the Puseyites' and it soon became evident that the Episcopalian party viewed his activities with similar anxiety. Both groups were dependent to a large extent on Livingstone's co-operation. Could he remain impartial? Would he not be more likely to favour a fellow Scot, encouraged by men whom Livingstone knew, with the promise of a Scots settlement to follow? It was natural to suppose that Bishop Gray would be eager to safeguard the priorities and rights of the mission for which he had been in part responsible, and that the arrival of Stewart would have caused him more than a twinge of anxiety and doubt. As it happened Stewart, rather to his surprise, liked the bishop and found his conduct of worship agreeable because it was not too near 'the cursed fooleries of Romanism'. After some discussion they agreed that the country was 'vast enough for all'. The bishop, however, was not equalled in his charitable outlook by the other members of the Episcopalian party in Cape Town. After initial difficulties, including involvement in what Bishop Mackenzie called the 'Ajawa Wars', the U.M.C.A. mission at Magomero had become more settled and was beginning to show results. Bishop Mackenzie had therefore decided to send for his sister, Anne Mackenzie and for the wife of Henry Burrup, his second-in-command. These women and a young curate, the Revd Edward Hawkins, were part of the group now waiting to proceed to the Zambezi, with servants, baggage, stores supplies, mules and carts. Miss Mackenzie, though she had not disliked Stewart, was more inclined than Bishop Gray to regard him as an intruder and a potential rival. 'I do hope he will keep his mission a long way from ours,' she wrote. It was between Stewart and Hawkins, however, that real personal animosity developed. In the months that followed they indulged in an ecclesiastical duel, doctrinal parry interspersed with petty denominational thrust, that spelt death to any growth of amity and trust based on common interest. Moreover both Miss Mackenzie and Hawkins became party to Rae's intrigue.

She disseminated stories of the 'scandal' and he cast doubts, whenever possible, on Stewart's right to travel with them on the *Hetty Ellen*.

Possibly under pressure from Miss Mackenzie, the bishop offered Stewart a free passage back to England. This offer, made from whatever motives, confirmed Stewart's worst suspicions about Rae and the bishop, but he was rescued by Mary Livingstone who declared that she would not move from Cape Town unless Stewart was permitted to go on the same ship. This declaration carried the day as there could, of course, be no question of arriving at the Kongone without the doctor's wife. Encouraged, Stewart wrote defiantly, 'I must go on though fifty Bishops were blocking up my path and as many Raes were doing their best to leave me in the lurch.'[21]

These verbal assurances of Mrs Livingstone's were not enough for Rae who, before they left Durban after another delay, asked her to sign a statement affirming that Stewart travelled to the Zambezi under her authority.

It was in this atmosphere of hostility and distrust that the journey continued and it is scarcely surprising that Stewart was obsessed by a sense of persecution and harrowed by doubts about everything. 'I am worried, wearied with anxiety, concerned not about great pay, but mere bread. I have my character slandered, my motives misconstrued and find myself loathed by a set of snarling arrogant Episcopalian curs.'[22] Shortly after leaving Southampton, Stewart had recorded misgivings about the prospects, particularly with regard to the opening up of the Ruvuma, to the hostility of the Portuguese and, indeed, to the justification for founding any kind of mission at all. In Cape Town he had been dismayed by the scepticism regarding Livingstone's claims for the Zambezi and discomfited to discover how 'that part of the world and Livingstone's connection with it, is systematically decried'.[23] His first glimpse of the Zambezi at the Luabo mouth did nothing to allay his pessimism. He was increasingly obsessed by the possibility of failure. Would that failure be of his own making? Or could the blame be laid at Livingstone's door? Even before meeting Livingstone his mind tossed with the alternatives. Either he had come on 'a wild-goose chase', 'careering over a whole continent in search of work I have marked out for myself' and, therefore, if he accomplished nothing, he would have to go home 'branded with the mark of ambition, with running where I was not sent . . .'; or, perhaps, 'Livingstone's work is not what it is supposed to be' and, if that turned out to be the case, 'If there is no entry into the country, if missionary and commercial purposes equally, the whole thing is a bubble, then let all the world know this; or all the world should know that we may not for ever be chasing a mere African will o' the wisp.'[24]

It is in the light of these experiences since leaving Scotland that Stewart's first meeting with Livingstone must be judged. 'I retreat backwards and am introduced to the Doctor. I shake hands and continue my backward progress under the awning. "I am glad to see you here, Mr Stewart" and "Thank you Doctor" was all my reply except the hearty good will and admiration with which I looked at the man.'[25] Of all the emotions which this tongue-tied adulation expressed, relief was probably uppermost. 'All the troubles and work of many years seemed compensated for.' This man, who had become for Stewart the only possible solution to his many difficulties, the only possible means for the realisation of his aspirations, had at least received him with courtesy and with pleasure. Two days later Stewart, in his first discussion with Livingstone, produced his letter of reference from Dr Candlish but Livingstone brushed it aside, assuring him that he was satisfied that he was the same man about whom Dr Tweedie of the F.M.C. had written. Stewart was further reassured when Livingstone, doubtless primed by his wife, went on to belittle the scandal and suspicions of the previous months, declaring that he thought the people concerned had acted in 'the most nonsensical way imaginable' and that such activities were 'part of the work of Auld Nick to keep men from doing good.'[26] These remarks appear to refer to the scandal concerning Stewart and Mrs Livingstone and also to rumours suggesting that either the U.M.C.A. would not welcome Stewart or that Stewart would gain preference over the bishop. Livingstone seemed prepared, in fact, to take Stewart as he found him, showed interest in his plans, discussed missionary subjects with him and according to Stewart they 'always agreed'.

George Rae and Miss Mackenzie, however, lost little time in bringing the members of the expedition up to date on the latest news. The scandal spread with all the rapidity of a virulent disease, breeding in such close quarters. Conjecture was rife about the behaviour of this new missionary and about the possibility that he might 'quite cut out the Bishop'.[27] Thus once again, Stewart found himself isolated, distrusted and suspect. One perceptive observer wrote that whereas he approved of Stewart making this exploratory journey, Stewart ought never to have come alone.[28] This was indeed the weakness of Stewart's venture. He had not the inner strength to withstand loneliness; and ostracism, while it did not break him, increased his propensity for self-pity and his tendency to be uncharitable. All might have been put in much better perspective if he had had a companion with whom to share mutual grievances and pleasures.

There is no evidence to suggest that Livingstone ever attached much importance to these rumours about his wife and James Stewart. When she died at Shupanga only four months after their arrival, Livingstone turned to Stewart for assistance and comfort, an impossibility if he had felt as others did that the scandal had been a contributory factor in her death.[29] For his part, Stewart felt that Livingstone's public acceptance of him had improved his standing with the other members of the expedition who considered him a mere 'nobody'; but he did not look on it as proof that Livingstone did not believe the rumours, presumably because he had no need to do so. It was only much later that Stewart seemed to consider that Livingstone might in some way hold him responsible for this episode, and in 1864 when both men were in Britain he sent Livingstone all the notes which Mary Livingstone had written to him on the voyage to Cape Town. He insisted that 'to Mrs Livingstone I always acted with the same ease and freedom as if she had been my mother'.[30] His tone was over-anxious, Livingstone's reply, magnanimous:

> Whatever may have been said or written, no variation as far as I was conscious, was made in my conduct either to the dead or the living. Generally I can forgive, and I prefer not to take unkind feelings towards anyone along the path of life. If we carry sunshine in our bosoms, why should we allow the silly sayings of the past to come back to becloud our joy?[31]

In contrast to this, Livingstone was sensitive to the possibility that a Presbyterian and Episcopalian wrangle might develop with Stewart's arrival. When he heard that Stewart had written a letter to the *Cape Advertiser and Mail*, implying criticism of Hawkins, Livingstone was fierce with him: 'I am sorry to gather . . . that you had written to the Advertiser against Mr Hawkins and thereby put yourself into a state of open warfare with our church brethren.'[32] In the event he need not have worried. Once Stewart had parted company with Hawkins and after Miss Mackenzie had left the party, his antipathy to the U.M.C.A. diminished: 'We are better friends now partly because . . . I have beaten the others who played their little game to prevent me seeing the country at all; and who went back to the Cape at the news of the first great disaster.'[33] When Stewart met Horace Waller at Shupanga it was 'like the visit of a friend at home'[34] and when he eventually reached Chibisa's he felt, ironically, completely at ease in the company of these Anglican missionaries. The rigid denominationalism which had been his inheritance was shown to be an irrelevance. This was one lesson of these months on the Zambezi which Stewart did not forget.

Nevertheless, it was with the fortunes of this embryonic mission that Stewart's hopes and ambitions were most intimately connected. If it could succeed then his own chances were immeasurably improved. For Livingstone, also, this was something of a proving ground. He had claimed that the area was suitable for such a settlement and had urged that such an attempt be made. Success here would cast a redeeming light on the apparent failures of this expedition. The cataclysmic event at this time, therefore, was the news of the deaths of the bishop and Mr Burrup. Stewart promptly asked Livingstone if this disastrous news would make any difference to his plans. Livingstone, despite his 'anxiety and heavy load of care' declared that he would not swerve in any way from his present position and, thus encouraged, Stewart vowed that, unless Livingstone expressly negated his plans, he too would go on. 'So far as I myself am concerned this event, sad as it is, would not move me from my intentions in the slightest degree. I do not think one would be justified in turning back on that account from the work proposed.'[35]

From this time, however, Stewart's earlier misgivings about his own prospects increased. He had already become critical of Livingstone's administrative ability concluding that it was all very well for the ox-wagon or 'untutored Makololo' but that it could not stand with people whose minds 'will think as well as himself'.[36] Small things irritated him; the threadbare condition of his coat, insufficient food, money, the haphazard approach to worship. Now the difficulties which he had entertained on the outward voyage reappeared, strengthened by the tragedy. The slow progress of the *Pioneer* had been a graphic illustration of the navigation problems of the Zambezi. 'The severest blow I have yet received and that which offers the greatest barrier to a successful prosecution of the scheme has been the proposal to make the locality of the mission on Lake Nyassa and neither on the Zambezi nor the Shire Rivers.'[37] The Zambezi had seemed to offer an easy entrance to the centre of the great African continent but was this really the case? A mission in the interior would have to be accessible or men would 'break their hearts before success came'. This would necessitate a small river steamer which would increase the overhead expenses. 'I sometimes have nightmares with the whole weight of a steamer resting on my breast.' Further, Waller had confirmed the reports of the war-like state of the country up river and of the flourishing condition of the slave traffic. 'For five yards of Manchester calico you can, in the region of the Lake, purchase a man.' To counteract this, the industrial side of the mission would have to be developed on a large scale and this raised the problem of the dues imposed by the Portuguese which were a barrier to commerce, not to mention the fact that Waller maintained that it was not possible to get enough cotton as 'would fill your hat' and, if this were true, then Stewart's recommendations to the Cotton Suppliers Association would have to be negative.[38]

Livingstone, unaware of this turmoil in Stewart's mind, considered that Stewart was 'especially well rigged up for the work and specially well adapted for it'. Other missionaries might come out prepared for hardship in theory but 'grumbling like mountains in the family-way when put about by things they did not expect' but Stewart was not like that and 'to such a man I would say "Go forward" '.[39] The divergence in outlook between the two men increased over the next three months from May to July, though it never became explicit. Stewart was bored and restless at Shupanga and he blamed Livingstone for not allowing him to go to Tete with Kirk and Charles Livingstone. 'At Shupanga where I remained five months waiting on Dr L. my patience was completely wrung out when I learned there was to be a wait of another two.'[40]

In spite of pleasant hours spent in Livingstone's company with the doctor 'peculiarly communicative and agreeable' Stewart became more and more critical of his optimism. A note from Waller announcing the evacuation of the mission from Magomero to Chibisa's and the opinion of Charles Livingstone and Kirk that the Portuguese were outspokenly dissatisfied with Livingstone, added to Stewart's gloom. 'How can it be soberly proposed to settle missions in a country where a man's life is only worth the leaden bullets in his gun, I do not well see. Gradually then and bit by bit, I must come to the conclusion that in coming out here I have made a mistake. What shall the future bring?'[41]

In an effort to overcome his boredom, Stewart planned a journey to Chibisa's and to Tete, alone. Before he left he had what he described as a 'remarkable conversation' with the doctor. Livingstone insisted that Stewart should carry on because if he showed that he was determined then the people at home would support him. 'You could not in the meantime do more than you are doing, acquiring the language and becoming acquainted with the people.' When Stewart raised tentative objections about the difficulties of communication, Livingstone's reply was to the magnificent effect that 'without risk there would be no credit'.[42]

This is a revealing incident. Stewart considered the conversation 'remarkable' because it showed him clearly that Livingstone was totally unwilling to face up to the problems as he, Stewart, saw them. Livingstone, intrepid, fearless, quixotic even with regard to Africa demanded of his fellows that they like him should retain the spirit of the possible even when all seemed impossible. His physical courage, which was so impressive, was dependent on a mental and spiritual attitude which had already conquered all dangers. Few men could equal this. It could not be said with any justification that Stewart was a coward but his caution took precedence over his mental courage or optimism. Charged as he was with the establishment of something useful and permanent, with responsibility for the health and welfare of men both black and white, with the development of church and industry, he was, of course, right in thinking that what one man alone could dare, what one man could risk, the average artisan or missionary or trader would neither dare nor risk, nor could he be called upon to do so. This was what made Stewart's relationship with Livingstone peculiarly difficult. Others had criticised Livingstone's lack of administrative skill, had grumbled about his readiness to listen to gossip, had threatened to leave him, had disparaged his unwillingness to share authority but no-one had attempted to hold him, no-one had attempted to temper his over-enthusiasm, no-one had tried to harness his inspiration and put it to the practical test, no-one that is until the bishop and Stewart had arrived on the scene. Stewart, impatient in his ambition to realise practical ends became disillusioned because Livingstone could not meet his demands; but Livingstone was as disappointed in Stewart as Stewart was in him. The bishop died too soon but his successor Bishop Tozer failed, even more than Stewart, to match Livingstone's expectations. A man like Waller, who had a vision of himself as a knight on horseback, freeing Africa from the curse of slavery, 'a Philanthropist at heart of the most florid order'[43] became and remained a close friend of Livingstone's because he was attuned to his idealism. Stewart and Livingstone, in contrast, made demands on one another which neither could fulfil and, without understanding on Livingstone's part and without charity from Stewart, the relationship was permanently impaired.

By the time he reached Chibisa's in early August, the report which he would have to make to the Committee was very much on Stewart's mind. His attitude was still ambivalent. To a friend he wrote that, 'stubborn facts . . . have wrought certain changes in my own mind as to the final result. . . . Still if the Committee would undertake the work, I would remain here.'[44] But later he noted in his journal that it 'would not be possible or rather wise and expedient to found a mission just now'. His enjoyment of the company of the missionaries at

Chibisa's temporarily mellowed his anxiety and he almost envied their 'world-forgetting and world-forgotten sort of life' but successive tours of the surrounding areas with Waller, Rowley and Procter merely underlined their impression that the Yao were virtually masters of the Shire Highlands. Discussion was still heated at the mission on the question of responsibility for their earlier quarrel with the Yao and Stewart came to agree with Rowley that Livingstone's plan for the release of slaves had forced the mission to take military action, and that violent reaction to this event at home had caused Livingstone to absolve himself from blame, stating that his actions were defensive as opposed to the offensive actions of the missionaries. Moreover the mission, though they now wished after their initial involvement to remain detached from local politics, were finding it difficult to affirm their neutrality. This was in part due to the actions of the Makololo who were a thorn in the side of the mission, freeing slaves and then plundering to support the increased population. Even Waller was critical of Livingstone in this respect. Stewart again accepted the missionaries' strictures on the Makololo and added that to his list of grievances against Livingstone. 'The sum of the matter is the Makololo are not all the specimens of men they are represented in Dr L's book to be.' Finally, although the country was fertile, there was often the 'greatest possible difficulty in finding food' and this again raised the question of communications, simply for survival.[45]

It is strange to think that this little group, arguing, debating, criticising, worrying, night after night in the remote, troubled, war-ravaged Shire Highlands, formed the spearhead of what would become an intensive and extensive missionary and political enterprise. They themselves, however, saw little hope of success and, with one or two exceptions, felt themselves misled or deceived. On the night before he left, Stewart summed up the general opinion as one of strong feeling against Livingstone for his mis-statements. 'His accursed lies have caused much toil, trouble, anxiety and loss of life, as well as money and reputation and I have been led a dance over half the world to accomplish nothing.'[46]

Stewart's contrary and ill-humoured observations about the country as he found it applied no less to the people who occupied it. In general, he was repelled by their appearance, dress and manners and made no secret of his opinion. 'You used to be hard on me,' wrote Waller years later, 'because I could see so much good in the Natives and never felt that great wide gulf between Civilisation and Savagedom that is ordinarily supposed to exist.'[47] For Stewart, this kind of opinion was 'little else than affectation' but, though he later became more

98

tolerant of manners and customs, he had never anything but contempt for ignorance and idleness, which he considered would 'drive a man into a state of drivelling imbecility'. The overwhelming impression of the people on Stewart was of the emptiness of their minds and the equal emptiness of their hands:

> The greatest kindness to them is to increase their wants – not their mere desires; these are strong enough already but their necessary wants; to give them nothing that is not wrought for and so by slow steps lead them to reach what hardly any of them have yet reached, a supply of things necessary for this life by their own exertions put forth and sustained in an honest way.[48]

Stewart became convinced that the African should be given nothing for nothing, materially or educationally. What he paid for he would value. Therefore doctrinal teaching must be linked with industrial and agricultural training so that the African could be brought to an appreciation of the cardinal virtue of labour. If Stewart had thought vaguely in these terms before, his experiences in central Africa marshalled his thoughts and gave them coherent form. It was of immense importance for his future approach to education and mission in Africa. He judged a man, black or white, by the work he did. Of the African as he saw him on this Zambezi journey, Stewart could only comment in amazement, 'he must enjoy his laziness in order to endure it.' It could be said that in his attitude to the African, as with his attitude to Livingstone, Stewart's restless energy and obsession with organisation, made him intolerant and unappreciative of those whose style of life was so different to his own.

In the last few months of 1862, Stewart had the satisfaction of seeing Tete for himself and of going on to the Cabora Bassa rapids. Part of this journey he accomplished alone, part in the company of young Richard Thornton, a geologist who had just rejoined the expedition having left it in 1859 after repeated disagreements with Livingstone. Though Thornton died so soon after Stewart left central Africa, this brief friendship had some repercussions. Thornton wrote to his sister Katherine that, as he had come to know Stewart, he had found him to be 'a much superior man to any of his denouncers, a very clever sociable and desirable companion and good-hearted, though his judgement is rather severe on some points. . . . I asked him to visit you. . . . When he comes receive him as one of my best friends.'[49] Stewart did visit the Thorntons and entered into a fairly vigorous correspondence with the Thornton sisters who felt that they had no cause to be grateful to Livingstone after his treatment of their brother. Thornton's letter shows that the tide of personal animosity had at last begun to turn for Stewart. Even Kirk wrote, begging his pardon for 'having been misled and so far misjudged you before I had the chance to know you personally.'[50] But all this was too late for Stewart as in the months from October to April of 1863 he grew progressively more miserable, 'almost beyond endurance', and more savagely critical of his surroundings and of Livingstone. Successive bouts of fever made him 'irritable to an excessive degree' and every day he felt he was getting weaker and more weary. In this mood he parted with Livingstone finally on 10 January, claiming that he had 'no wish whatever to meet him again'.[51] In an agony of physical and mental distress he sat with Procter one night and tore the doctor's reputation to shreds, declaring that he was not fitted for his position, that he was quite careless of human suffering and that, in some respects, he must be held responsible for the bishop's death. The final blow came on the following day when they heard the news of Scudamore's death, depleting the mission yet again and making it a matter of time before the remnant would have to move. It was under the influence of this destructive conversation and seemingly unnecessary death that Stewart took Livingstone's book, 'fragrant with odours of . . . earnestness' and flung it into the Zambezi river, that river which had promised so much and now apparently offered so little.[52]

It would be a mistake to judge Stewart on these outbursts. This was private hysteria, fever-flavoured and distorted, transcribed in a private journal. There is no evidence that Livingstone ever knew the depth of Stewart's disillusionment and despair. Two months later in Mozambique, Stewart received letters from the missionaries, Kirk and Livingstone which served to put him in better heart and gave him information which 'altogether changed the spirit of my dream'. Stewart was consoled by the tone of the letters from his friends and their assurances that 'fold by fold all this wicked malignity is being wrapped up',[53] but it was the letter from Livingstone which gave him the most satisfaction. Evidently when Stewart had met Livingstone at Shupanga in January and had given him his report on the state of the country, he had refused to believe it, but as Stewart wrote to a friend, 'He credits it now. Four days ago I had a letter from him in which he admits the disorganisation of the country and finds it I think much worse than I found it.'[54] The letter certainly gives that impression. 'The country is completely disorganised and a new system must be introduced with a strong hand. We have counted thirty-two dead bodies floating down the stream. . . . I never witnessed such a change.

It is a desert and dead bodies lie everywhere.'[55] Stewart commented that Livingstone considered that drought, famine and war had done this but that he himself was not convinced. Stewart was never prepared to accept that Livingstone had been telling the whole truth about the country as he saw it in 1860, despite the assurances of Waller and Kirk that the political condition of the country had indeed drastically altered in the intervening years.

Although Livingstone in this letter agreed that the state of the country was disorganised, yet it is apparent that he was still eager to see a settlement made in this area and that he had no idea that Stewart's mind was set on giving a discouraging report to the Committee. Not only did he ask Stewart to be sure and let him know how the Free Church brethren would react 'to the important question you will bring before them' but he offered to pay Stewart's expenses back to the Zambezi, plus £150 per annum on condition that the government refunded the money that he had spent on the *Lady Nyasa*.[55] In the event, Livingstone was not recompensed and the scheme did not materialise. Moreover, the offer was made before he had heard an account, at least in part, of the accusations Stewart had made. He was aware that Stewart had spoken of 'hindrances' as he had written to Waller saying that these were 'imagined'. One night in June 1863, however, when Livingstone was near the Mission and Waller was visiting, the conversation aboard the *Pioneer* turned to cotton. It was Rae who supplied the information that Stewart had vowed that he had seen only *five* cotton bushes in all his travels. Livingstone was furious and said 'Mr Stewart was down at the ship with me and never spoke to me on the subject'. He demanded to know if Stewart had then gone up to the house at Shupanga and, behind his back, called in question all his affirmations about cotton-growing. Stewart's friends who were present, Waller, E. D. Young and Meller, rushed to his defence. Waller stated that Rae was mistaken, that he had misunderstood Stewart's meaning but Young went further and swore that it was a 'purgering lie' (sic).[56] Whether Livingstone was mollified or not is left unanswered, but his anger could be attributed to the fact that Stewart had not confronted him with these differences of opinion and that he had therefore been deceived into thinking that Stewart was still in favour of a settlement in central Africa. At a time when he had recently learned that the expedition had been recalled it was one more blow for his dreams for the African continent. 'Had Scottish enterprise and perseverance been introduced it might have reacted on the Universities Mission and prevented their abandonment of the Zambezi and placing the Headquarters of their mission at Zanzibar.'[57]

Stewart gradually recovered his strength and equanimity at Mozambique and by the time he sailed on the *Gorgon* on 30 April 1863 he could write that his prospects had already changed for the better. Nevertheless he remained convinced that he could not give any favourable report. 'I assure you no amount of willingness can alter these grim facts and consequently . . . I am not very proud of the result. I wake every morning with the sense of the disgrace of failure on my mind.'[58] He had been asked by the Convener of the F.M.C. if he would visit their South African missions at Lovedale, Burnshill, Pirie and Macfarlan in Kaffraria on his return journey to Scotland. The missionaries there pressed Stewart to consider Lovedale as a field of work and John Buchanan in Durban urged him to come to 'populous, peaceful, thriving, healthful, hopeful Natal',[59] so that the prospect of employment in Africa was never far from his thoughts. He discussed these prospects with a friend in Cape Town before sailing for home. 'I admit you would have opened up to you, in Caffraria a whole sphere of influence and you would be called to labour in a work . . . dear to your heart. But I think . . . that you should go to an enlightened congregation.'[60]

For a brief period he did, in fact, go to the congregation of Free St John's in Glasgow as assistant to Dr Roxburgh, and later to Glasgow University to complete his medical degree. But he was quickly entangled in the network of African connections in Britain, communicating, visiting, lecturing, writing articles, editing books. The Thorntons, for instance, were trying to piece together Richard's sketchy and very scientifically-oriented journals; Kirk was in Brentford, where he wrote to Stewart, complaining of Livingstone's duplicity and 'ungratefulness'; Rowley was in Oxford, preparing his book on the history of the mission. By July Waller was in London, in September Procter arranged to meet Stewart in Edinburgh. Even Charles Livingstone had visited Stewart late in 1863, prior to his departure for America.[61] David Livingstone himself, the focus of all their thoughts, had arrived in July after his legendary journey to Bombay in the *Lady Nyasa*.

Stewart had visited the Thorntons soon after his arrival in England and continued to correspond with them. They sought his advice on the many questions concerning Richard's journals and he, evidently, relied on them for consolation and justification for the decisions he had made in the past. 'Indeed, Mr Stewart,' wrote Octavia Thornton, 'we do not think you severe in your judgements. On the contrary we were often struck with your moderation in speaking of the members of the Expedition: the treatment you received at their hands was at variance with the laws of both Christianity and humanity.'[62]

If he spoke harshly in private, however, Stewart was more cautious in printed articles. He sent the Thorntons a copy of his article in the *Daily Review* and was commended by them for the 'inconsistency' in what he said and what he wrote:

> Dr L . . . is a great and wonderful man but from his lack of fellow-feeling and kindliness he has proved himself rather an hinderer than a helper of others – if your better coin does not arouse in him a feeling and an expression of remorse for the past, one will not be able to give him credit for possessing much of either generosity or justice. He has done or permitted to be done great wrong to yourself, Richard and Mr Baines and the Mission party also – whether he is fully alive to the suffering he has caused is not known.[63]

There was, however, a growing duality in Stewart's attitude to Livingstone. He needed the defence of such dedicated champions as the Thorntons who sympathised, perhaps for romantic reasons, with his wounded pride and self-justification. Yet, he had already written to Livingstone, describing the report he had made to the Committee but emphasising that, despite its lack of encouragement, he was 'very far from giving up hope'. He then went on to give reasons for his own behaviour, the direct outcome of the 'storm of slander' which had assailed him and which had influenced him 'to an extent which I cannot describe'.[64] It was a clumsy and rather embarrassing attempt to remove the barriers between them, in the unspoken hope that they might start afresh. It was the most that Stewart's pride could allow, that he, and not Livingstone, should make an 'expression of remorse for the past'.

Throughout the spring and summer of 1864, Stewart was under increasing pressure from William Govan, Principal of Lovedale Institution, to consider returning to Lovedale as a member of the staff:

> You must be aware that it is from the Colony that the influence is to go forth that is to Christianize and civilize Southern Africa. And I venture to think that here in the Colony and the Lovedale Seminary . . . you may exert an influence as potent and as extensive as you could do in any other position in which you could be placed.[65]

In this he unconsciously echoed Livingstone's own words to Stewart when he had declared that if he were a young man he would go in for 'this new field of missionary labours'. 'The effects of mission are cumulative. You here begin a work which will go on increasing to the end of time. . . . Africa must be Christianized from within outwards.'[66] The need to make a decision was accelerated by the return of Dr Alexander Duff[67] from a visit to Kaffraria. He had decided that Lovedale required to be set on a new course and had come to the conclusion that Stewart was the man to do it. As the new Convener of the F.M.C. of the Free Church, Duff added his considerable weight to the demands already being made by Govan.

Stewart prevaricated; the Lovedale appointment was ill-defined, the salary was inadequate, the work was not heavy enough. In fact, Stewart was still waiting to see whether or not Livingstone had any plans for the Zambezi region in which he might be included. On 10 September Livingstone visited him in his Glasgow lodgings:

> Today at 11 Dr Livingstone came. A long talk. He does not see his way. He is in the same position I was in last November. When he is speaking of the need of his presence at home for the family the direction of the current is apparent. He asked what is to be done. Would the Free Church do anything?[68]

There was nothing in this interview to give Stewart hope. He was convinced that Livingstone was 'cool' towards him and, perhaps brooding on the cause for this, it was at this stage that he decided to return Mary Livingstone's letters, written four years earlier. 'I believe that we have both been defooled and good work in consequence spoiled. It is in the conviction of this as possible at least that makes me write now as I am doing.'[69] Then, mentioning that Dr Duff was pressing hard for his answer, he questioned Livingstone on his future plans, asking whether he intended to set up a commercial rather than a missionary enterprise on his next venture to Africa.

Livingstone's reply, courteous and forgiving, must nevertheless have disappointed Stewart. The past was behind them, his future plans were still undefined, but one thing was certain – next time he would go alone. 'I should only attempt to open up the way and I would undertake nothing that would as lately separate me from constant contact with the natives.'[70] After settling several points with the Foreign Mission Committee, Stewart agreed in late November to go to Lovedale.

Further correspondence between Livingstone and Stewart dealt almost exclusively with proofs of Livingstone's book and Stewart's articles in *Good Words*. In August Livingstone left for Bombay. A letter from his friend Dugald Boyd, minister in Bombay, told Stewart that 'Livingstone hoped to see you yet in Central Africa'[71] but from that time all contact between the two men ceased and Stewart was dependent on Horace Waller for personal news and information about Livingstone.

Having completed his medical degree in 1866, Stewart with his wife sailed for Lovedale in November of that year. Stewart's marriage was also to prove important for the future of Scottish missions in Africa. His wife was one of the Stephens of Linthouse and through her brother, John, much money was diverted to Lovedale and Livingstonia. Privately Stewart had decided to give four years to Lovedale.[72] He would carry out Duff's reforms to the letter and then do something else, as yet unspecified.

From Waller in 1867, Stewart learned of determined efforts by influential people, led by Sir Fowell Buxton, to 'get up an agitation on the slave question'. There were rumours also that Livingstone had been murdered and that a search party would be sent out under E. D. Young, though it was Waller's private opinion that 'Livingstone himself would never have cared to go a mile to look at any man's grave.'[73] It was from Blair, however, one of the original members of the U.M.C.A., now working with the Zululand Mission, that Stewart heard of a proposed expedition to central Africa by a certain Captain Faulkner of the 17th Lancers. Faulkner planned to spend £4,000 on this journey to the Zambezi region and to take a small steam launch with him. This rumoured activity stirred all Stewart's desire to return to central Africa. Urgently he wrote to Robert Macfie, the Lancashire business man who had so generously aided him in 1860, asking him to consider financing him again. He deplored the 'spending of £4,000 by Irish officers for mere hunting and exploring expedition when . . . so difficult to get men and money for higher purposes.' Stewart outlined a plan whereby, using Lovedale as a base of operations for the project, he would bring fifteen or twenty young men from the Zambezi region to be educated at Lovedale, thus producing a 'trained native force to begin a Zambezi mission'. He assured Macfie that he had never deviated from the plan formed years ago and that though he had been obliged to come to Lovedale 'no step in my life has been taken without some reference to that projected mission.'[74] He repeated these statements in his letter to Dr Duff, claiming that if he had not come to Lovedale he 'should have tried to find means of returning at once'. Almost in panic he begged Duff to consider that this proposed Faulkner expedition would be 'powder and shot' and would 'ruin prospects for thirty years'. He himself had done nothing for the past nine years that had not been 'induced or modified by the purpose of going to Central Africa'. Finally, he added, in a revealing statement, 'I wish to be first. . . . To introduce the gospel into a region where it has never been is *the ambition that moves me*. I would not care to follow after the path had been opened.'[75]

For Duff there was no question of allowing Stewart to carry out his 'meditated flight to Central Africa'. He had been sent to Lovedale for a purpose and only he could see that the Committee's plan was 'carried into accomplishment'. Once that was done however the Committee would be under obligation to Stewart to further his 'grander enterprise'. Then, promised Duff, 'I shall do my utmost to raise for you the means of transporting into Central Africa.'[76]

For the next few years Stewart was absorbed in Lovedale affairs. Waller felt that there was a good chance of establishing a 'sort of Sierra Leone under a good earnest Englishman' on the east coast and that this might provide an opportunity for Stewart to carry out his old plans.[77] It was not until 1874, however, when his going home to Scotland on Lovedale business coincided with Livingstone's burial in Westminster Abbey, that Stewart's chance finally came. The resolve was made to reopen the question of the Central African Mission and this time to give it the form of a memorial to Livingstone. Stewart recalled the birth of the idea years later in a letter to his brother-in-law:

> Do you remember one night we sat late in the drawing room at Shieldhall in May 1874. . . . I remember exactly the way we were sitting and the position of our chairs to the fireplace . . . I put a certain question to you wishing your opinion. . . . You did not know with what anxiety I waited for your answer. At length you said 'Yes I would do so'. From that time the Livingstonia idea went on.[78]

Looked at in the light of all subsequent events it can be seen that Livingstonia was a natural consequence of the ambition and energy which had driven Stewart to make his first attempts to go to central Africa. The possibility of establishing a mission in that region remained a challenge which he could not ignore. While he was alive Livingstone could not have been the means or instrument of the realisation of Stewart's ambitions, but once dead, the name of the great man could be used to further a grander enterprise than Stewart had ever envisaged. Even here, however, Stewart was prevented from 'being first' and when he finally wrote *Livingstonia: Its Origin* in 1894, it was to make public the part he had played in bringing the mission into being as his initiative was in danger of being obscured. Stewart's commitment to Lovedale and the Livingstonia Committee's feeling that the leader of the first party should be familiar with boats, meant that Stewart, most reluctantly, had to yield his place to E. D. Young. 'The strain upon you I know has been great,' sympathised Waller. 'Already there was the old boat-song in your ears, the mist on the rivers and the old loved hills in view on the Shire, when you had to resign your place to another.'[79] Stewart would not have expressed it in this way but he, like Waller, was emotionally bound to 'inconsequent Africa'.

When Stewart eventually reached Livingstonia a year later, much of the pattern of the previous expedition repeated itself. The work was done but at tremendous cost, not only of lives, but of time and temper and good relations between men. 'Fever poison has the tendency to make men quarrel in the most remarkable degree' observed Waller.[80] Perhaps if he could have remembered that and been more lenient in his judgements and opinions, Stewart would not only have achieved great things but have been remembered for the greatness with which he achieved them.

For a man who was so prolific a writer Stewart made significantly little reference to Livingstone in the years after 1874. In a letter to William Blaikie, written to congratulate him on his recently-published biography of Livingstone, Stewart ventured his personal summary of Livingstone's character:

> From what I know of Livingstone . . . and I saw him in a great many trying positions – I think you have given to many who did not know him a truer idea of the man than any previously presented. I recognise the truth of the portrait at many points – so far as a man can be represented by lines of type. He was like the rest of us, not perfect; and by this I do not mean of course anything but what the words convey – for I think he kept his temper with others and his trust in God unshaken when hundreds of others would have failed . . . or thousands. With all the honours that were heaped upon him there remained about him to the last, that which I can only call a kind of sanctified naturalness.[81]

If Stewart had ever idealised Livingstone in the past, he certainly did not join the hero-worshippers of a later date. It was typical of his attitude that he would console himself in a difficult situation with words which Livingstone had spoken to him on the Zambezi in 1862; 'I am not one of these blessed fools who never make a mistake but I have acted for the best.'[82]

Notes

1 J. P. R. Wallis (ed.), *The Zambesi Journal of James Stewart 1862–1863*, London, 1952 (Oppenheimer Series). Hereafter referred to as ZJ. The original MS from which Wallis omitted several sections ST 1/2/1, Rhodesian Archives, will be referred to as SJ.

2 H. A. C. Cairns, *Prelude to Imperialism*, London, 1965, p. 84; Owen Chadwick, *Mackenzie's Grave*, London, 1959, p. 119; B. Ransford, *Livingstone's Lake*, London, 1966, p. 33.

3 Chadwick, op. cit., p. 119; Ransford, op. cit., p. 75; W. Blaikie, *The Personal Life of David Livingstone*, London, 1881, p. 271.

4 J. Stewart, *Livingstonia: Its Origin*, Edinburgh, 1894, pp. 1–4.

5 Stewart to Foreign Mission Committee (F.M.C.), 20 August 1860, ST13/3 Rhodesian Archives, R.A.

6 Stewart to St Andrew's Students' Club, 2 November 1860, ST13/1, R.A.

7 Minutes of the F.M.C., 17 October 1860, Church of Scotland Offices (CS), Edinburgh.

8 Stewart, op. cit., p. 9.

9 Livingstonia Mission established 1875 by the Free Church of Scotland in Central Africa. Lovedale Institution: Seminary for the education, primarily of Africans but also of Europeans, established in Kaffraria, South Africa in 1841 by the Glasgow Missionary Society. Stewart became its second principal in 1870.

10 SJ, 16 October 1861.

11 Stewart to John Stewart, 21 June 1860, ST13/3, R.A.

12 Mission supported by the Universities of Oxford, Cambridge, Durham and Dublin. Set up as a response to Livingstone's appeals in 1857, the missionaries reached the Zambezi early in 1861.

13 R. Foskett (ed.), *The Zambezi Journal and Letters of Dr John Kirk* (hereafter referred to as KZJ), London, 1965, p. 440. 4 May 1862.

14 KZJ, p. 568. John Kirk to Alexander Kirk, 25 July 1862.

15 SJ, 11 November 1861.

16 Blaikie, op. cit., p. 257. Mary Moffat to David Livingstone.

17 KZJ, p. 415, 3 February 1862.

18 Ibid., p. 559. John Kirk to Alexander Kirk, 10–14 December 1862.

19 This section is based on Stewart's journal and on Chadwick's account of Stewart's relations with the Episcopalian party, op. cit., pp. 113 ff.

20 Blaikie, op. cit., p. 238. Livingstone to Moore.

21 ZJ, 31 October 1861.

22 SJ, 19 December 1861.

23 Ibid., 31 August 1861.

24 ZJ, 30 December 1861.

25 Ibid., 1 February 1862.

26 Ibid., 3 February 1862.

27 KZJ, p. 415. 3 February 1862.

28 W. Cope Devereux, *A Cruise on the Gorgon*, London, 1869.

29 KZJ, p. 439. 27 April 1862.

30 Stewart to Livingstone, 4 October 1864, ST 1/1/1, R.A.

31 Livingstone to Stewart, 7 October 1864, ST 1/1/1, R.A.

32 Livingstone to Stewart, 30 July 1862, ST 1/1, R.A.

33 Stewart to D. Boyd, 1 August 1862, University of Cape Town Stewart Collection (S.C.).
34 Horace Waller, member of the U.M.C.A., life-long friend and correspondent of Stewart.
35 Stewart to Candlish, 10 April 1862, ST 13/3/1, R.A.
36 ZJ, p. 12. 15 February 1862.
37 Stewart to Candlish, 10 April 1862 (as 35).
38 The Cotton Suppliers Association had supported Stewart in this venture and had asked for a report on his return. Cf. Clegg to Stewart, 11 March 1861, ST 13/2 R.A.
39 Livingstone to Candlish, 12 March 1862.
40 Stewart to J. Stewart, cousin, 1 August 1862, Private Collection (P.C.).
41 ZJ, p. 67. 27 May 1862.
42 Ibid., pp. 78-9, 6 July 1862.
43 Waller to Stewart, 18 October 1864, P.C.
44 Stewart to D. Boyd, 1 August 1862, S.C.
45 ZJ, 16 August 1862; 24 August 1862; 14 September 1862.
46 Ibid., p. 125. 17 September 1862.
47 Waller to Stewart, 8 June 1871, P.C.
48 ZJ, p. 113. 5 September 1862.
49 Ibid., p. 219. Richard Thornton to Katherine Thornton, 15 March 1862.
50 John Kirk to Stewart, 25 February 1863, ST 1/1/1 R.A. (ZJ, p. 222).
51 ZJ, p. 187. 10 January 1863.
52 Ibid., p. 189. 1 February 1863.
53 Waller to Stewart, 25 February 1863, ST 1/1/1 R.A. (ZJ, p. 221).
54 Stewart to Buchanan, 4 April 1863, S.C.
55 Stewart, op. cit., pp. 26-8. Livingstone to Stewart, 19 February 1863.
56 E. D. Young to Stewart, 16 July 1863, ST 1/1/1, R.A.
57 David and Charles Livingstone, *Narrative of an expedition to the Zambesi and its tributaries; and of the discovery of Lakes Shirwa and Nyassa, 1858–1864,* London, 1865.
58 Stewart to Buchanan, 4 April 1863, ST 13/3/1, R.A.
59 Buchanan to Stewart, 1 June 1863, S.C.
60 Abercrombie to Stewart, 21 December 1863, S.C.
61 Waller to Stewart, 2 July 1864; Procter to Stewart 23 September 1864 ST 1/1/1 R.A.; Annabel Thornton to Stewart, 13 November 1863, P.C.
62 Octavia Thornton to Stewart, 23 March 1864, P.C.
63 Annabel Thornton to Stewart, 4 May 1864, P.C.
64 Stewart to Livingstone, 5 April 1864, ST 1/1/1, R.A. (ZJ pp. 228–30).
65 Govan to Stewart, 14 March 1864, S.C.
66 Stewart, op. cit., p. 30. Livingstone to Stewart, 24 December 1862.
67 Alexander Duff, missionary of the Free Church of Scotland in India until he returned from there in 1864 to take up the office of Convener of the F.M.C.
68 SJ, 10 September 1864.
69 Stewart to Livingstone, 4 October 1864, ST 1/1/1 R.A.
70 Livingstone to Stewart, 7 October 1864, ST 1/1/1, R.A. (ZJ, pp. 232–3).
71 R. Boyd to Stewart, 18 December 1865, S.C.
72 Stewart to Duff, 19 February 1869, ST 13/3/1, R.A.
73 Waller to Stewart, 9 April 1867, P.C.
74 Stewart to Macfie, 11 November 1868, ST 13/3/1, R.A.

75 Stewart to Duff, 19 February, 1869.
76 Duff to Stewart, 8 February 1869, ST 13/3/1, R.A.
77 Waller to Stewart, 4 July 1873, P.C.
78 Stewart to John Stephen, 3 March 1885, S.C.
79 Waller to Stewart, 4 July 1875, P.C.
80 Waller to Black, 22 May 1875, P.C.
81 Stewart to Blaikie, 14 March 1881, S.C.
82 Stewart to John Stephen, 6 March 1882, S.C.

5 Livingstone and the Mang'anja Chiefs

J. M. Schoffeleers

Livingstone had been in contact with the Mang'anja people for a period of nearly five years, from January 1859 to the close of 1863, during which period he undertook some seven journeys through the whole or part of their country. None of the Malawi peoples did he come to know so well as the Mang'anja and on few other African people did his travels have so much direct effect. Furthermore, on no other part of his second great expedition is there so much documentation. Livingstone himself left two extensive accounts, one in his journals, the other in a book which he published after the expedition. In addition to this, we also have in published form the journals of two of the men who for whole or part of the expedition were with him. In its later years the expedition was joined by the first representatives of the Universities' Mission to Central Africa, who also established themselves in Mang'anja country and had constant dealings with Livingstone. The missionaries seem to have been equally prolific authors. Again, we have two journals in published form as well as one account in book form. Much of this documentation bears on the political situation of the Mang'anja area and on the interaction between the Europeans and the Mang'anja chiefs.[1]

This chapter has a double purpose. It is an attempt at reconstructing the political situation as it was during Livingstone's time and at assessing Livingstone's influence on it. While the first of these purposes relates mainly to local history, the second may be of wider interest as it highlights a side of Livingstone's personality of which little is known as yet. The formal study of Livingstone's interaction with the peoples he visited has yet to begin. One of the reasons for this is that such studies require intimate knowledge of regional histories, which in many instances are absent. In other cases, where such histories are sufficiently

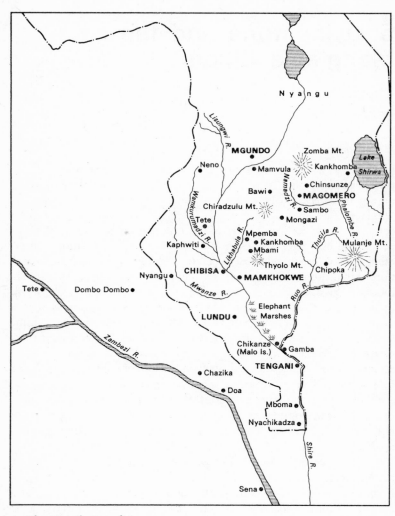

5 The Mang'anja polities

well known, Livingstone's own information is too scant to allow for fruitful use. Only rarely are the two requirements fulfilled, and the Mang'anja case seems to be one such instance.

The Mang'anja polities during Livingstone's time

The Mang'anja are the south-eastern section of the Chewa population, traditionally occupying the lower and middle valleys of the Shire river and the adjacent highlands. The earliest Chewa speakers were in occupation of large parts of this area by a date which is theoretically put at *circa* 1200 A.D., but it was only towards the sixteenth century that a centralised state system emerged under the impulse of a wave of immigrants known as the Phiri-Maravi, one of whose early settlements in the valley has recently been carbon-dated 1420 A.D. ($\pm$18).[2]

The Maravi state system developed from a widespread proto-Chewa structure in which village groupings constituted the effective political units. These consisted of a number of lineage-oriented villages, interrelated by ties of kinship and marriage, which united for economic, ritual and religious purposes. Characteristic of this organisation was the *nyau* brotherhood which provided the ritual and religious services within the cluster, and which forged close links between the adult men. The overall unity of the proto-Chewa population was experienced in a common language, culture, history and clan organisation and, more directly, in a network of territorial shrines with Kaphiri-Ntiwa in the Dzalanyama mountain at its centre.[3]

The Phiri-Maravi from the late fourteenth century onwards spread through this proto-Chewa territory, settling initially in relatively unoccupied country but gradually extending control over the proto-Chewa themselves. Occasional violence is mentioned but on the whole this seems to have been a process brought about by peaceful means. The centralising efforts of the Phiri-Maravi were only partially successful as they seem to have been incapable of obtaining direct control of the proto-Chewa village organisation, which remained intact as distinctive units within the later system. Consequently the resulting system showed a considerable degree of duality which was, *inter alia*, expressed in the clanship of the rulers, the senior headmen being mainly of proto-Chewa stock, and the higher echelons of power being occupied by the Phiri-Maravi. In the course of time the political duality came to be matched by an opposition in the religious organisation between territorial shrines, which were particularly associated with the ruling houses, and the *nyau* societies, which came to represent the interests of the village organisation.

For a period of about one hundred years, between the middle of the sixteenth and seventeenth centuries, the Maravi polities expanded their territory beyond the original proto-Chewa boundaries, in the south-west under Undi, and in the south-east under Lundu. Alpers reckons that the mysterious Zimba who wrought havoc in the Zambezi valley and along the east coast at the close of the sixteenth century were part of Lundu's campaigns.[4] Portuguese records also mention an attempt by the Karonga Muzula ('the Uprooter') in the latter half of this period to conquer Mutapa's lands south of the Zambezi. Lundu, one of the Maravi conquerors in this period, broke away from Undi and Kaphwiti and founded his own kingdom which came to include the highlands east of the Shire, the lower valley of that river and most of the country between the Zambezi, the Shire and the east coast, known to the Portuguese as the kingdom of Bororo. In consequence the Mang'anja group came to form two politically distinct units: a western section remaining under Undi and Kaphwiti and an eastern section under Lundu. This breakaway movement was different from earlier secessions in that Lundu aimed at total independence from the Maravi confederacy. Unwilling to recognise even the overall religious organisation which periodically brought the Maravi rulers together, he established an influential countercult with headquarters at the present Nsanje.[5] He was, however, unable to obtain total success. His political and religious reforms met with little support from chiefs in the northern section of his kingdom whose senior representative was Mankhokwe, and in 1622 Lundu was successfully challenged and defeated by the combined forces of the Karonga Muzula and the Portuguese, after which the kingdom became nominally part of Karonga's.

From the beginning of the seventeenth century onwards Undi's influence began to spread eastwards, and in time it challenged both the Karonga and the Lundu polities.[6] In the eighteenth century his was the most powerful Maravi kingdom in existence, and the northern Lundu chiefs under Mankhokwe had openly shifted their allegiance to Undi. The last quarter of the eighteenth century was a particularly fateful period for Lundu's state. Apart from the separatist tendencies among the northern chiefs, it had to face massive ethnic movements, occupation of tribal land by *prazeiros* and Portuguese rebels, and an increasingly aggressive trade system which involved direct contact between traders and local population without the intermediation of the chiefs. The greatest threat in terms of ethnic movements was posed by the Lomwe-Makua peoples, who had once belonged to the conquest area of the kingdom but had since become independent and had begun to move westwards. Lomwe communities were already found in several parts of the Mang'anja territory and, in two places, the Lake Chirwa and the Ruo areas, massive invasions were on the point of erupting. To the west of the valley the Nyungwe group, originating from around Tete, had already moved east in large numbers and established a sizeable settlement at Mikolongo in the Chikwawa district. The *prazos* and robber kingdoms of some Portuguese rebels posed another threat since they had begun to cast their eyes across the Zambezi as a result of increasing official resistance against their independent operations and the discovery of a largely untapped slave potential in the Mang'anja area. By *circa* 1800 the former Lundu kingdom consisted of little more than the lower valley. The king himself was reduced to insignificance and actual government was carried out by the senior chief Tengani who was able to rally the southern chiefs around him in the face of the Lolo and Portuguese threats.

Mankhokwe who in former years had successfully challenged Lundu, had a larger and more complex area to administer in which centralised control had become virtually impossible. His power collapsed after 1830 when political fragmentation had thrust effective authority back into the hands of the senior headmen. This meant in a sense a return to the early pre-Phiri system, and in some quarters it was indeed perceived as a reaction to the Maravi rule, but there were significant differences. Village groupings had become primarily defence units, each trying as best it could to ward off raids by the others.

The slave trade had developed both in terms of quantity and method of acquisition. When the first demands arose, headmen and lineage elders had responded by selling into slavery unwanted persons such as convicted witches and other criminals and any unprotected refugees they could lay hands on. In time, however, demands became more frequent and more specific. The coastal slave trade demanded able-bodied men, and the tribes along the Zambezi which had been subjected to the Ndebele raids asked the Portuguese for large numbers of women and children in exchange for ivory. Tete developed into an active trade centre and, although we have no figures for the preceding period, some idea of the extent of this trade may be gained by a report that in the period between October 1858 and June 1859, 5,782 elephant tusks were acquired and sold by the merchants of Tete alone.[7] Buying parties of Lomwe-Bajana employed by the merchants of Quelimane roamed the eastern highlands, while the Tete traders employed Chikunda retainers for the same purpose in the western part. The shortage of supply and the easy profit to be gained from this type of commerce led to inter-village raiding by the more enterprising headmen. Village clusters now began to concentrate in strong stockades surrounded by virtually impenetrable *euphorbia* hedges. On the valley floor the villages, ordinarily situated along the banks of the Shire and its perennial tributaries had been moved to clearings in the thick forest some distance away which could only be reached by long and narrow tunnels whose entrances were cleverly concealed.[8]

By the time of Livingstone's arrival, the Mang'anja country could be said to consist of four distinct areas according to the political situation prevailing in each.

The first to be considered is the south-western area, roughly between Tete and the present Chikwawa, through which ran the historical trade route into the Shire highlands. In this area three categories of people with political and military power were operating. One group consisted of a small number of Goanese and Portuguese rebels who had established outposts on the north bank and from there raided northwards for slaves. Another category consisted of Mang'anja middlemen in the slave trade who dealt particularly with the Tete merchants but who also had relations with the rebels. Their ultimate aim was to carve out small principalities after those of the rebels, with groups of retainers who would engage in raiding. Their most pressing problem was the acquisition of guns which they could not purchase in sufficient numbers to establish a firm power base. Finally, there were the traditional chiefs, the most important of these being Kapichi whose area had shrunk to almost half its original size and who could survive only by an uneasy truce with the rebels and the middlemen. Of the latter the most prominent was Chibisa who was eventually to play a crucial role in Livingstone's interaction with the Mang'anja.

Chibisa's original home was at Mikolongo where his lineage was related to the local chiefs.[9] He served in the household of one of the Tete merchants until some time after 1840 when he made a claim to the spirit mediumship of the chiefdom. After having passed the traditional test he was officially installed in that capacity. Soon it became clear, however, that he had aspired to that office in order to gain a political platform. This was a most unusual thing to do in terms of the Mang'anja tradition concerning spirit mediums, but he was successful in that he gained the support of the Nyungwe refugees. In the years which followed he extended his influence towards the Zambezi, mainly in Nyungwe area but, having twice suffered defeat at the hands of the Portuguese rebels Dombo-dombo and Chisaka, he was temporarily driven back to the east. After a brief sojourn near Lake Chirwa he was finally permitted to establish himself and his followers at Chikwawa where he made contact with Livingstone. His new village was strategically situated on the major trade route from Tete to the highlands, almost exactly in the geographical centre of Mang'anja territory. It was an ideal place for Chibisa whose ambition it was to rally the scattered Mang'anja forces around his person. His efforts, however, met with only moderate success since the very process of fragmentation which had allowed his rise to prominence prevented him from translating it into effective leadership. The divisions among the chiefs had already developed past the stage of reconciliation. Nothing less than ruthless force would be able to reunite the Mang'anja and neither Chibisa nor anyone else could apply such force. Despite all this, he was able to win the support of some of the chiefs who professed themselves willing to throw in their lot with him. These were mostly the chiefs of the eastern highlands, which is to be considered as the second of the four areas. The immediate threat in this part came from two sides: the Bajana slavers who acted on behalf of the Quelimane merchants and the Chikunda traders who acted for the Tete people. In it a situation of inter-village raiding had arisen on account of a number of headmen who wanted the profits from the trade and who like Chibisa wanted to make themselves independent of the chiefs. However, actual independency had not reached the stage that it had in the Tete-Chikwawa area. Traditional authority was still acknowledged, although only nominally, it being on the verge of collapse. The chiefs were looking among themselves for a person to give their loose confederation some new vigour and who would be able to check the abuses of the slave trade and the threatening incursions by the Yao. Their first choice was Mankhokwe, but he was both unable and unwilling, which made some of them turn to Chibisa.

The other two areas to be considered are the south-eastern area under Tengani and the north-western area under Mgundo Kaphwiti. These differ considerably from the former two in that each of them had a powerful leader to check fragmentation at least for the moment. In addition both were similar in that they made up the heartland of the former paramountcies.

This then was the political situation in which Livingstone found himself – a centuries' old state system which under the influence of progressive geographical contraction had, in two of its territories, the eastern highlands and the Tete-Chikwawa area, become increasingly subject to internal fragmentation. The pattern of fragmentation was determined by the historical division between the senior village headmen and the higher echelons of power. It led the senior headmen to seek independence from the chiefs and establish a power base of their own. Opportunities for this were provided by the escalation of the slave trade in which headmen frequently became middlemen, and in which the more successful among them were able to obtain guns and become slave raiders in their own right. The chiefs by and large had abstained from this kind of action and among their numbers attempts were made to counteract the segmentary process by inviting their senior representative Mankhokwe to assume overall leadership. Mankhokwe's unwillingness to accede to their attempts was probably the logical consequence of his assessment of the political situation. As a matter of fact he concentrated on the defence of his own area and refrained from allying with anyone unless forced to, as he ultimately was. Those among the highlands chiefs who were most immediately threatened were prepared to accept Chibisa as an alternative, but their number was too small and their authority too insignificant to provide Chibisa with any effective power.

In the territories of Tengani below the Ruo confluence and of Mgundo Kaphwiti above the Shire rapids conditions were less critical and the ruling chiefs had been able to keep their headmen under control. It was Tengani who had organised the most effective defence system, and it was through Tengani's area that Livingstone had to pass first.

The realities of the European presence

Livingstone's expedition had been planned as more than a mere exploratory journey; it was definitely associated with schemes of settlement and civilisation. This was already clear from the statement of the Chancellor of Exchequer when he justified his government's contribution to the expedition by pointing out that it might lead to important consequences particularly with regard to the cotton industry. Livingstone further clarified this idea in his instructions to Kirk, economic botanist and medical officer to the expedition, when he wrote that the chief aim of the expedition was to explore the mineral and agricultural resources of east and central Africa, and to engage the inhabitants to exploit these resources with a view to exporting raw materials to England and by so doing to help kill the slave trade. Among other things this would mean the maintenance of some permanent base station where experiment on crops could be carried out for the benefit of the population.[10] The official documents, moreover, do not disclose Livingstone's more private ideas, which went considerably further, envisioning colonies of Englishmen in the healthier regions of central Africa, which would function as centres of 'civilisation'.[11] He further

118

assumed that it would be possible to win the influential chiefs over to this idea, and he therefore instructed the members of the expedition to treat the leading men of villages with great respect and to do nothing that would weaken their authority. Peaceful persuasion and non-interference were thus to be the major guidelines of his policy which, however, suffered from two kinds of weakness. One was the assumption, already mentioned, that his industrial and colonial propositions were attractive enough to be accepted by the chiefs and the local population. The other was that Livingstone had a strong urge to succeed in view of the high expectations which he had generated among industrialists, church people and others. Failure of his plans carried with it the possibility of general disillusionment on their side and disgrace on his own. As a matter of fact, the expedition came already close to failure even before it entered Malawi, when the Cabora Bassa rapids in the Zambezi proved impassable. An entry in his diary, dated 1 September 1858, shows his particular feelings at this moment when he writes that 'the high position I have been raised to is not of my seeking, nor was the éclat which greeted me at home a matter of my choice'.[12] True as this may have been, it did not do away with the fact that the high and the mighty had placed their trust in him and that he had accepted that trust. Nor were physical obstacles the only ones he had to overcome: there were also the chiefs whom he intended to persuade including those who did not wish to be persuaded. Rapids and rocks were one thing, people were another, since their attitudes struck at the very heart of his avowed ideals. The test came as soon as he entered the Shire and reached Tengani's village.

Tengani, as we have seen, was one of the most powerful Mang'anja chiefs who had been able to retain firm control over his area. This he had managed by rigorously keeping out all Portuguese traders who had proved to be the main disruptive element elsewhere. Not long before Livingstone's arrival, his armed men had managed to turn back a Portuguese ship. Livingstone had heard the story at Sena and he knew that he would be far from welcome. His party was hailed by a band of warriors whom Kirk estimated at between 400 and 500 and whose weapons were superior to anything they had seen on the Zambezi. Peaceful persuasion was of little help, for Tengani's people were not prepared to make a distinction between English and Portuguese, had they been able to. Confronted with their continuing threats Livingstone finally reacted by having his party's arms loaded and showing them to the chief's trembling deputy with the announcement that if Tengani's people were ready to fight, so was he.[13] Permission to proceed was reluctantly given, and the ship continued its course with an unhappy and morose Livingstone aboard. In his conversations with Portuguese traders and officials he had learned that they were in the habit of asking a chief's permission to pass through his territory and that they even paid dues for this privilege. He had been frankly appalled as he thought this to be a serious weakness on the side of the Portuguese, and he was determined that no such tricks should be played on him. Now he was indignant not because he had used the threat of arms to force his way through, but because the impression had been created that he had asked permission to pass on. He realised very well that he had broken a carefully maintained blockade but he thought that it was his deserved right to do so since Tengani had no business to halt rightful trade or peaceful exploration. Only much later did it dawn on him and Kirk among others that much more was involved and that by forcing their way in they had inadvertently opened the door to the slave traders who everywhere began treading in their footsteps.[14] Tengani in his turn felt a keen resentment against Livingstone and he remained deeply suspicious of his aims. This was not even dispelled when during the second ascent of the river two months later, Livingstone was finally able to see the chief himself and explain the purpose of his travels. For one thing, the purpose did not become clear, because the interpreter, mixing up cotton with Christianity, managed to tell the chief that the Book said that he had to plant cotton and sell it to the English. For another thing, Tengani had quite different worries, chief among them the growing pressure from the slave traders. At Tengani's court the incident is remembered to this day in a rather garbled fashion. Confusing the earlier incident with the Portuguese ship and the later attacks by Livingstone's Kololo from the north, they maintain that they had managed to turn his ship back by pelting it with stones. Only Livingstone had one better on them by returning to the Zambezi, then called 'Sand River', and sneaking into the country from the north. It was thus that the 'Sand River' was renamed Zambezi or Zembezi from the root -zembez- ('to hide something as a thief').[15] Although treachery, as implied in this story, was totally alien to Livingstone's character, it was what people chose to remember because of the later Kololo episode. Had it not been for these men, Livingstone would probably have gone down in Mang'anja oral history as some mythical visitor from distant lands who came to converse with their ancestors. As it was, the two men were not to see each other again. While continuing with his first ascent Livingstone had become quite withdrawn. He sailed by the town of the Paramount Mankhokwe, possibly because he was not aware of his status, and it was only after some urging by Kirk, who feared that the expedition had already acquired a bad

Livingstone's operating bag

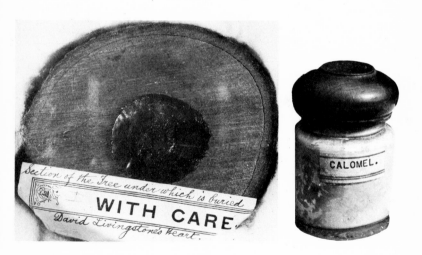

Left: Section from the tree under which David Livingstone's heart is buried. This is at Chitambo, Zambia. *Right:* Livingstone's last words, spoken to his servant, were 'Give me my Calomel bottle. You may go now.' It is probable that this was the actual bottle.

Upper left: Bishop Mackenzie. *Lower left:* Revd Horace Waller.
Right: Bishop W. G. Tozer.

The mission station at Magomero

name, that he began to speak to the people again. Near the Murchison rapids which brought his first exploration of the Mang'anja country to an end, he met briefly with the frightened messengers of a few inconsequential headmen to whom he made a small present. Little of lasting importance had been achieved, and the expedition returned to prepare itself for a second attempt.

Two months later Livingstone was back on the Shire and this time he brought himself to spend the night at Mankhokwe's village. The following morning the party was told to wait a little while for the chief to make his appearance but Livingstone left in a huff, declaring that this was only done to impress him with the greatness of the chief. He hoped that this would teach Mankhokwe and the likes of him a lesson, though what lesson it is difficult to see, unless that Englishmen did not wish to be treated as Portuguese were. On the next occasion Mankhokwe simply refused to see him, and only later did the two men meet face to face, but the breach was never healed. Yet another possible ally had been antagonised by lack of diplomacy. Livingstone could only, with some difficulty, bring himself to believe that Mankhokwe was the actual Paramount of the northern Mang'anja. He kept on enquiring from the chiefs whom he met but in that area the answer was always the same. He was told though that there was one more important person still, who in theory was the ruler of all Mang'anja, but this person he never met. Although the name of this supreme ruler is not mentioned, the reference is almost certainly to Lundu, who was then old, blind and powerless, and meeting him would have been of little advantage.

The hostility between Livingstone and Mankhokwe was definitely exacerbated when the explorer at long last found a friend in Chibisa. The reception was among the warmest: here were to be experienced none of the formalities of intermediaries and none of the suspicions which the expedition had met with everywhere else. All information that Livingstone asked for was given, although not all of it was equally reliable. Chibisa, very much the outgoing character, assured Livingstone that the only bad tribes were the ones that he had come across downstream but that from now on things would be well. People in the highlands were quite different. They were civil, like children, and somewhat less advanced, because they were still dressed in bark cloth instead of cotton. It is quite clear that for some reason or another Chibisa wanted Livingstone to begin his exploration of the highlands and to this end he was even prepared to tell a few lies, conditions in the highlands being possibly even worse than those in the valley as Livingstone was soon to experience. Without realising it, he had become a part of Chibisa's ambitious but naïve scheme to establish his authority in all the area between Chikwawa and Zomba. Initially, Livingstone fell for it and, when he finally realised what Chibisa was up to, he refused to dissociate himself from him, partly because Chibisa was the only influential ally in an otherwise hostile environment; partly because Chibisa's village occupied a strategic position as a port for the expedition's ship and as a base camp for the exploration of the highlands.

Realising that his association with Livingstone might estrange him from the other chiefs and fearing that they might retaliate after Livingstone's departure, Chibisa tried to play off both sides by informing them of Livingstone's intention to explore the highlands. There is no information as to which chiefs, apart from Mankhokwe, were notified, nor what their reply was, but it is not likely that their reaction was favourable because soon after the expedition had set out one of Chibisa's men was seized and nearly killed for having brought the English. What Chibisa wanted most urgently were guns and, if possible, the military backing of the English. This he revealed only after several days had passed and after telling Livingstone stories of how he had been attacked by some Mang'anja headmen from across the river. He now pleaded for the expedition's assistance to undertake a punitive action against them. The real truth dawned on Livingstone when he found out that the very first villages through which he travelled on his way to the highlands had been laid waste by Chibisa himself. Livingstone was also annoyed and at times acutely angered when some of Chibisa's deputies, following in his trail, made it appear to the local population that the expedition had been sent out by their master in order to lay claim to all the country it passed through. One day, he had even occasion to fear for his life on their account. On the whole, the reception in the highlands was decidedly cool, if not hostile, and quite in contrast to the picture of the innocent people that Chibisa had conjured up. The political situation was in Kirk's words very much that of every man to himself. No one person seemed to be in control of a large area like Tengani and Mankhokwe, and the expedition received a welter of contradictory information as to the traditional or actual status of individual chiefs and headmen. From all appearances what counted was the right of the strongest.[16] Going towards Lake Chirwa, the aim of this second journey, hostility, if anything, kept increasing. Signals were transmitted from village to village and cries of defiance and intimidation were shouted in their ears. Kirk even mentions that the local people made an attempt to drown them in the lake.[17] If Livingstone had found his healthy highlands where exemplary

Englishmen would thrive, it was certainly not the place, not for the moment at least, where they could survive without first mastering the power game. Yet it was in this situation that the first mission was to begin only two years later when the situation had even further deteriorated, and the very first problem with which the missionaries were faced was precisely that of their place in the power game.

Later in the year, on his journey to Lake Malawi, Livingstone was spared the nuisance of Chibisa's ministrations, for he had left Chikwawa where, in the absence of Livingstone, he had come to fear for his life. Moving to Doa, his Zambezi village, he had resumed his role of middleman for the slave traders, leaving his headman Chechona behind at Chikwawa to keep up his claim to the place. Chechona, however, had little power to provide the expedition and its members with any measure of protection. Some other arrangement was needed if the expedition was to retain its base in the face of an unsympathetic Mankhokwe. A solution ultimately presented itself when Livingstone had to dismiss his Kololo porters for a serious breach of discipline and decided to settle them at Chikwawa until he could take them again to their country. This event heralded a significant change in Livingstone's policy of non-interference. To be sure, there was a semblance of conformity, because permission was sought from Chibisa. On the other hand, one may equally regard it as contrary to Livingstone's avowed policy, since it was clearly done against the will of Mankhokwe who could not fail to see in it an immediate threat to his position. The Kololo had guns, that most coveted of possessions, given them by Livingstone to gain a living by hunting and to protect themselves. But guns could be put to other uses as well and before Livingstone appeared again on the scene with his first missionaries in June 1861, his former porters had already become headmen in their own right with a prosperous community to look after.

The Universities' Mission to Central Africa had been founded after Livingstone's visit to Cambridge and Oxford. Its purpose was 'to found a little agricultural village which should show the natives how to export cotton, which should show them the truths of the Christian religion, and display in its corporate life the model of a Christian and civilised community; and thus, by their presence, their example, and their economy, would begin to destroy slavery.'[18] It was a plan devised for an area and for living conditions of which nobody had any idea. Their only guide to go by was Livingstone, whose optimism seemed for once to be greater than his sense of realism. Otherwise it is hard to see how he could have possibly encouraged the foundation of a mission at that time and that place. In the nine months that the mission held out in the highlands virtually everything went wrong. The issue of interference in tribal affairs had already come up before they marched off to their new station. When they arrived at Chikwawa they found a Mang'anja embassy from Zomba on its way to ask for Chibisa's assistance against the Yao. Its claim, incorrect as it turned out, was that the Portuguese were supplying the Yao with guns to enslave the Mang'anja. Rowley, one of the mission party, assured them that God was angry with such evil people, and that the mission would bring peace once it was settled in Zomba. Rowley was duly edified when he saw tears rolling down their cheeks, but, unbeknown to him, 'the poor fellows' had interpreted his pacifist words as a promise of possible armed support. And armed support they got. On three occasions the missionaries decided to use fire-arms against the Yao, and once they gave a solemn undertaking to the assembled Mang'anja chiefs that they would support them against the Yao if they themselves forsook slaving activities from then onwards. Their decision to make use of guns can to some extent be traced back to Livingstone. They had discussed the matter with him, Bishop Mackenzie being more than loathe to carry a gun, but Livingstone had assured them that they were 'the greatest pacificators in the world' and that he would not hesitate to use them against 'marauding savages'. As if to make the point clear he himself gave the order to fire when the mission party had gone out to meet the Yao for the first time. After guiding the mission to Magomero, he took leave, saying rather incongruously that they should not take part in any tribal war, but fortify the mission and make it into a place of refuge, which advice the missionaries took to mean that he approved of the use of fire-arms for defence but not for attack. The dividing line between the two proved to be a rather thin one, and their support of the Mang'anja predictably enraged the Yao. The mission also found out that the Mang'anja were at least as guilty as the Yao, when a count of 'liberated slaves' at the mission station revealed that fully three-quarters were Yao instead of Mang'anja. In the end, when tribal warfare flared up again in April 1862, they were prepared to draw the only logical conclusion which was that they themselves were pawns in local intrigue. They had in Chadwick's words, only two courses open to them. They could set up a little English kingdom, based on a few English guns, with all that this would mean, depriving local chieftains of their rights, or they could abandon the region altogether. Their soul-searching led them to admit that, in a manner, they were already little kings and that their community had already become a kind of theocracy. The dilemma was starkly clear: either to assume full secular power and survive, or decline and go.

or needed the whole yr. round

Also → agric. paymt. + unempl? in hid ie rising prices +
inflation? Gives subsistence bhu labourer + pauper
vanished. Whereas fore farm laun actes for the
landed interest.

Pay decreases when Speenhamland sys. intro'd
Poor Law made assistance cheaper to be a
deterrent to the lazy (always)

All in blbyd of coming of industrializat⁻

3. The village wartes
Came for many was perish occasionally ventures
to fairs. Inn the meeting place in the village, + also
centre for politics + discussion

wealth? 1830 was to attempt to win back than
d? rights.
The labourers were rioters wanted money + employ⁻
not land.

HOBSBAWM + RUDE   Captain Swing

Not peas. econ. at what

3 classes :   landowner
              farmer
              farm labourers

(effects) enclosures on last 2 groups
i. The Rural Poor

- Yanga 'servants' (wh. they became when c.25-30 Live) at "living" Fairs or Maps
- labourers
- wage: even in good growing said different to the farmer + labr
- poor : wh. of pop = agrarian rev'n in (78 but
a permanent surplus of labour where the fastest V side
notably swing system occurred where the fastest
population. OTD system g employ't decline the
servant. Gt. shattering g contract hire in (18
Expansion g cereal crop. + → casual labourers

They opted for withdrawal and left the highlands on 25 April 1862. The time allotted to them was too short to begin evangelising and the political circumstances were so adverse that the industrial side of their mission was also a complete failure. They now went to live near another 'little English kingdom', the settlement of the Kololo, who had solved the same dilemma in their own way.

The black 'English' chiefs

Technically, the Kololo were only granted hospitality at Chibisa's village, but to all intents and purposes they had become headmen and prosperous ones at that. Rowley, who was not unsympathetic to their cause and who as their neighbour had plenty of opportunity to observe them, wrote that they were:

> ... revelling in all good things that part of the world could procure, masters of the village, monarchs of all they surveyed. They had cattle by the score, fowls by the hundred; they ate the finest corn and drank the best of pombi (beer). They and their numerous wives were clothed and decorated without regard to cost. They had sprung all at once from poverty to wealth, from a condition little removed from bondage to that of lords of creation.[19]

The Kololo considered themselves and were considered by the Mang'anja as 'Englishmen', which idea found ritual expression in their habit of greeting each other in English. In keeping with what they had come to see as the main preoccupation of their erstwhile master they went about freeing slaves and giving protection to numerous companies of refugees whom they fed from the spoils of their raids, but whom they also set to work in their large fields. While in the years 1862–3 all other parts of the Mang'anja country suffered from a catastrophic famine caused by the combined effects of drought and war, the Kololo settlement prospered among its lush river gardens. Thus they brought to fruition yet another English ideal, that of an industrial community. Had Livingstone asked them to organise the cotton plantations of his dreams, they would in all probability have set out to do this, such was still their veneration for him. Thus it came as a shock when they heard that the English in the persons of the U.M.C.A. publicly disowned them.

The conflict began soon after the missionaries had set up house about a mile away from the Kololo. While at Magomero they had been on the most friendly terms. The Kololo gave a hand when the mission was being put up and rendered numerous other services from their settlement on the Shire. Once, when the mission had run out of cloth, then the general means of barter and payment, the Kololo gladly supplied them from their own stock awaiting a new shipment. There was disappointment on the mission side when the Kololo were found to have relationships with some of the liberated women slaves, but even that did not really harm their good relationships, though the bishop bade them go. The nearness of the two encampments at Chikwawa however, changed all this, since the missionaries were from now on identified with the Kololo and whatever mischief the Kololo did was put at the mission's door. Having only just taken the decision to abstain from all interference in tribal affairs, and having sacrificed their first mission station for this purpose, they were once more being accused of the same thing. The Kololo being to the valley what the Yao were to the highlands, the missionaries were now, from the Mang'anja viewpoint, siding with the enemy. Mankhokwe made the strongest representations to help him remove the Kololo, but wise from bitter experience the missionaries did not give in. Instead, they laid their own and the chiefs' complaints before Livingstone who was, however, little inclined to believe them. He intimated to the missionaries that they were probably being used by some unscrupulous Mang'anja and thus they found themselves under attack from all sides.

If the missionaries' attitude had shocked them, the Kololo were in for a further disappointment, this time from Chibisa. When he gave permission for the Kololo to settle in his village at Chikwawa, he did so partly to please Livingstone whose friendship still meant something in terms of status and protection. He may also have thought of the Kololo settlement as a means of checking Mankhokwe and of the Kololo themselves as possible allies in his intermittent feuds with the Portuguese freebooters. The Kololo themselves probably regarded Chibisa as the one who would ultimately emerge as the strong man of the valley. Accordingly, they went to his assistance twice, but on the second occasion they met an angry and defeated Chibisa on his way back to Chikwawa. Once again the mission was asked to provide guns and ammunition, and once again they refused, although they accepted an elephant tusk from him wherewith to buy powder from Livingstone. Ultimately they managed to get it from a Portuguese trader but only after Chibisa had made his way back to the Zambezi in a desperate last stand. Frustrated on all sides and in possession of a curt message from Mankhokwe to dismiss the English, Chibisa decided on a fresh approach. He invited a number of Mang'anja chiefs and headmen to a meeting at which he denounced the Kololo for their violence and depredations and the missionaries for having brought them in. The missionaries feared that violence might break out at any time and the Kololo, now seemingly deserted by all, decided to move their village to a safer place. On the point of doing this the rumour went round, spread by Chibisa's headman, that the missionaries intended to exterminate the Kololo. Although Rowley, as the mission's spokesman, officially denied this, there was some truth in this rumour as his colleague Waller had decided on his own account to supply Chibisa with firearms against the Kololo.

After Chibisa's departure and the move of the Kololo village peace returned for a while. Livingstone had also come upstream to attempt the transportation of a ship past the rapids, and his presence did much to soothe tempers on both sides. The famine had come to an end, although it had decimated the population. The missionaries were now thinking of returning to the highlands where the Yao conquest was almost complete. But it proved to be the lull before a storm. In March 1863 both Tengani and Chibisa were killed and the valley was now open to invaders from the south and the west. The U.M.C.A. decided to withdraw from the country in June and around the same time Livingstone's expedition was recalled. The time had come for the Kololo to act or to perish. With Livingstone and everyone else out of the way they decided to act. In a series of swift strokes and aided by Yao gunmen and Mang'anja retainers, they first secured the defences to the south and west and then proceeded to the systematic extermination of the Mang'anja chiefs. Kapichi, Mgundo Kaphwiti and Lundu were among the first victims. Only Mankhokwe proved unconquerable for a number of years, but finally he, too, was defeated. Wars ensued with the Massingire *prazo*, and these most dangerous of all enemies were finally driven back behind the Ruo.[20] In a very real sense the Kololo thus became the saviours of the Mang'anja for without them the Mang'anja would probably have been wiped out, although the present Mang'anja will be the last to concede this. The ruthless force that the Mang'anja needed to unite again in the face of total onslaught was ultimately provided by Livingstone. His men organized a fully centralised polity, a feat that the lines of the murdered Phiri chiefs had never been able to perform. This success was partly due to their guns but in a very real sense also to their intuitive understanding of the historic duality in the Mang'anja political system. They destroyed the aristocratic leadership together with their shrines, but they spared the senior headmen and the *nyau* societies of which they took control. Their absolute rule lasted only a quarter of a century but this was long enough to enable the English to return and for the country of the Mang'anja to become a British Protectorate.[21]

Conclusion

It seems clear that from the very beginning Livingstone placed himself
in a dilemma by stressing a policy of non-intervention and respect for
established authority. He solved it in fact by abandoning these principles when the necessity arose. He may not always have been aware of
this but he felt the occasional need to justify himself by disparaging
his antagonists. One might suggest that his breach of principles was
only caused by the abnormality of the situation, but few would accept
that his far-reaching plans could have possibly been carried out without
the application of moral and physical force. Livingstone was not free
from the colonial presumption that European-Christian civilisation
was superior, and that its introduction elsewhere was desirable, even
when the potential recipients did not immediately understand this.
In addition, he was possessed of a strong sense of mission which was
one of the major driving forces behind his explorations.

As it was, Livingstone used the threat of arms against Tengani;
he spurned the authority of Mankhokwe; he lent support to the
upstart Chibisa; he fired on the Yao; and he settled the foreign Kololo
in the heart of the country. Whatever their justification, these were
deliberate acts of interference, although inevitable if the expedition
was to survive. From the viewpoint of the Mang'anja he came at a
time when in large sections of their country aristocratic leadership
was breaking down and a type of fragmentation was coming into
existence. This brought enterprising headmen and traders into prominence. It was typical of that situation that Livingstone was in conflict
with such members of the aristocracy as were still in authority and
that he was on friendly terms with chiefs definitely on the way out
and headmen on the ascendancy. While these people tried to use
Livingstone and his associates to salvage or boost their political power,
Livingstone in his turn used them to promote his own cause. The
expedition's permanent base and the first and second mission station
were all in the territories of such men. It may have been the easier
solution but it was fraught with potential conflict and virtually doomed
to failure. There were unending demands for arms and armed assistance on the expedition and the mission and, whatever the decision,
it always caused discontent and in the end it always reflected negatively
on the Europeans.

The expedition and the mission could have chosen two alternatives which would have given them a greater chance of success and survival. One of these would have been to place themselves squarely under the authority of the chiefs still in power; the other was to establish themselves as political overlords. The first alternative was rejected following a clash of personalities; the other was rejected because of a clash of principles. In the end, only the second alternative remained, and it was left to the Kololo to take it up.

Notes

Part of this paper is based on fieldwork carried out between 1966–68 with financial aid from the Nuffield Foundation, London, to whom grateful acknowledgement is made. I am also indebted to Mr E. C. Mandala, student at Chancellor College, University of Malawi, for his assistance with the documentary research and his comments.

1 For the Livingstone expedition's writings see:
   J. P. R. Wallis (ed.), *The Zambezi Expedition of David Livingstone, 1858–1863*, London 1956;
   David and Charles Livingstone, *Narrative of an Expedition to the Zambesi and its Tributaries and of the Discoveries of Lakes Shirwa and Nyassa, 1858–1864*, London, 1865;
   R. Foskett (ed.), *The Zambesi Journal and Letters of Dr John Kirk, 1858–1863*, Edinburgh, 1965;
   E. C. Tabler (ed.), *The Zambezi Papers of Richard Thornton*, London, 1963.
   For the U.M.C.A.'s writings see:
   N. R. Bennett and M. Ylvisaker (eds), *The Central African Journal of Lovell J. Procter, 1860–1864*, Boston, 1971;
   J. P. R. Wallis (ed.), *The Zambezi Journal of James Stewart, 1862–3*, London, 1952;
   H. Rowley, *The Story of the Universities' Mission to Central Africa*, London, 1866.

2 The samples for this radio-carbon dating were taken from what appeared to be one of the earliest middens at the original shrine of the Kaphwiti chiefs near the court of the present Chief Chapananga in the Chikwawa District. I am indebted to Professor Desmond Clark who kindly consented to carry out archaeological research *in loco* in August 1968, and to Drs Recher and Rainer Protsch of the U.C.L.A. Radio Carbon Laboratory who undertook to process the samples.

3 Cf. J. M. Schoffeleers, 'The Chisumphi and M'bona cults in Malawi: A Comparative History'; paper presented at the Conference on the History of Central African Religious Systems, Lusaka, Zambia, 1972.

4 Cf. E. Alpers, 'The Mutapa and Malawi Political Systems to the Time of the Ngoni Invasions', in T. O. Ranger (ed.), *Aspects of Central African History*, London, 1968, pp. 21–2.

5 Cf. Schoffeleers, op. cit.

6 An account of the history of Undi's kingdom appears in H. W. Langworthy, 'Chewa or Malawi Political Organisation in the Pre-colonial Era', in B. Pachai

(ed.), *The Early History of Malawi*, London, 1972, pp. 104–22.

7 Rowley (op. cit., p. 112) relates how the Tete merchants exchanged slaves for ivory with the Banyai tribesmen who had lost most of their women and children in the Ndebele raids and wanted them replaced. Part of this supply came from Mang'anja country. The figures on the Tete ivory trade are taken from Livingstone's journals; cf. Wallis, *The Zambesi Expedition of David Livingstone*, p. 117.

8 Cf. Kirk's testimony in Foskett, op. cit., p. 164.

9 The best source on Chibisa are Rowley, op. cit. and Bennett and Ylvisaker, op. cit.

10 Cf. R. Coupland, *Kirk on the Zambesi. A Chapter of African History*, Oxford, 1928, pp. 76, 103–8.

11 Cf. an entry in Livingstone's journal, probably written in October, 1859. 'Colonization from a country such as ours (ought to be looked upon as) . . . the performance of an imperative duty to our blood, our country, our religion and to human kind.'

12 Wallis, *The Zambesi Expedition*, p. 39.

13 Ibid., p. 78. This account is to be compared with the one in D. and C. Livingstone, *Narrative*, p. 76, which gives an entirely different impression and describes the meeting as a highly satisfactory one. The *Narrative* appears to be a highly structured account in which the first and later years of the expedition are placed in contrast to each other.

14 Cf. Coupland, op. cit., pp. 193–4; D. and C. Livingstone, *Narrative*, pp. 355–6.

15 This tradition was recorded at Tengani's court, April 1972.

16 Cf. Foskett, *The Zambesi Journal of Dr John Kirk*, pp. 183 and passim.

17 Ibid., pp. 194–5.

18 O. Chadwick, *Mackenzie's Grave*, London, 1959, pp. 17–18.

19 Rowley, op. cit., p. 277; Chadwick, op. cit., p. 157.

20 For an account of the relationships of the Kololo with the Massingire, cf. M. D. D. Newitt, 'The Massingire Rising of 1884', *Journal of African History*, XI, 1, 1970, pp. 87–105.

21 For an account of the role of the Kololo in the genesis of the Central African Protectorate, cf. P. R. Warhurst, 'Portugal's Bid for Southern Malawi, 1882–1891', in Pachai et al. (eds), *Malawi Past and Present*, Blantyre, 1971, pp. 1–19.

6 David Livingstone, the Arabs and the Slave Trade

Melvin E. Page

The name of David Livingstone has been since his own time inexorably bound up with the campaign to end the East African slave trade. For many, both then and now, this has also meant Livingstone's opposition to the Arabs of East and Central Africa who were, more often than not, the principal generators of this traffic in human beings.[1] Clearly, the last twenty years of his life were spent in efforts, often agonising, largely aimed at ending the slave trade. Less than a year before his death he confided to his daughter:

> No one can estimate the amount of God-pleasing good that will be done, if by Divine favour this awful slave-trade, into the midst of which I have come, be abolished. This will be something to have lived for, and the conviction has grown in my mind that it was for this end I have been detained so long.[2]

Although he knew many were involved, Africans and Europeans included, he saw East Africa as 'the slaving field of the Banians and Arabs'.[3] And while the former were the Zanzibar-based financiers of the operations, it was the latter, the Arabs, whom he saw as both the perpetrators of the slave trade and the purchasers of its human produce.

It was easy for Livingstone's contemporaries and more recent historians to seize upon his descriptions of the Arabs as the chief villains of the slave trade.[4] On occasion he called them 'the vilest of the vile', and, in reference to their Islamic faith, 'the most cruel and bloodthirsty missionaries in existence'. Nor did he trust them. 'Falsehood seems ingrained in their constitutions,' he wrote; and he advised John Kirk that he 'must not trust to Arabs'.[5] Through such descriptions Livingstone's views seem clear. Yet he also saw these men as 'my Arab friends'.

They often treated him with 'the greatest kindness', and offered him their 'genuine hospitality'. They could be, indeed, 'gentlemen' and he often found that they 'traded with honour'.[6] Can these be the descriptions of the same men, written by the same man? This apparent contradiction has puzzled students of David Livingstone. One writer, perhaps overdramatising the matter, called this 'the amazing paradox of David Livingstone's career'.[7] Even the most knowledgeable scholars and careful biographers of Livingstone have found it difficult to reach a satisfactory explanation for this ambivalence in his views.[8]

Perhaps the puzzlement is really an outcome of the generalisations which followed in the wake of Livingstone's work. Many of these are best described as sweeping generalisations or exaggerations,[9] often promulgated with a single purpose in mind: enlisting support for the final abolition of the slave trade in East Africa. Such anti-slaverism, of course, became one of the cornerstones of British policy in the region.[10] And, as already mentioned, it has also been the principal focus of historical interest in Livingstone. It was true shortly after his death and by and large remains true today. It is equally true whether one is speaking of European historical writing[11] or of Africans in the villages.[12] But such an institutional emphasis in Livingstoniana has tended to blur the understanding of his relationships with individual Arabs. This chapter aims to correct this imbalance by looking more closely at David Livingstone and the Arabs and their involvement in the slave trade, and by examining their individual relationships with the explorer.[13]

Livingstone first met the slave trade of Central and East Africa during his initial journey to the Zambezi in 1851. At the court of Sebituane of the Makololo he and William Cotton Oswell were astounded to find that, according to their hosts, the slave trade had come into the region only the previous year. The principal traders Livingstone identified as Mambari, whom he incorrectly described as 'of the Ambonda family which inhabits the country southwest of Angola' and who were African agents of Portuguese merchants.[14] Although it has been suggested by one noted historian that Arabs were responsible for the introduction of the commerce in human beings,[15] Livingstone and Oswell clearly were aware that this was not the case. In fact, they suggested that Arab merchants from the east, about whom the Makololo had some limited knowledge, were prevented from entering the region by the large falls which they were told blocked passage on the Zambezi.[16]

Two years later, however, there was no doubt that Arabs had come to the lands of the Makololo. And there Livingstone had his first personal encounters with them. He recounts having met two Arabs

132

from Zanzibar, subjects of the Sultan of Oman, who also ruled Zanzibar. These men, Nyafman bin Chombo and Alim Minokombo, were members of a trading caravan led by Said bin Habib bin Salem el Afifi whom Livingstone was later to meet on numerous occasions. By way of introduction, Nyafman bin Chombo wrote in Livingstone's notebook, approximately as follows: 'O dear one who loveth us and who art noble, exceedingly noble, the noble one whom we hold dear; Livingstone may God and his Prophet give him help.'

Though the writing is clearly that of a barely literate Arabic speaker, the missionary was most impressed by the Arab's ability to write. And he seems to have struck up a friendship with the Arabs. They came one evening to pay him 'a friendly visit' and amicably discussed a number of topics through a combination of 'words and signs . . . with assistance [of] guessing'.[17] Livingstone managed to extract some geographic information, including a description of Lake Tanganyika. They also chatted about religion: the problem of Islamic dietary laws in the middle of Africa and a consideration of the relative merits of various prophets, including Jesus and Muhammad.

Such good relations continued even after Livingstone's return from his journey of nearly two years to Loanda. At this time his principal acquaintance appears to have become Said bin Habib himself, the leader of the Arab merchants. Having met Said briefly at Naliele after just setting out for the west coast, Livingstone renewed that friendship on his return. It was from him that the missionary obtained a description of the route to Zanzibar, including the lake and river systems which crossed the path to the east coast. At one point he contemplated the offer of the Arab to travel along that route, where he might 'discover Tanganyeta or Lake Nyasa', but he rejected the temptation feeling 'it will not be right to go with Rya Syde [bin Habib] for the sake of the fame of discovering another lake'.[18] He was willing, however, to trust his precious letters to Said, whom he called 'my Arabian post-office man'. Livingstone seems to have been most pleased by this attention and quite unexpectedly impressed with the candour of his Arab friends. He wrote to William Thompson, the London Missionary Society agent at the Cape. 'The Arabs . . . strike up great friendships with me wherever we meet, calling me "father", &c., and telling the people how much we hate the slave trade in which they are engaged.'[19]

It was precisely this, the slave trade, that initially caused Livingstone some doubts about his new friendships. Although he realised that 'Portuguese, Mambari and Arabs were all intent on the slave trade',[20] he also knew, as he told an audience at Cambridge in 1857, four years later, it was a form of commerce 'of which the poorer people have an

133

unmitigated horror'.[21] The involvement of the Arabs in this traffic obviously troubled him deeply. But other reasons as well led him to admit that he was 'not possessing much confidence' in Said bin Habib and his fellows.[22] Even in their quests for ivory, the Arabs used their guns to disrupt and often kill the African populace rather than trade freely and openly. It seemed, too, that they were encouraging the Makololo to adopt similar practices. Livingstone also objected to the growing intervention of the Arabs into local commercial activities. Said bin Habib's agreement to conduct a party of Makololo to Loanda brought a prophetic note in his journal: 'It is difficult not to entertain doubts of his sincerity.'[23] His missionary tendencies also caused him to object to the marriage of Said to Sebituane's daughter. 'This is the plan the Arabs adopt for gaining influence in a tribe,' he wrote, fearing that it would gradually allow them 'to draw all the tribe over to their religion'.[24] Thus he could write of these new friends, 'Shame upon us if we are to be outdone by slaver traders ... Arabs from Zanguebar.' The answer he developed to this challenge was to be the criterion for all his subsequent geographic and missionary efforts: the introduction of European 'legitimate' commerce and the propagation of the Christian gospel. So he resolved that 'In pursuance of a nobler object than theirs, I have determined to try and fulfill the second part of my enterprise, viz. to open up a way to the coast.'[25]

That journey, to Quelimane on the Indian Ocean, brought Livingstone tremendous fame and notoriety on his return to Britain. But it also served as a springboard to bring him back to Africa in 1858, this time as a secular missionary, 'Her Majesty's Consul at Quilimane for the eastern coast and the independant districts of the interior, and commander of an expedition for exploring Eastern and Central Africa.' Though usually known as Livingstone's Zambezi expedition, these explorations focused more on Lake Malawi and the Shire river. And during this period of travels, it was not until he reached the regions of the lake that Livingstone encountered Arab traders from the east coast.

The slave trade, however, was more readily found. On the Zambezi itself Livingstone met a number of slave merchants, all subjects of the king of Portugal. They openly talked of their work, largely to supply the demands of 'free emigrant' labour for the French islands of the Indian Ocean. But of Arab slave dealers he heard nothing until he reached the Shire. On the lower river he was told that beyond the cataracts, 'The river is ... smooth, and navigated by Arabs from Zanzibar in canoes.'[26] Once past the Shire highlands, the Arabs he expected were not to be found. Instead, there were Yao slavers, who 'were evidently goaded on by Portuguese agents from Tette'[27] into buying slaves for sale at the various Indian Ocean ports of Mozambique. Livingstone was able to learn little about their activities, as they eluded his party. Groups of Yao engaged in the slave trade would 'persuade the villagers to mislead us, so that we could not see their traffic'.[28] Even as far north as Zomba mountain no Arabs were encountered. At Lake Chilwa the explorers were told, according to John Kirk, 'The Arabs are not known here but [are] masters of the slaves of the other lake to the north.'[29]

It would appear that it was not until Livingstone and his party reached the confluence of Lake Malawi with the Shire river in September 1859 that they might have met Arabs. In a letter shortly after the event, Livingstone described the encounter:

> We met a large east coast slaving party here coming from Cazembe's country, with an immense number of slaves and elephant's tusks. ... A more blackguard looking set I never saw: they appear to be the people of the Angotia river, but not Arabs, though somewhat like them.[30]

Writing the *Narrative* of the expedition some years later Livingstone was far more definite, recounting that, 'A large slave party, led by Arabs, were encamped close by.' By this later recollection, they were 'a villainous-looking lot' who 'when told we were English, showed signs of fear, and decamped during the night'.[31] Was this his first encounter with Arabs on Lake Malawi? Their behaviour is not altogether the same as that he found later, but it is possible that these were Swahilis from the *mrima* coast opposite Zanzibar, or perhaps more likely, *waungwana*, agents of Arab merchants. As such, they might have been more suspicious, more careful with goods and slaves not their own; this might account for their somewhat hostile behaviour.

There can be no doubt, however, of his meeting with Arabs, near Nkhota kota, in 1861 and again in 1863. On his first exploration of the lake, in a four-oared gig from the *Pioneer*, Livingstone heard from the peoples he met of 'three Arab traders in two Dhows in front of us: they are buying slaves and ivory'. The party seems not to have met these merchants; one dhow was sent across the lake 'full of slaves and ivory, and one remains to carry on the business'.[32] Livingstone, perhaps recalling the behaviour of the slave party he had met previously at the south end of the lake, interpreted this as an attempt to flee from the English explorers. But John Kirk, the expedition's botanist, noted in his journal that the remaining trader was simply avoided: 'We passed the Arab and the chief he is living with.'[33]

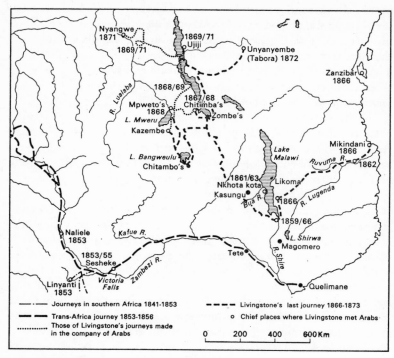

6 David Livingstone's contacts with the Arabs

The small band sailed beyond Nkhota kota and landed their gig near the mouth of the Kaombe river. There they met two Arabs, Juma bin Saidi and Yakob bin Arame, 'from Katanga, where they have been living for 14 years'. They had come to the lake, they told Livingstone, to buy cloth and then return to Katanga. After seeing their establishment, and noting slaves as only a minor item of exchange, he concluded that, 'The Arabs must be driving a good trade.' He was, however, not at all pleased with the geographical information which they gave him, dismissing it 'simply as a piece of Arab geography'.[34] Although they seemed friendly enough, Livingstone was willing to suspect them immediately when a theft occurred, the first he had experienced in any of his African travels. And when the party was robbed again on the return journey down the lake, the doctor was sure of the cause: 'We never suffered from impudence, loss of property, or were endangered, unless among people familiar with slaving.' Quite naturally, then, his 'suspicions fell on some persons who had come from the East Coast'. It was perhaps this incident that led him to remark in one dispatch shortly thereafter, 'A very marked deterioration was observed when we came within the sphere of the Arab vessel.'[35] Whatever Livingstone had intended by this remark, when he returned to Nkhota kota in 1863. this time travelling by land, he was amazed at the increased population in the area under Arab control. His explanation for this was that through the possession of firearms the Arabs were seen as protectors, and had hence attracted a sizeable following.

On this subsequent visit to the Arab centre, Livingstone again met Juma and Yakob who evidently had chosen not to return to Katanga. Again the 'Arabs were very civil when we arrived, and came forth to meet us, and presented us with rice, meal and sugar-cane.'[36] As Juma was 'evidently the chief person' in Nkhota kota at the time, the Europeans were invited to his village, a short distance from the lake. And Juma, sensitive to Livingstone's views regarding the slave trade, removed a number of chained slaves from the vicinity.[37] Despite the avowed purpose of the visit, to verify reports from Zanzibar that most of the slaves sold there came from the Lake Malawi and Shire river areas, no such hard data was collected. Instead, Livingstone seemed most interested in the failure of the Islamic community to proselytise among the Africans. This, he was sure, was all to the advantage of the indigenous peoples. None the less he was impressed, both at the lake and as far west as Kasungu, with the adoption of Arab forms of currency and measurement as an aid to trade.

Apart from a brief encounter with a slave caravan led by one Birkal bin Yaobo on the Ruvuma river in 1862, these were the only meetings between Livingstone and Arabs during his Zambezi expedition. But two other incidents during this time help to assess his attitude towards these Islamic merchants. The first involves Said bin Habib, whom he had met amongst the Makololo during his great journey across the continent. When he returned to Sesheke in 1860, Livingstone was appalled to find that Said had never returned from the trading expedition he had undertaken in the company of ninety-five Makololo five years previously; what is more, none of the Africans had returned either. Livingstone, his initial scepticism on the wisdom of the venture now proven, wrote a dispatch on the matter to the British Foreign Secretary, Lord John Russell, accusing Said of abducting the Makololo.[38] The matter might have ended there had not Juma bin Saidi and Yakob bin Arame told Livingstone, during his first visit to Nkhota kota in 1861, that Said bin Habib had 'gone back to Sekeletu's with the Makololo carrying 3 guns, cannons, 50 barrels of powder and 57 muskets'. The explorer was pleased to add, 'He has been stirred up by our consul at Zanzibar.'[39] Coincidentally, on his second visit to the

Arab entrepot on the lake two years later, Livingstone missed meeting Said bin Habib, who was returning to Kilwa, by only one day.

The second incident involves Livingstone's attempts to discover information about Albrecht Roscher, a German explorer who also had been engaged in an attempt to open up the Lake Malawi regions. Roscher joined an Arab caravan at Kilwa and journeyed across the Ruvuma towards the lake, reaching it on 19 November 1859, about two months after Livingstone. Reportedly ill even on his departure from Zanzibar, Roscher suffered throughout his travels; he was murdered on the return trip from the lake. During a journey up the Ruvuma Livingstone inquired about Roscher, but was able to find nothing. In fact, on at least one occasion he was told by a local ruler 'that he heard nothing of any white man having gone to the lake – that we are the first'. Livingstone concluded that, 'Poor Roscher must have identified himself in dress with the Arabs and left no trace of his own individuality in the country.' His repetition of this theme on several occasions would indicate that Livingstone was troubled deeply about the problem of relations with the Arabs.[40]

Having expressed these views it is perhaps ironic that Livingstone's final African venture was characterised by close relations with Arab merchants. But given the region of these last travels, largely along and across the trade routes that dominated Lake Tanganyika, it was perhaps inevitable. Certainly the intent of the British government, which nominally financed the expedition, was to use their cordial, if sometimes strained relations, with the Sultan of Zanzibar as the key to Livingstone's mission inland. Thus, in early 1866 the doctor was dispatched from Bombay in the recently refitted *Thule*, which was being presented as a goodwill gift to Sultan Majid bin Said. Livingstone's status was not lost upon the Zanzibar ruler, who received the explorer with great courtesy and promises of support for his endeavours. The Sultan wrote to the governor of Bombay concerning Livingstone: 'I will show him respect, give him honour, and help him in all his affairs.'[41] To this end a letter of introduction was written to all the subjects of the Sultan travelling or resident in the interior, commending Livingstone to them and seeking their aid in his travels. Despite this outwardly courteous treatment, Livingstone was troubled by his short stay in Zanzibar, calling the island 'a great slave emporium'.[42] The first difficulty was his visit to the famous slave mart where he observed about three hundred slaves being sold, most of whom he believed to have come from the region of Lake Malawi. And later, having travelled from the coast to the shores of the lake itself, he had deep second thoughts about what cooperation might be expected from the Sultan and 'his bigoted Mahometans'.[43]

Such an attitude was probably intensified by the experiences of the journey from Mikandani to the lake. The people he met near the coast did not impress him: 'They are low-caste Arabs, three-quarters African ... [they] come down to the native ways, and make no efforts to raise the natives to theirs; it is better that it is so, for the coast Arabs manners and morals would be no improvement on the pagan African!'[44]

Following the Ruvuma river inland, Livingstone met at least one Arab caravan, although he reported that most of the merchants avoided contact with him. Observing that there was little Arab proselytising, he wrote that 'some Arabs asserted that it would be useless, for the Makonde [among whom he was then travelling] had no idea of a Deity';[47] perhaps these were the 'bigoted' Moslems whom he later wrote about. Far more than this, however, he was appalled at the evidence of the slave trade which he saw. Not only burnt villages and abandoned slave sticks were to be seen but the corpses of abandoned slaves, murdered or left to die as they became ill, were frequently visible as well.

This pattern remained little changed as he approached and then travelled around Lake Malawi for what was his last visit to the region. Again he reported that Arab merchants fled at his approach. This behaviour became more and more disconcerting to Livingstone. 'The fear which the English have inspired in the Arab slave-traders,' he observed, 'is rather inconvenient.' Even passage across the lake was hindered, as he believed that 'the owners of the two dhows now on the lake kept them out of sight lest I should burn them as slavers'.[46] He also faced the difficulty of making use of the letter of introduction which he had been given by Sultan Majid. Contrary to his expectations based upon previous experiences, the Arabs were more often than not unable to read the letter. 'Very few of the coast Arabs can read; in words they are very polite, but truthfulness seems very little regarded.'[47] Yet despite these difficulties and unfavourable impressions, Livingstone appears to have spent some time with Arabs on the west shore of Lake Malawi and to have met their trading caravans near Mponda's further south on the lake. And their friendliness and even trustworthiness seem to have been well established by both his own experiences and his inquiries of Africans in the area.

Setting off overland from the southern end of Lake Malawi, Livingstone marched north, towards Lake Tanganyika. His next eighteen months often put him in intimate contact with Arabs and left him with mixed feelings about these friends, as well as slavers. Stanley's conversation with Livingstone gave the reporter the impression that during this period 'Arabs conspired against him ... false Muslims betrayed him ... [and] he was detained ... by wars between Arabs and natives.'[48] In fact, much of this did happen. As he neared Lake Tanganyika, Livingstone again made contact with Arabs. He also began to get reports of some sort of conflict between these merchants and a powerful African ruler in the vicinity. He was even warned that should he travel alone he might be mistaken for an Arab and killed. Reaching Chitimba's however, he found 'a large party of Arabs, mostly black Suahelis'.[49] This time his letter from Sultan Majid seemed to do some good; the traders were friendly and seemed to be most concerned about his safety, if only to insure their own position with the Sultan. Thus the doctor was practically forced to remain with them until the difficulties were resolved and safe passage west assured, a frustrating experience for him. Although a number of the leaders would have preferred to achieve this through peaceful means, ultimately force was required. And, in fact, there were other times during this period when force was used by the Arabs to achieve their ends.

Livingstone, as might be expected, denounced such actions, complaining that the Arabs 'bully as much as they please by their firearms'. He saw the disruption this caused to the areas in question and realised that it could only turn the Africans against the Arabs. This he feared would reduce the supply of ivory, the main trade item, and ultimately 'Those Arabs who despair of ivory invest their remaining beads and cloth in slaves.' Indeed, slaves could easily be found. In the region between Lakes Tanganyika and Mweru he observed that they were sold 'in the same open way that the business is carried on in the Zanzibar slave-market'. This entire process, it seemed to him, was further abetted by the Islamic faith of these men, who in practice used it as an excuse to do what they pleased. Though all of this caused him great inconvenience and delay, it also deeply upset him since it touched at the heart of his interests in eastern Africa. In his journal for 28 July 1867 he confirmed that 'slavery is a great evil wherever I have seen it', adding nearly a year later, 'even in its best phases, I would not be a slave dealer for the world'.[50]

Despite his complaints of delays, disruptions and their disastrous consequences, Livingstone saw another side to this year and a half of journeying. The Arabs whom he met did 'seem sincerely religious, according to the light that is in them'. After reflection on their gifts and the services they provided for him, he did admit that 'they have been extremely kind'.[52] Certain individuals among them came in for special praise. Among these was Hamed bin Muhammed el Murjebi, better known as Tippu Tip. He and his close followers went out of their way to accommodate Livingstone, as both the explorer and the Arab recognised, and 'in acknowledgement of his good services' Tippu Tip was given a letter of thanks by Livingstone which was obviously intended to provide him with an introduction to the British powers in Zanzibar.[52] Another of those whom Livingstone favoured was his old acquaintance, Said bin Habib, whom he seems to have completely forgiven for earlier activities. Even though Said was one of the chief offenders in disrupting the African population, his kindness was not forgotten: he offered to take Livingstone in when most of the others were afraid of what he might write to Sultan Majid; he was hospitable under the most trying of circumstances; and he provided canoes to transport an ailing doctor across Lake Tanganyika. But of all these men, perhaps none was more appreciated than Muhammed bin Gharib, usually called Bogharib by Livingstone. Muhammed cooked for him and escorted him through much of the region between Kazembe's and Lake Tanganyika. More importantly, however, it was Muhammed bin Gharib who nursed Livingstone through a serious illness, probably pneumonia, back to health.[53] Of Muhammed and the others, then, he could write: 'These Zanzibar men are very different from the slavers of the Waiyau country' near Lake Malawi. And in a draft dispatch to the Earl of Clarendon he went so far as to proclaim:

I am glad that I was witness to their mode of trading in ivory and slaves. It formed a complete contrast to the atrocious dealings of the Kilwa traders, who are supposed to be, but are not, subjects of the same Sultan. If one wished to depict the slave-trade in its most attractive, or rather least objectionable, form, he would accompany these gentlemen subjects of the Sultan of Zanzibar.[54]

In March 1869 he gradually began to regain his strength and arrived in Ujiji, ending this period of his journey. There the explorer looked forward to receiving the supplies which had been sent on to that Lake Tanganyika settlement to await his arrival. But almost none of the hoped for provisions were to be found. They were either spoiled, never sent, or stolen in transit. And when the Arab agent who had been entrusted with the care of the merchandise returned from Unyanyembe with a few meagre loads, the doctor was able to extract his merchandise only after paying again for its pre-paid transport. Disappointing as this may have been, Livingstone also found that his friends seemed less and less friendly. Said bin Habib refused to carry letters to the coast, and others followed suit. 'I suspect they fear my exposure of their ways more than anything else,' he wrote.[55] Though he finally did persuade them to carry a packet of his letters to Zanzibar, his fears that it would not arrive proved well founded. In one of only two letters written at this time which reached the coast, he confided to John Kirk that 'The people here are like the Kilwa traders haters of English.' His journal entry was more piercing: 'They are nearly all miserable Suaheli at Ujiji, and have neither the manners nor the sense of Arabs.' But he tried to make the best of the situation, assuring Kirk 'I am good friends outwardly with them all.'[56]

If the experiences at Ujiji had begun to change his opinions of the Arabs in east Africa, his next two years of travelling in the eastern Congo to and from Manyema certainly completed the process. There were some instances of kindness, to be sure, especially on the part of Muhammed bin Gharib, with whom he travelled over a part of his routes. Livingstone could on occasion still speak of 'my Arab friends'.[57] He even engaged in discussions with them as of old, debating the merits of their respective religions. And he seems to have understood and accepted, at least in part, their occasional reluctance to carry his letters. He confided to his old friend Oswell, late in 1869, that: 'when an Arab party is met with going to the coast, the headman can scarcely be expected to feed 200 or 300 people for 2 or 3 days, merely to let a foreigner pen words which may be against all Arabs in general, and himself in particular.'[58]

But by and large this portion of his final expedition was characterised by a gnawing doubt about the Arabs. He seemed to have a growing sense, probably more real than paranoiac, that he was distrusted in their company, 'that they hated having a spy in me on their deeds'.[59] Judging from what he observed, it is little wonder that they might have felt thus about him.

Although Livingstone had known of Arab atrocities before, what he came in contact with in Manyema was far more blatant. One party attached to Thani bin Sulaiman met the doctor after having burned several villages and killed a number of Manyema. They made no attempt to hide their activities, and upon reproaching them Livingstone was astounded when the leader pronounced boldly, 'We are sent to murder.' This was not an isolated instance; scenes of past devastations and African fears of new attacks greeted him all along his route. He could only conclude 'This is the usual course of Suaheli trading; it is murder and plunder.' He wrote to Kirk, 'It is not slave trade, it is slaking thirst for blood and catching free people.'[60] Much to his consternation, reports reached him of such deeds committed at the hands of men in the entourage of his closest Arab associate, Muhammed bin Gharib: the cold blooded shooting of men and the capturing of their terrified women and children. Of this news, Livingstone confided to Kirk:

The episode I mention was by Mohammed Bogharib's people and he being the best man of all who have come to trade in Manyema you may, if you can, imagine the conduct of the people of the worst. . . . With all his goodness I have no doubt but he knew of the plan and will receive his full share of the captives.

Unable to escape the reports and evidence of such activities all around him, Livingstone wrote, obviously in great distress, 'I never imagined that human or Muhammedan nature rather, could be so atrociously vile.' [61]

But an even worse shock was to come. Staying for a short time at Nyangwe, the westernmost Arab centre in Manyema, it was his habit to frequent the local market which he found fascinating. One day in July 1871, as he strolled to the market, he was an unwilling witness to the coldblooded massacre of, by his own estimate, 330 to 400 Africans. Carried out by the unquestionably undisciplined followers of some of the principal Arabs, the attack was ostensibly to punish the local population for befriending and trading with an upstart slave of Said bin Habib. At this outrage, the vituperation which had been welling up in Livingstone could no longer be contained. He wrote in his journals of the 'Nigger-Moslems' responsible for the massacre, calling them 'inferior to the Manyema in justice and right'. A few days later, reflecting on the experience, he added: 'Men are worse than beasts of prey, if indeed it is lawful to call Zanzibar slaves men.' [62] Writing to Thomas Maclear, the Astronomer Royal at the Cape a few months later, he likened these men to the Griquas, whose illtreatment of Africans he had deplored while a more sedentary missionary in South Africa. And their masters, he observed, were 'Arabs in whom Satan has full sway'. [63]

The effect of this incident upon Livingstone went far deeper than his emotions. Despite all the assistance they had rendered, and might still render, him, the explorer resolved to avoid travelling with the Arabs. He set out on his own, with a small party, for Ujiji hoping to find supplies which would enable him to finish his work without their further help. But again he was disappointed. This time his supplies had been sold by the Arab agent in charge of them, Sherif Basheikh bin Ahmed. Although others in the Muslim community at Ujiji offered to make at least partial restitution, Livingstone demurred, probably acting on his resolve made in Manyema. And through Sherif his now hardened image of the Arabs was preserved. It was with great relief, then, that he welcomed the arrival of Henry Morton Stanley to whom he could turn for the aid and assistance which he would no longer accept from the Arabs.

For Livingstone, however, the period of respite with Stanley at Ujiji and later Unyanyembe was all too short and he was left again with only the Arabs and his few loyal followers. Still, he was unwilling to turn to the merchants. He even acknowledged that the key factor in this persistent changed attitude was the killing he had witnessed at Nyangwe. 'That massacre,' he wrote, 'turned my heart completely against' the Arab friends he had made.[64] His hostility grew and he gradually began to speak of 'a slave trading ring or coterie' based at Unyanyembe, which was bent on hindering his travels. This conspiracy, as Livingstone saw it, was nearly all pervasive, not just of Arab origin but also involving the Banians in Zanzibar, non-Muslim Indian subjects of Britain who were the chief financiers of Arab commercial ventures in the interior. Of their support for Arab activities he complained bitterly to the authorities in London, Bombay and Zanzibar. This new conspiracy theory completely dominated his thinking on the Arabs and the slave trade in the last months of his life. Even those Arabs who were kind to him had to be explained in terms of it: they were outside the ring, not a party to its nefarious schemes.[65] Having no direct contacts with Arabs after leaving Unyanyembe in late August 1872, there was little that might have altered this conception. Thus, this was the final image of his relationship with the Arabs, the one which he carried with him to the end of his journeying in May 1873.

Even as he died, then, Livingstone seems to have been caught in his own inability to characterise clearly the Arab merchants around him. He would have liked to condemn them all but was unable to do so; he could recognise that there really were differences among them. Although it was not always so clear to him, there were distinguishable differences between the various actions of nearly each one of the Arabs whom he knew. For him these disparities between both individual actions and separate personalities were not always so grossly drawn as in his final few months. Rather, he seems throughout his last journeys at least to have attempted several evaluations of these complex men.

Livingstone offered the first of these after his experiences among the Arabs between Lakes Tanganyika and Mweru. Though unable to condone all their actions, he found them to be helpful and kind, and even called them gentlemen. In his view, their behaviour set them apart from the Arabs he had met, along the Ruvuma and elsewhere, who carried their goods to Kilwa, as well as from the Yao slave traders to the south and the 'Portuguese from Tette'. It was the location of their homes, therefore, that set the Arabs apart; the northerners from Zanzibar were acceptable, while the southerners largely from Kilwa were no better than 'ruffians'.[66] This easy, simple means of spotting the differences was not really adequate, however. It did not allow for the friendly and helpful men of Lake Malawi, Arabs from Katanga whose coastal trade was largely Kilwa-bound. It was able to explain neither the treatment he later received at Ujiji, a settlement of Zanzibar Arabs and their followers, nor the conditions he observed among the Zanzibar Arabs 'trading' in Manyema.

At first Livingstone tried to make his original distinctions apply, referring to those who made difficulties for him at Ujiji as 'like the Kilwa traders'. But he quickly seems to have created a more basic model to account for his new-found difficulties. By calling the Ujijians 'miserable Suaheli', he adopted a common nineteenth-century means of looking down on some because of their mixed parentage.[67] Although the term Swahili is a difficult one to define,[68] Livingstone's basic observation ('Suahelis . . . are the descendants of Arabs and African women.'[69]) would find a good deal of general acceptance today. For the missionary-explorer, the term became a convenient means of stereotyping. These 'Suaheli' were 'degenerate' and 'not fully committed Muslims',[70] thereby set apart from his Arab friends. On at least one occasion he labelled them inferior to Africans. It was very easy, therefore, to blame them for the troubles which beset him. They also made convenient scapegoats for the pillage and destruction he observed as he entered Manyema and which he called 'the usual course of Suaheli trading'. The racial tone of this approach was clear as he inveighed against the Swahili as 'Nigger-Moslems'. Again, such simplistic divisions proved unsatisfactory. First, it became obvious to Livingstone himself that even the Arabs whom he had set apart were indeed, as has been seen, implicated in the atrocities observed in Manyema. And secondly, he seems not to have applied the racial distinctions in a way at all recognised by his companions. Thus when he was previously among the gentlemen 'Arabs' near Lake Mweru one of their number termed his companions 'swahili'.[71]

Perhaps consciously unaware of the failure of his models of Arab behaviour, but undoubtedly frustrated at attempting to understand them, Livingstone at last tried to see them in terms of the slave trade. His complaints of a 'slave trading ring or coterie' were no more successful than his previous attempts at understanding; the arbitrary nature of the classificatory system was obviously strained. The Arabs could not all be seen as either good or evil; neither could any one of them be explained in contrasts of either/or. It might appear, therefore, that Livingstone faced a paradox as well. And possibly in his last year he did, as the weariness of nearly constant travel and the renewed loneliness after Stanley's departure heightened his sense of mission against the slave trade. This Livingstone, of the last few months, of course, must not be seen to override the broader and in many ways more representative man of previous years. It is to those earlier days of his travels that we must turn to understand Livingstone and the Arabs. The answer, too, goes deeper than the simple explanations which he appears to have constructed.

Despite its occasional moralistic and even racialist content and a frequent arbitrariness in his generalisations, it is in Livingstone's character that the key to his confused, at best ambivalent, views towards the Arabs may be found. A glimpse of this side of Livingstone can be seen in his own defence against charges that, despite his own previously well-known feelings on the matter, he had been living amongst and was closely associated with Arabs for long periods during his last travels. His reply to Earl Granville was direct: 'I have been reported as living among the Arabs as one of themselves; that only means that I am on good terms with them all. They often call me the "Christian", and I never swerved from that character in any one respect.'[72] That his claim was substantially correct there can be little doubt. Even those whom he roundly condemned saw him in such terms. Said bin Majid, an Ujiji-based merchant, wrote matter-of-factly to one of the wealthy Banians in Zanzibar mentioning Livingstone: 'Letters have come from the people of Menama [Manyema], from Mohamed bin Gharib and his people, and they have got good prices, such as please them; the Christian is in their company.'[73]

This is understandable when we realize that from his first meetings with Arabs he had resolved upon such conduct. He wrote in his journal on 23 September 1855, as he set out down the Zambezi towards Quelimane, 'A missionary following conscientiously the principles we hold is soon seen to be of a superior race to that of the wonderfully selfish Arabs.'[74] There is very little, if any, evidence to suggest that he strayed from such a course on any of his journeys. And by following this predetermined path, even while befriending the very Arabs whose actions he condemned, he stood above them. It was as an 'Anglesi', and not as an Arab that Livingstone was described to E. D. Young while he was searching for traces of the explorer along the southern shores of Lake Malawi.[75] The people there had not confused him with the Arabs. Nor did the Manyema, whom Livingstone himself reported as 'telling each other that I am the "good one". I have no slaves.'[76]

The same principles which enabled Livingstone to maintain his identity also helped him to see the Arabs and the slave trade as separable, independent of each other and therefore worthy of independent judgement. In this way he could, though he seems often not to have realised it, get beyond the slave trade and its horrible effects, as others were, and have since been, unable to do. It is not surprising, then, that the Arabs had a good and helpful side which, as can be seen, came through clearly in his writings. Each one was seen, and was treated, as an individual. 'Consciousness of my own defects makes me lenient,' he wrote on one occasion, explaining, if only to himself, his genuine affection for one whose actions he could not countenance. With such views, an unusual detachment sometimes crept in and allowed him to make judgements with more understanding than might be expected. Occasionally he would remind himself when angered or disappointed with them that the Arabs should be 'judged by the East African Moslem standard . . . and not by ours'.[77]

The source of this understanding and its accompanying acceptance of individuals, of course, went deep into his religious character, the Christian missionary in him which could not be effaced though he no longer remained in missionary employ. Perhaps it was H. M. Stanley who observed this best, albeit in words to impress the readers of the *New York Herald*:

> Dr Livingstone is truly a pious man – a man deeply imbued with real religious instincts. . . . His religion . . . is of the true, practical kind, never losing a chance to manifest itself in a quiet, practical way – never demonstrative or loud. It is always at work, if not in deed, by shining example. . . . It governs his conduct towards his servants, towards the natives and towards the bigoted Mussulmans – even all who come in contact with him.[78]

Not surprising praise for a missionary, perhaps. But in the case of David Livingstone, worthy of repeating. For when we come to consider Livingstone all too often moral judgements on the slave trade have tended to obscure his nature and to prevent an understanding of his true feelings towards the Arab merchants of East Africa.

Notes

I wish to acknowledge the constant encouragement and patient assistance of Professor Bridglal Pachai, without which this chapter would not have been written.
  1 These were not all, strictly speaking, Arabs; many were Swahilis and some even their partly-Islamicised followers. As Livingstone generally used the term Arab, it has been adopted here. See below, however, for a discussion of Livingstone's variations in terminology.

2 Livingstone to Agnes, 15 August 1872, quoted in George Seaver, *David Livingstone: His Life and Letters*, London, 1957, p. 610.
3 Livingstone to James Young, n.d., quoted in W. G. Blaikie, *The Personal Life of David Livingstone*, London, 1880, p. 443.
4 See, for example, E. F. Berlioux, *The Slave Trade in Africa in 1872*, London, 1872, reprinted 1971, p. 56.
   R. Coupland, *Livingstone's Last Journey*, London, 1945, passim. In his many works on East African history, Coupland almost uniformly refers to the 'Arab Slave Trade'.
5 H. Waller (ed.), *The Last Journals of David Livingstone in Central Africa*, London, 1874, vol. II, pp. 11, 92, 108.
   R. Foskett (ed.), *The Zambesi Doctors: David Livingstone's Letters to John Kirk, 1858–1872*, Edinburgh, 1964, pp. 148–9. Livingstone to Kirk, 25 March 1871.
6 Waller, *Last Journals*, I, p. 348, II, p. 43; Livingstone to Kirk, 30 May 1869, in Foskett, op. cit., p. 138. Livingstone to Bartle Frere, July 1867, quoted in J. Martineau, *The Life and Correspondence of the Right Hon. Sir Bartle Frere*, London, 1895, p. 116.
7 O. Ransford, *Livingstone's Lake*, London, 1966, p. 130.
8 See J. I. Macnair, *Livingstone the Liberator*, 1940, reprinted London 1958, pp. 322–3; and Seaver, op. cit., p. 490.
9 For recent historical comment in this vein, see G. Shepperson, 'The African Abroad or the African Diaspora', and N. R. Bennett, 'The East African Slave Trade', both in T. O. Ranger (ed.), *Emerging Themes of African History*, Nairobi, 1968, pp. 156 and 146 respectively.
10 See B. Pachai, 'Christianity and Commerce in Malawi: Some Pre-colonial Aspects', in B. Pachai et al. (eds), *Malawi Past and Present*, Blantyre, 1971, p. 43.
11 See Macnair, op. cit., p. 318; and O. H. Robertson, 'Trade and the Suppression of Slavery in British Central Africa', *Nyasaland Journal*, 13, 2, 1960, p. 16.
12 This has been and is true of Malawians. See. A. G. MacAlpine, 'A Central African "Livingstone Centenary",' n.p., MacAlpine Papers, University of Edinburgh Library, Manuscripts: Gen. 766/2. Such views appear even today in the collection of oral data; testimonies of V. H. Chipala, age seventy-two, and Binti Msusa, age ninety, collected at Nkota kota, Malawi, 6 and 7 February 1972 by Mr J. B. Mkandawire. I am indebted to Professor B. Pachai for placing this information at my disposal.
13 Such an approach has been recently suggested, but not explored, by Norman R. Bennett, 'David Livingstone: Exploration for Christianity', in R. I. Rotberg (ed.), *Africa and its Explorers*, Cambridge, Mass., 1970, p. 56.
14 David Livingstone, *Missionary Travels and Researches in South Africa*, London, 1857, p. 218. The 'Mambari' were neither a tribe nor a group of 'half-castes', but rather people of double allegiance, followers of the Portuguese in West Central Africa; see John T. Tucker, 'Livingstone's Travels in Africa', *Africa*, 26, 1956, p. 187.
15 R. Coupland, *Kirk on the Zambesi: A Chapter of African History*, Oxford, 1928, p. 45.
16 D. Livingston(e) and W. C. Oswell, 'Latest Explorations into Central Africa beyond Lake Ngami', *Journal of the Royal Geographical Society*, 20, 1852, pp. 168–71.
17 I. Schapera (ed.), *Livingstone's Private Journals 1851–1853*, London, 1960, pp. 227–8.

18 I. Schapera (ed.), *Livingstone's African Journal 1853–1856*, London, 1963, pp. 295–6.
19 Livingstone to Thompson, 13 and 27 September 1855, in I. Schapera (ed.), *Livingstone's Missionary Correspondence 1841–1856*, London, 1961, pp. 283–4. See also 'Narrative of Said bin Habeeb, an Arab Inhabitant of Zanzibar', *Transactions of the Bombay Geographical Society*, 15, 1860, p. 148.
20 Livingstone to Jean Fredoux, 28 September 1853, in I. Schapera (ed.), *David Livingstone: Family Letters 1841–1856*, London, 1959, vol. II, p. 225.
21 William Monk (ed.), *Dr Livingstone's Cambridge Lectures*, 2nd edition, Cambridge, 1860, p. 165.
22 *Missionary Travels*, p. 501.
23 Schapera, *African Journal*, p. 296.
24 *Missionary Travels*, p. 508.
25 Livingstone to Arthur Tidman, 24 September 1853, in *Missionary Correspondence*, p. 250.
26 Livingstone to Lord Malmesbury, 14 February 1859, in 'Extracts from the Dispatches of Dr David Livingstone', *Journal of the Royal Geographical Society*, 31, 1861, p. 263.
27 David and Charles Livingstone, *Narrative of an Expedition to the Zambesi and its tributaries; and of the discovery of Lakes Shirwa and Nyassa, 1858–1864*, London, 1865, p. 363.
28 J. P. R. Wallis (ed.), *The Zambezi Expedition of David Livingstone*, London, 1956, p. 100.
29 R. Foskett (ed.), *The Zambesi Journal and Letters of Dr John Kirk*, Edinburgh, 1965, p. 195.
30 Livingstone to ?, 10 October 1859, in *Cambridge Lectures*, p. 376. Livingstone used nearly identical language to describe the incident in a letter to Admiral Sir Frederick Grey, 28 October 1859; manuscript collection, Royal Commonwealth Society Library, London. I am grateful to the Librarian of the Society and to Professor B. Pachai for making photocopies available to me.
31 D. and C. Livingstone, *Narrative*, p. 124.
32 Wallis, *Zambezi Expedition*, p. 199.
33 Foskett, *Zambezi Journal*, p. 378.
34 Wallis, *Zambezi Expedition*, p. 210; D. and C. Livingstone, *Narrative*, p. 389.
35 D. and C. Livingstone, *Narrative*, pp. 378, 380; Wallis, *Zambezi Expedition*, p. 404.
36 David Livingstone, 'Explorations to the West of Lake Nyassa in 1863', *Journal of the Royal Geographical Society*, 34, 1864, p. 247.
37 D. and C. Livingstone, *Narrative*, pp. 511–12. It would appear that Livingstone again failed to meet the reigning Jumbe, Salim bin 'Abdallah. Since no mention is made of this man in Livingstone's accounts, it is possible the Jumbe was away, having left the affairs of the community in the hands of a subordinate. The uncertainty in describing Juma bin Saidi's position ('evidently the chief person here') would also suggest this. Such an interpretation might account for the lack of traditions concerning Livingstone's visits among the East Coast Islamic community at Nkhota kota; testimony of Sheikh Nkhungula, age ninety-six, 6 February 1972, collected by Mr J. B. Mkandawire.
38 Livingstone to Russell, 6 September 1860, in Wallis, *Zambezi Expedition*, pp. 392, 394.
39 Ibid., p. 210.

40 G. Shepperson (ed.), *David Livingstone and the Rovuma*, Edinburgh, 1965, pp. 99, 161; D. and C. Livingstone, *Narrative*, pp. 123–4, 562–3.

41 Majid bin Said to Governor of Bombay, 18 February 1866, quoted in Waller, *Last Journals*, vol. I, p. 6.

42 Livingstone to Earl of Clarendon, ? 1868, quoted in (Mrs) Charles E. B. Russell, *General Rigby, Zanzibar and the Slave Trade*, London, 1935, p. 209.

43 Livingstone to Professor Sedgwick, 24 August 1866, quoted in Seaver, op. cit., p. 476.

44 Waller, *Last Journals*, vol. I, pp. 13, 24.

45 Livingstone to ?, 18 May 1866, in *Proceedings of the Royal Geographical Society*, 11, 1866–67, p. 17.

46 Waller, *Last Journals*, vol. I, p. 94; Livingstone to Sir Roderick Murchison, 2 February 1867, in *Proceedings of the Royal Geographical Society*, 12, 1867–68, p. 175.

47 Waller, *Last Journals*, vol. I, p. 91.

48 N. R. Bennett (ed.), *Stanley's Dispatches to the New York Herald, 1871–1872, 1874–1877*, Boston, 1970, p. 57.

49 Waller, *Last Journals*, vol. I, p. 209.

50 Ibid., pp. 222, 225–6, 232, 302.

51 Ibid., pp. 242, 298.

52 Ibid., p. 270; translated W. H. Whitely, *Maisha ya Hamed bin Muhammed el Murjebi yaani Tippu Tip kwa Maneno Yake*, Nairobi, 1966, sec. 32; Livingstone, Introductory letter written for Tippu Tip, 12 September 1867, in Foskett, *Zambesi Doctors*, p. 137.

53 Michael Gelfand, *Livingstone the Doctor*, Oxford, 1957, pp. 248–9. Other Europeans came to share Livingstone's debt to Muhammed bin Gharib, for example the L.M.S. lay missionary, Edward Coode Hore; J. B. Wolf (ed.), *Missionary to Tanganyika, 1877–1888*, London, 1971, p. 128.

54 Waller, *Last Journals*, vol. I, pp. 217, 260.

55 Ibid., vol. II, p. 8.

56 Livingstone to Kirk, 30 May 1869, in Foskett, *Zambesi Doctors*, pp. 138–9; Waller, *Last Journals*, vol. II, p. 12.

57 Ibid., p. 43.

58 Livingstone to Oswell, October 1869, quoted in W. E. Oswell, *William Cotton Oswell, Hunter and Explorer*, London, 1900, pp. 108–9.

59 Waller, *Last Journals*, vol. II, p. 46.

60 Ibid., pp. 45, 79; Livingstone to Kirk, 25 March 1871, in Foskett, *Zambesi Doctors*, p. 145.

61 Livingstone to Kirk, 25 March and 14 May 1871, in Foskett, *Zambesi Doctors*, pp. 146, 151.

62 Waller, *Last Journals*, vol. II, pp. 133–8, 143.

63 Livingstone to Maclear, 17 November 1871, in *Proceedings of the Royal Geographical Society*, 17, 1872–3, p. 70; Waller, *Last Journals*, vol. II, p. 142. On Livingstone's views of Griqua ill-treatment of Africans, see his letters to Robert Moffat, 4 March 1850 and 14 April 1851, in *Family Letters*, vol. II, pp. 78, 125–6.

64 Waller, *Last Journals*, vol. II, p. 178.

65 Livingstone to William Thompson, November 1872, in D. Chamberlin (ed.), *Some Letters from Livingstone, 1840–1872*, London, 1940, pp. 272–3; Livingstone to Murchison, 13 March 1872, in *Proceedings of the Royal Geographical Society*, 16, 1871–72, p. 434. On the Banians, see R. G. Gregory, *India and East Africa*,

Oxford, 1971, pp. 24–5.
66 Livingstone to Lord Clarendon, July 1868, in *Proceedings of the Royal Geographical Society*, 14, 1869–70, p. 10.
67 See M. D. Biddis, *Father of Racist Ideology: The Social and Political Thought of Count Gobineau*, London, 1970, p. 67.
68 See the discussion in Marcia Wright and Peter Lary, 'Swahili Settlements in Northern Zambia and Malawi', *African Historical Studies*, 4, 1971, p. 547.
69 Waller, *Last Journals*, vol. I, p. 280.
70 Livingstone to Earl Russell, 16 October 1862, in Shepperson, *Rovuma*, p. 161; Waller, *Last Journals*, vol. II, p. 209.
71 'The History of Abdullah ibn Suliman', A. Roberts (ed.), *African Social Research*, 4, December 1967; p. 251.
72 Livingstone to Granville, 1 July 1872, in *Proceedings of the Royal Geographical Society*, 16, 1871–2, p. 439.
73 Said bin Majid to Ludda Damji, n.d. (about November 1870), in *Proceedings of the Royal Geographical Society*, 15, 1870–71, p. 206.
74 Schapera, *African Journal*, p. 300.
75 E. D. Young, *The Search after Livingstone*, revised H. Waller, London, 1868, pp. 133, 147, 150.
76 Waller, *Last Journals*, vol. II, p. 105.
77 Ibid., vol. I, p. 287, vol. II, pp. 75–6.
78 Stanley, *Dispatches*, p. 97.

7 Searching for Livingstone: E. D. Young and Others

P. A. Cole-King

For the last twenty years of his life Livingstone was one of the heroes of Victorian Britain, a nation much given to idolising the men who brought honour to its name, especially if at the same time their work was devoted to improving the lot of those they considered less fortunate. Livingstone was seldom at home to enjoy his hero status, which in any case he found somewhat irksome. To be a great man satisfied a curious streak of vanity in his otherwise modest and retiring nature, but it also involved a round of receptions and addresses, and the writing of lengthy accounts of his travels, all of which he disliked. From 1853, when he set off on the journey across Africa which first brought him fame to his death in 1873 he spent only two years (1857 and mid-1865 to mid-1866) in Britain. For the rest he was away, wandering in the great continent he loved, mostly on foot and mostly without any companions of his own race.

The pioneers of today, who cross oceans alone in small boats, or climb mountains, or penetrate the few remaining unknown parts of the globe, do so with all the benefits of modern communications. It is hard to imagine any of them being truly lost. Livingstone spent a large part of his life in a state of what we should regard as lost, cut off from all communication with his fellow countrymen; it was one of the accepted hazards for a nineteenth-century explorer. From time to time, however, Livingstone became so very lost, or was even reported dead, that others were prompted to go and look for him. The most celebrated searcher for Livingstone was H. M. Stanley, whose historic meeting with the great explorer in 1871 at Ujiji ('Dr Livingstone I presume?') needs no emphasis. Less well known but equally deserving of attention, if only because of the contrast between him and Stanley, is E. D. Young, a Gunner (Warrant Officer) in the Royal Navy. Stanley was a journalist,

James Stewart and his party before leaving for Livingstonia

Livingstone in the Zanzibar slave market

Lake Nyassa Lat. 12° 31' S.
Long. 35° — E.
23 Sept. 1861.

My Dear Sir Roderick

We happen to be navigating this Lake in a small boat we carried past the Murchison cataracts at an untoward period of the year for the equinoctial gales set in so strongly from the East then turn round to the North that we are either driven ashore or make but little headway with the oars — Like all narrow seas a heavy swell gets up in a few hours — three days ago we were nearly lost by a tremendous sea being raised in about 20 minutes. The breakers equal those off the ~~Tongone and astonish the seamen~~ we being with us though he has been in most parts of the world. I cannot give you many particulars about the Lake yet — We have followed the Western shore and find that to be remarkable for its numerous bays — one of these runs in about 20 miles southward and makes with the portion we saw on its discovery a sort of forked extremity We have named the bold rocky promontory which juts out between the two tails of the Lake Cape Maclear after our good friend Sir Thomas Maclear the Astronomer Royal at the Cape — In going round this Cape we could find no bottom with our sounding line at 35 fathoms or 210 feet. Where we are now no one attempts to cross but there are four places at which they do. In one they spend about six

[left margin, vertical:] Italy on the map — not unlike the boot & shape of Italy on the map

[left margin:] x

sent by the *New York Herald* to find Livingstone, with instructions to make as big a story out of it as possible. He did. Not only had he a powerful press behind him but he was also a man well able and willing to blow his own trumpet. Young carried out his search for Livingstone smoothly and efficiently, with a minimum of fuss, as befitted a British sailor who knew how to keep to his station. He was the last man to blow his own trumpet and it is unfortunate for him that few since have seen fit to blow it for him.

Early in 1864 rumours of Livingstone's death in the latter part of the previous year appeared in the British press. At a meeting of the Royal Geographical Society in February, the President, Sir Roderick Murchison, declared that he believed these rumours to be unfounded and that, as he understood it, 'Dr Livingstone had received some injury in the foot when landing on the shores of Lake Nyassa.'[1] In fact the whole thing turned out to be without any foundation at all for in June the society received a dispatch from Livingstone describing an overland journey he had carried out, between August and November 1863, in the country to the west of the lake, a typically Livingstonian final fling to the not very successful Zambezi expedition after he had received notice from the Foreign Office of the expedition's recall. During the journey he had encountered, quite harmlessly, a band of the dreaded Ngoni warriors and apparently news of this had somehow got around, becoming magnified into reports of his death. While he was away, the two men who were to play the leading parts in the drama to follow were left with the expedition's steamers, *Pioneer* and *Lady Nyasa*, at the foot of the cataracts on the Shire river: they were the villain of the piece, Musa, one of a number of men from the Comoro Island of Johanna in the Indian Ocean who were employed as crewmen, and the hero, Gunner Young, who had been seconded from the Navy to take charge of the *Lady Nyasa*. Musa and Young got to know one another well – to the latter's complete disenchantment.

The Zambezi expedition over, Livingstone returned to Britain, via Bombay, in July 1865, to spend a little more than a year there before setting out once more for Africa on what was to be his last journey, in the official but unpaid capacity of British consul. He reached Zanzibar, again via Bombay, at the beginning of 1866 where he collected stores and recruits for his expedition. Foremost among the recruits was Musa, re-engaged on the strength of his former service, along with nine other Johanna men. At the end of March, H.M.S. *Penguin* took Livingstone and his entourage to the mainland near the mouth of the Ruvuma river. On 5 April, after parting with the officers and crew of the British warship, the last Europeans bar one that he was to see for the rest of his

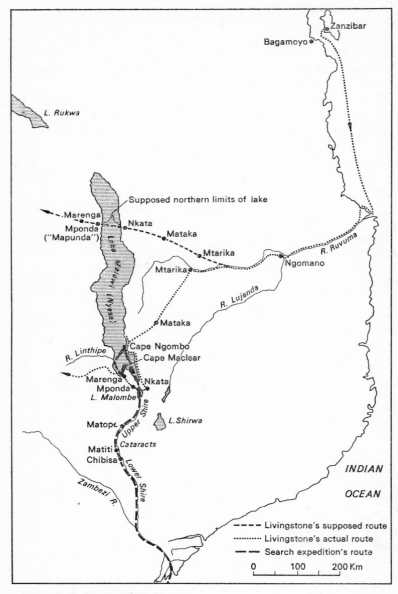

Zanzibar

Bagamoyo

L. Rukwa

Supposed northern limits of lake

Marenga
Mponda
("Mapunda")

Nkata

Mataka

Mtarika

R. Ruvuma

Lake Marawi (Nyasa)

Mtarika

Ngomano

R. Lujenda

Mataka

R. Linthipe

Cape Ngombo
Cape Maclear

Marenga
Mponda
L. Malombe

Nkata

L. Shirwa

Matope

Upper Shire

Cataracts

Matiti
Chibisa

Lower Shire

INDIAN

Zambezi R.

OCEAN

— — — Livingstone's supposed route
· · · · · · Livingstone's actual route
— — Search expedition's route

0   100   200 Km

7 The search for David Livingstone

life, Livingstone headed for the interior.

His intended course was to follow the Ruvuma as far as possible towards Lake Nyasa (it might even flow out of it, a point he had been unable to settle during the Zambezi expedition) and then make for the north end of the lake to find out how far it extended. Afterwards he would go on towards Lake Tanganyika, to see whether there was a river connecting it with Nyasa and to establish a base at Ujiji on its eastern shore from which he could set about solving the riddle of the whole central African system of lakes and rivers which was still puzzling geographers. Perhaps he would even find the ultimate source of the White Nile which, in spite of the work of Burton, Speke, Grant and Baker, and the discoveries of Lake Victoria and Lake Albert, was still an open question, some believing it to be Tanganyika itself.

Livingstone's party numbered sixty, which he considered excessive but which was modest by the standards of other contemporary explorers. There were his own personal servants, Susi and Amoda, local men who had worked for the Zambezi expedition, and Juma and Wakotani, young men who had been released from a slave gang by Livingstone in the Shire highlands in 1861 and later employed by him. As general attendants and carriers were twelve Sepoy volunteers from the Bombay Marine Battalion under a *havildar* (sergeant), nine young Africans from a school at Nassick, near Bombay, the ten Johanna men, and twenty-four porters recruited on the coast by the Ruvuma. In addition there was Livingstone's menagerie: six camels, three Indian buffaloes and a calf, two mules and four donkeys. The animals were taken partly as beasts of burden and partly as an experiment to see how they would survive in areas infested with tsetse fly. And finally there was Livingstone's pet poodle Chitani, later to prove a valuable means of identification.

The sixty men and seventeen animals disappeared into the interior of Africa and for seven months nothing was heard of them. Early in November a letter from Livingstone reached the Royal Geographical Soviety via the British Consul at Zanzibar. It had been written on 18 May, at Ngomano, the junction of the Ruvuma and the Lujenda rivers, 150 miles from the coast, where Livingstone said he intended to make his headquarters 'till I have felt my way round the north end of Lake Nyassa'.[3] Then on 5 December who should appear at Zanzibar but Musa and eight of the Johanna men, with a detailed and circumstantial tale of disaster. They recounted it to Dr G. E. Seward, the British acting-consul and Dr John Kirk, who had been Livingstone's staunch second-in-command on the Zambezi expedition and was now surgeon and vice-consul at Zanzibar.

According to the Johanna men's tale Livingstone had stayed some time at Ngomano before continuing westwards along the Ruvuma, reaching Mtarika and then Mataka where he stopped again for a while. Before leaving Mataka the Sepoys, who had proved useless, were dismissed, and the reduced party, which had also lost nearly all its animals, carried on to Nkata:

> ... one day distant from the border of a lake [where] they obtained four canoes and, embarking in the morning, were all landed on the opposite shore by midday. ... The canoes were propelled by means of poles, and paddles were seldom used. The water was not deep; the opposite shore was of white sand, with plains to the west, but no hills visible although high mountains appeared to the south.[4]

Having crossed the lake they came to a village called Mponda where Wakotani and the *havildar* deserted. Two days' journey westward across flat country they reached Marenga, who received them well and ferried them over a swamp. One morning shortly after this, at about nine in the morning, Musa was marching at the head of the Johanna men some fifty yards behind Livingstone, his personal attendants and the Nassick men, when word was passed back that a band of Ngoni warriors was approaching. Musa ran forward in time to see the Ngoni charging. Livingstone fired his rifle, killing the foremost man, and those with him also opened fire. Before Livingstone could reload his rifle he was struck down by 'a blow from a battle-axe which severed the neck-bone, so that the head dropped forward and he fell instantly'.[5] Musa, who had seen all this from the shelter of a tree, now ran back along the path where he met his comrades preparing to abandon their loads at the sound of shooting, and make off into the bush. This they did, and remained in hiding until evening when they emerged to bury their leader's body, near which were those of two attendants and two Ngoni. All the remaining members of the party had vanished along with the stores and equipment; even Livingstone's body had been stripped of all but the trousers. Thankful for their own narrow escape the Johanna men then made their way back to Zanzibar.

It was a very plausible story. Seward and Kirk did their best to shake it, but the most crucial part rested on the evidence of Musa alone, and though the others gave confusing and contradictory accounts in matters of detail, they could not be shaken in the main substance: they had all seen Livingstone's dead body with the gaping wound in the neck and had assisted in his burial. Regretfully Seward and Kirk came to the conclusion that the story was probably true and began sending a series of official dispatches and private letters to Britain containing details of the news. Since Kirk was the only one who knew anything of the country around Lake Nyasa, Seward asked him to prepare a report on the geographical implications of Livingstone's route as recounted by the Johanna men. Kirk reckoned that Mtarika, Mataka and Nkata were all places on the way to Livingstone's first intended objective, the northern end of Lake Nyasa. He was puzzled by the Johanna men's description of the shallow crossing point, which took only a few hours and had level country around, for he knew the 200-odd miles up from the southern end of the lake as a result of his 1861 trip there with Livingstone; nowhere was it narrow or shallow enough to be crossed in a few hours in a canoe propelled by poles, and one of its features were the hills and mountains along its shoreline. Another puzzling point was the fact that Livingstone had crossed the lake at all since it was the northern extremity he wished to see. Kirk, after expressing a small doubt that it was Nyasa that the Johanna men were speaking of, eventually concluded that Livingstone must somehow have satisfied himself of its northern extent before crossing. As for the crossing point itself, Kirk could only suggest that the northern end of Lake Nyasa was shallow like its appendage Lake Malombe in the south, which would have fitted well with the Johanna men's description. The village of Mponda on the other side, sounded similar to 'Mapunda', one of the places at the north end of the lake which Kirk remembered hearing about in 1861. Marenga being two days beyond Mponda, and the place of attack a further three days beyond that, Kirk concluded that Livingstone met his death some forty or fifty miles west of the north end of Lake Nyasa, probably about the middle of July 1866. Seward's reckoning of the date was September. He also differed from Kirk when, having sent off their first round of reports to London, the two men visited the Arab centre of Kilwa on the mainland to try to obtain news from caravans returning from the interior; Seward found that the information he gathered at Kilwa 'tends to throw discredit on the statement of the Johanna-men', whereas Kirk found 'nothing to encourage us in hope'.[6]

The first news to reach Britain was in a brief letter from Kirk to the Assistant-Secretary of the Royal Geographical Society which arrived early in March 1867, was published in *The Times*, and read at the fortnightly meeting of the society on 11 March. Sir Roderick Murchison, observing that better evidence than the apparently unsupported testimony of the Johanna men was needed, refused to abandon hope for Livingstone. By 25 March a whole sheaf of documents from Seward and Kirk, addressed to the Foreign Secretary and Sir Roderick Murchison, had arrived, and these were read in all their wealth of detail to the society's meeting that day and discussed by the distinguished company present. Of those who spoke Sir Roderick Murchison, Captain Sherard Osborn and Thomas Baines still had doubts about the story; Sir Samuel Baker, of Nile fame, and Mr J. Crawford considered it to be true; and Mr Horace Waller was plainly undecided in his opinions and preferred to sit on the fence. Everyone was impressed with the fact that Kirk, who knew Livingstone, the country and the people, had clearly come round to believing the story; the weight of his experience counted for much. The doubts of Seward, the other man on the spot, who now believed it possible that the Johanna men had simply deserted and told their story as a cover-up, were ignored. Several of the speakers suggested further inquiries in Africa and Sir Samuel Baker offered to lead any expedition that might be sent.[7] Public opinion was less informed and less sceptical than the learned members of the society. Victorian Britain loved sensation just as much as we do today and if it was the Death of a National Hero in Darkest Africa so much the better. The story found widespread acceptance and engendered a good deal of genuine dismay.

At the Royal Geographical Society's meeting on 8 April positive steps were announced:

Before commencing the business of the evening, the PRESIDENT announced that the Council of the Society had drawn up the following Resolutions with regard to Dr Livingstone:

'The Council are of opinion that it is highly desirable that a tentative expedition or expeditions should proceed, whether from Zanzibar to the head of Lake Nyassa, or from the Zambezi to that point, with a view to ascertaining the fate of Dr Livingstone; and that the Expedition Committee be requested to report upon the measures advisable to be adopted.'

It was also resolved:

'That the President be requested to communicate this Resolution to Lord Stanley, with the expression of a hope that Her Majesty's Government will see fit to adopt such measures as may appear to them most conducive to the end in view, in which not only Geographers, but the public at large, take so deep an interest.'

The PRESIDENT further stated that a large number of applications had been received from persons qualified to carry out, or to assist in this expedition, and that the desire was very general to set this question completely at rest.[8]

Among those who had offered their services was E. D. Young who, knowing Musa as an inveterate liar, suspected his story of being a cover-up for desertion. He consulted with Sir Roderick Murchison, found him of like mind, and then went to his friend of Zambezi expedition days, Horace Waller, who also remembered Musa as utterly untrustworthy. Waller now committed himself to the view that Livingstone might be alive after all, and he helped Young draw up a scheme for a search expedition to go to Lake Nyasa. Young went back to Murchison with the scheme and offered to lead the expedition. From then on things moved fast. At the society's meeting of 13 May Sir Roderick was able to announce that the government had provided funds for the expedition, which would consist of Young as commander with three other members, and would be provided with a special steel sailing boat; two weeks later the boat was nearing completion and arrangements had been made to transport the expedition to Cape Town and thence to the mouth of the Zambezi. On 11 June the Livingstone Search Expedition set sail from Plymouth aboard the Union Steam Packet Company's ship *Celt*. 'Livingstone Search Expedition' is something of a misnomer, for it is clear from the instructions issued by the Council of the Royal Geographical Society to Young that it was not anticipated that he would ever meet Livingstone in person; if he was alive he would by now be hundreds of miles from the place of his supposed murder. All the expedition was required to do was to make for the north end of Lake Nyasa and collect evidence as to the truth or falsehood of the Johanna men's story, and if possible bring back some relic of Livingstone.[9]

The men Young chose to accompany him were both old shipmates; Patrick Buckley, who had been with him on anti-slavery patrols on the east coast, and John Reid, the former carpenter on Livingstone's *Pioneer*. After Young had been appointed leader a certain Lieutenant Henry Faulkner applied for the post. Faulkner was on leave from India where he was serving with the Northumberland Fusiliers, having formerly been with the 17th Lancers. On learning from Sir Roderick that he was too late to lead the expedition he offered to accompany it as a volunteer. Murchison tried to dissuade him, doubtless feeling that it would be improper for the holder of Her Majesty's Commission to serve under a Gunner. Faulkner, however, was determined to go. He sold his commission and Murchison asked Young to take him along as a volunteer.[10] Both Young and Faulkner kept diaries of the expedition which they afterwards published in narrative form. While Young never has anything disparaging to say about Faulkner, the latter loses no opportunity to point out, with a superior air, the errors of judgement committed by 'Mr Young'; he evidently resented his position as second to a mere Warrant Officer. But apart from digs at his leader, Faulkner's account is the more accurate (and often amusing) record of the expedition, and it also gives detailed observations of wild life, as well as useful descriptions cf the country and its people. Young's book reads like the work of a less educated man, with occasional heavy humour, but contains valuable records of local ways, which he is able to interpret to some extent from his experiences of two years' sojourn in the country with the Zambezi expedition. It is a pity that both books should nowadays be very scarce collector's items. The long-winded sub-title of Faulkner's, *Elephant Haunts: Being a Sportsman's Narrative of the Search for Dr Livingstone, with Scenes of Elephant, Buffalo and Hippopotamus Hunting*, betrays his particular interest in accompanying the expedition, which gave him the opportunity to try his hand at hunting in Africa. At the age of twenty-nine he was fortunate in having private means to enable him to indulge his particular interest.

And what of Edward Daniel Young himself? He was educated at Greenwich School and began service with the Royal Navy as a boy entrant. He spent some years on anti-slavery patrols aboard H.M.S. *Gorgon* off the east coast of Africa, often being in charge of one of the small boats put off from the cruiser to chase Arab dhows among the mosquito-infested creeks and river mouths. Young was promoted Gunner in June 1858, shortly after Livingstone's Zambezi expedition reached the river, and was still serving on board H.M.S. *Gorgon* when he was seconded for duty on the expedition's steamers early in 1862.[11] Now at the age of thirty-five his experiences of the Zambezi and Shire route to Lake Nyasa singled him out as the man to head the expedition in search of news of his former leader.

The boat with which the expedition was equipped, appropriately named the *Search*, had been built to Young's design in the Admiralty dockyards at Chatham. She was thirty feet long, eight in beam, and drew eighteen inches of water; was fitted with sails (cutter-rigged) and oars; and was specially constructed in steel sections, so that she could be easily dismantled and carried by porters overland past the cataracts on the Shire river.

The expedition reached Cape Town aboard the *Celt* on 12 July and spent a few days transferring to H.M.S. *Petrel* which was to take them to the Zambezi delta. Young took the opportunity to recruit four Africans, John Brown and Antonio, Kroomen from Freetown, Sierra Leone, and Chinsoro and Sinjeri, who had been liberated from a slave gang in the Shire highlands by Livingstone in 1861, and were now engaged as interpreters. Before Young left London fresh reports had arrived from Kirk at Zanzibar of Arab traders who spoke of a white man in the neighbourhood of Lake Tanganyika. At Cape Town there was no further news and just before H.M.S. *Petrel* reached the Zambezi delta an American ship from Zanzibar passed and signalled 'No news of Dr Livingstone'. This was a considerable relief for 'It would have been provoking to come so far on a useless errand; now, this uncertainty was most opportunely dispelled, and we felt we had a fair start.'[12] The spirit of the search had obviously got into Young and he was undoubtedly thinking ahead to the time when he would reach the north end of Lake Nyasa, to complete the survey of the lake which Livingstone had failed to do in 1861.

H.M.S. *Petrel* reached the Zambezi delta on 25 July and three days later, having unloaded the *Search* and put her together, the Livingstone Search Expedition was off on its own up the broad river. With two whaleboats to carry stores as far as the cataracts on the Shire, and another sailor named Stacey, who was seconded at Young's request from the *Petrel*, the expedition, as Faulkner impolitely puts it, 'was now increased to five Europeans, four niggers and three boats'.[13] Local crews were recruited for the various stages of the river journey and on 16 August the expedition reached Chibisa (nowadays Chikwawa), where Livingstone's Kololo followers had remained behind when the Zambezi expedition withdrew in 1864. With the prestige of Livingstone's name, backed up by their possessions of firearms, the Kololo had established a considerable settlement and were extending their power in the lower Shire valley, taking advantage of the prevailing unsettled conditions. They were evidently pleased to see the newcomers and 'rushed into the river to drag our boats to shore, calling out continually "Our fathers the English are come again! Here is Mr Young! Mr Young! Mr Young!" They were wild with delight.'[14]

After much parleying twelve Kololo, led by their chief, Mloka, at last agreed to accompany the expedition to the lake, 'in consideration of the fabulous wages of eight pieces of cloth each for the job, three to be paid in advance'.[15] They had doubts about leaving their settlement at the time, for Ngoni raiding parties were believed to be coming down from the north, and it was only Young's promise to leave guns and ammunition with those remaining behind that finally induced the twelve to go. The *Search* and the two whaleboats were now taken to Matiti, the village at the foot of the cataracts twelve miles up the Shire from Chibisa, where Livingstone had made a base for his abortive effort to transport the steamer *Lady Nyasa* to the lake in 1863. Here a camp was set up and the *Search* dismantled. The Kroomen, Antonio and John Brown, were left in charge of the two whaleboats and stores, with instructions to return to the coast if the expedition had not returned by

15 November, and report to the British warship which was due to be there by 1 December.

Further Ngoni alarms delayed departure from Matiti until 24 August, when the expedition set off on their forty-mile overland journey through the rugged terrain beside the Shire cataracts. Over two hundred porters were needed to carry the sections of the boat, plus stores and equipment, but the whole cavalcade reached the upper Shire at the head of the cataracts (near modern Matope) in four days, without the loss of a single item. The porters were paid off and, in view of the continued reports of Ngoni raiders coming down from the north, Buckley was sent back to Matiti to reinforce the two Kroomen left there, with repeated instructions as to what to do in the event of the non-return of the rest of the party from the lake. This left the four Europeans, two interpreters and twelve Kololo with three servants, a total of twenty-one persons to be crammed into a thirty-foot boat with all their stores and equipment. Two days were spent reassembling the *Search*, a process watched with great curiosity by local villagers. Even more curious from the expedition's point of view was the story of a European with a small dog who had been seen some time ago at Lake Malombe, the appendage to Lake Nyasa about fifty miles ahead. Another version of the story was heard on 3 September by which time the expedition had only managed to make thirty miles along the upper Shire due to unfavourable winds and the demoralising effects on the Kololo oarsmen of repeated reports of Ngoni raiders in the offing.

Having heard the same story twice from widely separated sources, neither Young nor Faulkner was now inclined to doubt that a stranger, probably European, had been in the vicinity of Lake Malombe sometime in the not too distant past, but that it could be Livingstone seemed impossible as everyone believed he had gone to the north of Lake Nyasa, according to his expressed intentions. On 6 September, when the expedition passed through Malombe and the short stretch of the Shire joining it to Nyasa, heavy seas, thick reeds on the shore and then hostile crowds at the landing places prevented any useful communication being established, so the riddle of the mysterious European was left unsolved for the moment. The expedition sailed on to Lake Nyasa and camped on Boadzulu Island, Young concluding that the people they had seen that day would have been unlikely to give any useful information anyway.

Next day the *Search* encountered a gale and ran some forty-five miles before it to reach, in the evening, the shelter of a bay north of Cape Ngombo. Here, and at various other places on the same stretch of coast during the next week, the expedition collected abundant evidence of a visit by a man who could only be Livingstone sometime the previous year. Not only was he himself accurately described by those who had seen him, together with his attendants (Musa, Wakotani and Juma being remembered by name), his equipment and the little dog Chitani, but several people also produced presents of obvious British manufacture that he had given them. He had come from Mataka, to the north-east, and tried to cross the lake, but failing to get a passage he had gone south to Nkata and Mponda.

It was now clear that for some reason, Livingstone had not gone to the north of the lake, but had turned southwards. Musa and the Johanna men had correctly stated the order of places passed through, Mataka, Nkata and Mponda, but not being versed in the use of the compass had not been clear in their directions north or south. The shallow lake they had crossed with Livingstone was Malombe, not the north end of Nyasa. Kirk, interpreting the places in the light of Livingstone's intention to go north, and struck by the similarity of Mponda to the 'Mupunda' he had heard of at the north end of the lake, had nicely confused the trail, with all the weight of his experience behind him. It now remained for the expedition to cross over to the other side of the lake and try to pick up Livingstone's trail from there.

Accordingly on 15 September the *Search* crossed to a point near the mouth of the Linthipe river and the expedition again began making enquiries there. A similar story emerged: a European, with a number of followers and a small dog had passed to the south of the lake and stopped at Marenga, at the end of the south-western arm. Marenga was the place a short distance beyond where Livingstone was reported to have been murdered. The most valuable testimony came from some men who had acted as carriers for the European from a place five days' journey inland from the lake: he had come to their village with his dog, accompanied by only eight followers. The conclusion was obvious: Musa and the nine Johanna men must have deserted before this, while Livingstone went on unharmed. Young and Faulkner told their informants that they had come to investigate a report that the European had been murdered by the Ngoni. This gave rise to much amusement and they were informed that he had avoided the Ngoni and gone far westwards to the Bisa country around Lake Bangweulu.

The next step was to visit Chief Marenga, himself a member of the much travelled Bisa people, the noted traders of the period. Faulkner amusingly describes his and Young's arrival amidst the normal routine of court life at Marenga:

On the outskirts of this village, which was very extensive, was the

163

enclosure occupied by the chief. Within it were some six huts, and one or two large trees. Under one of these trees, reclining on a mat, and using one of his wives as a pillow, while thirty-nine more sat closely packed around him, lay Marenga, very drunk. He gave us a hearty welcome, shaking us long and violently by the hands. He is a man about six feet in height, and stout, with a debauched and bloated appearance, and covered with scurvy. Having arranged a mat for us, and seeing that we were comfortable, Marenga's first question was, 'Where is your brother that was here last year?' He was told that we had come to look for him, and should be obliged if he would tell us all he knew about him. He said he would, but he must have some pombe first, as he had much to tell. Having changed the wife against whom he was leaning for another, apparently a stronger one, a large pot of pombe was brought to him, and held by one of his wives, who sat by his side while he drank the beer through a Bamboo about one foot and a half long. Invariably, whenever he took a pull, which was generally a long one, one or other of his forty wives tickled his chest and stomach, ceasing the operation only when he took the bamboo from his mouth.[16]

In spite of a certain difficulty in expressing himself, what Marenga had to say was perfectly clear. Livingstone, whom he had seen before during his 1861 trip on the lake, had come to his town from Mponda the previous year accompanied by several men, including Musa, and stayed a day. Marenga had then lent him canoes in which to cross over the marshy tract at the end of the south-western arm of the lake, thus saving a long detour by land. A day or two after he left, Musa and some of his companions returned to Marenga saying that their service with Livingstone was finished, as they were not willing to venture into dangerous country. Marenga gave them a house for the night but where they had gone after leaving he could not say. He next sent for one of the carriers who had gone five days' journey with Livingstone, beyond the point where the Johanna men deserted, and he also produced several things Livingstone had given him, including some stomach powders wrapped up in pages torn from the *Nautical Almanack* for 1866 He ridiculed the idea that Livingstone could have been murdered within a considerable distance of his town without his hearing of it.

Young now believed that he had, according to the Royal Geographical Society's instructions, obtained 'reliable information of Dr Livingstone's fate' and he had to decide what to do next. His instructions stated that he must not allow 'geographical research nor the collection of objects in natural history . . . under any circumstances . . .

to interfere with the main purpose of the expedition'.[17] The expedition had already achieved its purpose – at the southern end of the lake and much quicker than anticipated. It was then 19 September; there were over two months before the appointed meeting with a warship at the Zambezi delta and Young considered making for the north, as had been the original intention: it could hardly be interfering with the 'main purpose' of the expedition since that had been achieved. The matter was settled for him by the attitude of the Kololo who, now that news of their former leader had been obtained, were concerned only with getting back to Chibisa and refused to go further.

Leaving Marenga on 20 September, the *Search* reached the head of the cataracts on 2 October, Young having made a short detour inland from Lake Malombe to visit Mponda, where he got further confirmation of Livingstone's journey: Wakotani had indeed left him there, as the Johanna men said, to join relatives. Since time was now of little object, Faulkner was able to go off on long expeditions to pursue his own destructive brand of natural history while the boat made its way down river. To an age desperate to conserve the vestiges of wild life in the country, Faulkner's records of the abundance of game in 1867 and of his own kills sound both tantalising and sickening. Young got the parts of the *Search* down to Matiti at the foot of the cataracts on 11 October. A week later she was reassembled and Young set off with her and one of the whaleboats, Faulkner taking the other to make his own way down to the Zambezi delta, stopping *en route* for more hunting forays. All arrived at the sea together on 11 November, and then had to spend three weeks waiting for H.M.S. *Racoon* to take them to Cape Town, where they were fortunate to catch the mail steamer *Celt*, in which they had sailed from England six months previously.

The Livingstone Search Expedition reached Britain on 21 January 1868. It had carried out its task according to plan, without the loss of a single man, European or African (a remarkable record in days when other African expeditions suffered alarming death-tolls) and in the time allotted – though this was to some extent the result of not having to sail all the way to the north end of Lake Nyasa. Six days after his return Young presented his report to the Royal Geographical Society and earned the acclaim of men well able to appreciate the efficiency with which he had led his expedition. He was given a gratuity of £100 by the society, which also recognised the excellent services of John Reid, who had been in charge of the *Search*, with a gratuity of £50. Apart from another £10 given to Faulkner for collecting-apparatus, all the expenses of the expedition were met by the government.[18]

Both Young and Faulkner had been vastly impressed with the lake, the latter regretting especially that he had not had a chance to see its northern end and making 'a firm resolution to return, if possible, at some future period'.[19] In 1869 he returned to the Zambezi and Shire having fitted out an expedition at his own expense. Whether he reached the lake again is not known, for all his journals were destroyed when he was killed sometime in 1870, having got himself involved in the turmoil of the Kololo rise to power in the lower Shire valley.[20]

Young was struck by the stretch of coast southwards from Cape Maclear to the Shire, today one of the two main areas of tourist development on Lake Malawi. 'For a settlement nothing more could be desired,' he writes. 'A little colony here would command a flourishing ivory trade, and it would hold the outlet from the lake, being situated so close to the spot where the Shire makes its exit from its waters.'[21] In 1875 he returned as leader of the pioneer party of the Livingstonia Mission of the Free Church of Scotland which, with the help of a small sectional steamer, he settled at Cape Maclear itself. After spending two years as leader of the mission he returned to Britain to resume his duties as Inspecting Officer, coastguard, to which he had been appointed after his return from the search expedition. He retired from the Navy in 1891 with the rank of Honorary Lieutenant and died in 1896. The best tribute to Young is the title on an article about him written some years ago – 'A Sailor who did his Duty'.[22]

As for Musa, whose story had been the cause of so much trouble, he was handed over to the Sultan of Johanna and spent eight months in irons, 'a severe punishment in a Johanna gaol', according to Professor Coupland.[23] The search expedition had revealed that the story told by Musa, and corroborated by his companions, had cleverly stuck to the truth in all matters except the death of Livingstone. Its purpose had been two-fold: to cover up for their cowardice in desertion and to enable them to claim back-pay from the time they left Livingstone. Fortunately Consul Seward at Zanzibar had been wise enough to withhold payment until the story was confirmed, so the Johanna men gained nothing by it.

Young presented his report to the Royal Geographical Society in January 1868. In April the first news from Livingstone himself arrived in the form of letters addressed to various persons and dated February 1867, two months after the Johanna men had returned to Zanzibar with their tale. At the Annual General Meeting of the Society in May, Sir Roderick Murchison was able to announce: 'Glorious indeed have been the tidings we have received . . . in relation to the great South African traveller.'[24]

But Young's expedition was only the beginning of many Livingstone relief and search expeditions. For the rest of his life the solitary, ailing explorer wandered amid the central African lakes and rivers, making many new discoveries but never really solving any of the outstanding geographical puzzles, and always virtually cut off from contact with his fellow countrymen. Reports that he was missing, or dead, appeared frequently in the press and searching for Livingstone became almost a popular pursuit amongst young men, mostly naval officers, with a taste for adventure. Even the reports that he was alive were conflicting, and he was located in all manner of places, if not completely erroneously then at least many months out of date.

As might be expected it was the British Agency at Zanzibar that

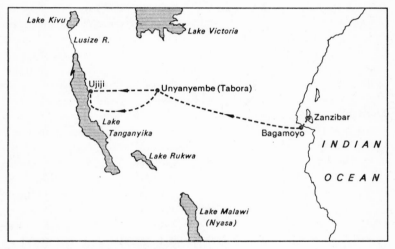

8 The route of the expeditions to Ujiji

became the base for Livingstone relief operations and Dr John Kirk, in his position as surgeon and vice-consul, who did much to maintain contact with his former leader, and send him help and supplies, in spite of Stanley's controversial allegations to the contrary. Ujiji, on the shores of Lake Tanganyika, was the objective of most relief parties since it was Livingstone's intended base and the one place at which, from the scanty information available, he did turn up from time to time. He himself had arranged for a caravan of supplies to be sent to Ujiji to await his arrival before he left Zanzibar in 1866. In July the same year, months before Musa's story burst upon the world, Consul Seward sent off further supplies to Ujiji. In January 1868, H. A. Churchill, who had replaced Seward, received a letter from Livingstone, at the time

167

Young's expedition was returning to Britain, requesting supplies, especially medicines, but Churchill inferred from the letter that by the time a caravan could reach Ujiji Livingstone would have passed beyond there, so he did nothing. In August he received further requests and this time he complied with them, sending off a substantial stock.[25]

As it turned out Livingstone did not reach Ujiji until March 1869, when there should, by all accounts, have been plenty awaiting him. But he found only a sorry assortment of things: some were useless, some had been stolen, and some, including the vital medicines, had been left not at Ujiji but at Unyanyembe (Tabora), 220 miles east on the route to Zanzibar. A further complication was that the enormous vested interests in the slave trade on this route made Livingstone's presence at Ujiji highly undesirable. He was a British consul, and Britain was dedicated to the elimination of the trade, hence the Arabs at Ujiji, though many of them remained courteous and friendly to Livingstone personally, closed their ranks when it came to relief parties reaching him from the coast and even more so to allowing dispatches from him, revealing details of the extent of slaving activities, finding their way to Zanzibar. Livingstone, however, wrote numerous letters from Ujiji and one of these addressed to Kirk and dated May 1869 managed to get through to Zanzibar in October. Kirk acted upon it and the same month sent off fourteen men, who were to stay with Livingstone and act as porters for his future explorations, under the leadership of a man named Sherif. They took with them a large consignment of necessary supplies for Livingstone, as well as goods of their own, for they intended to turn the expedition into a trading venture on their own account. Soon after reaching the mainland they were hit by a cholera epidemic. Five died, but the rest struggled on, stopping frequently to trade, and it was not until December 1870 that they got to Ujiji by which time Livingstone had crossed Lake Tanganyika and gone off into the country to the west. Sherif and nine companions, having reached their immediate goal and found Livingstone gone, proceeded to live off his supplies which they had brought. When word came from Livingstone that they were to join him west of Tanganyika, Sherif refused to go, preferring the life of luxury he was living at Ujiji. Instead he sent seven of the men off who eventually joined Livingstone and remained very unwillingly with him until he himself returned to Ujiji in October 1871. Sherif had in the meantime expended all Livingstone's supplies and trade goods, so that he found nothing awaiting him except a few things which he had, with unusual care for the future, left in the charge of an Arab he could trust before setting out two years earlier. It was one of Livingstone's most depressing experiences and he was near despair when, on 28 October his faithful Susi came running to him with astonishing news: 'An Englishman! I see him!'[26]

Livingstone's long overdue arrival at Ujiji in March 1869, news of which did not reach the outside world until the end of the year, had again given rise to speculation as to his whereabouts and possible death. In October of that year, when Kirk was preparing the Sherif caravan, Henry Morton Stanley, a journalist employed by the *New York Herald*, was given an assignment by his editor covering some of the more sensational areas of the world at the time. It included the opening of the Suez Canal, Sir Samuel Baker's Nile expedition, Jerusalem, the old battlefields of the Crimea, Persia and India. But the climax of this vast programme was to find Livingstone, dead or alive, and bring back proof, one way or the other.

While Stanley was engaged on the first part of his assignment the Foreign Office in London decided, as a matter of public concern, that its unpaid consul in central Africa deserved some assistance and in May 1870 gave £1,000 'in the earnest hope that the sum may be the means of promoting his return in safety to this country'.[27] Announcing this to the Royal Geographical Society, Sir Roderick Murchison said that it was not the present intention to organise another search expedition but that the money would be sent to Consul Churchill at Zanzibar who would arrange yet another relief caravan. This he did, sending off seven men with a caravan of supplies in November. In February 1871 Kirk learned that some of the men were still at Bagamoyo, on the mainland opposite Zanzibar; he immediately went there, sorted out the causes of delay, and despatched the caravan on its way with considerable vigour.

The previous month Stanley had arrived at Zanzibar to carry out the final part of his assignment. It took him four weeks to put together all the stores and equipment he needed and then, having crossed over to Bagamoyo, it took him a further six weeks to recruit all the necessary porters. His expedition set off in five sections, the first on 18 February, the last, with himself in charge, on 21 March. The full complement was 192, including two other Europeans beside Stanley himself, W. L. Farquhar and J. W. Shaw, whom he had picked up in Zanzibar. Both turned out to be useless, were rejected *en route* by Stanley, and subsequently died. On reaching Unyanyembe in June, Stanley found Kirk's relief caravan already there – and the way to Ujiji blocked by Mirambo, a local chief who had decided to oust the Arab slavers. Stanley wasted three months assisting the Arabs to try and overcome Mirambo, but to no purpose, and in the end he had to reach Ujiji by making a big detour south-west which avoided Mirambo altogether.

Stanley was almost defeated first of all by the difficulty of getting porters at Unyanyembe, and then by their mutiny on the way, but at last on 10 November 1871 he reached Ujiji. He was an emotional man and wanted to display something of what he felt as he walked towards the emaciated figure in the consul's cap with the gold braid around it, standing amidst the crowds that had turned out to see the new arrival in Ujiji. Instead he was possessed by something which, for him, passed for shyness, and he came out with that masterpiece of British understatement: 'I am shaking hands with him. We raise our hats, and I say, "Dr Livingstone, I presume?" and he says, "Yes."'[28]

For Stanley, although an American citizen, was British by birth and Susi had not been entirely wrong when he announced to Livingstone that an Englishman was coming, albeit under the Stars and Stripes rather than the Union Jack. Stanley's arrival put new life into Livingstone. He gave him news of the outside world, he bought much needed supplies and told him of the generous provision of £1,000 by the British government, the results of which were awaiting him at Unyanyembe, and he gave him something which until then Livingstone had not really missed – the companionship of one of his own race. The two men remained together four months, during which time they travelled to the north end of Lake Tanganyika to find that the Lusize river flowed *into* the lake not *out* of it: so Tanganyika could not connect with the Nile system that way, though there might be another outlet which did. The problem of the Nile source still unresolved, Livingstone and Stanley returned to Ujiji and then set off for Unyanyembe, again on a detour to avoid Mirambo. Although the supplies provided by the £1,000 had been badly pilfered, Stanley's stores left behind at Unyanyembe contained more than enough to make good the deficiencies and keep Livingstone going, he reckoned, for about four years. Keeping only what he needed for his return to Zanzibar, Stanley gave him everything else. He also undertook to enlist fifty men when he got to the coast and send them back to help Livingstone on his next journeys, as porters were impossible to obtain at Unyanyembe owing to the Mirambo war. Their parting on 14 March 1872 deeply affected both men, between whom a considerable bond had grown up during the months of their association, in spite of their enormous differences in character. For his part Livingstone was deeply grateful for the help and companionship he had received from the younger man (Stanley was thirty), while Stanley could not but admire the stubborn devotion to Africa in the ailing explorer, aged more than his fifty-nine years, who would not consider returning home before his work was complete.

Stanley reached Bagamoyo on 6 May 1872 to be greeted by Lieutenant

W. Henn, a member of yet another Livingstone search expedition, sent to do what Stanley had just accomplished. This latest venture had started in December the previous year when the first news reached Britain of the war between the Arabs and chief Mirambo around Unyanyembe, blocking the road to Ujiji. The conclusion to be drawn from the news was obvious: Livingstone was cut off in Ujiji and Stanley would be unable to get to him, so a full-scale expedition must be sent to his relief without delay. The Royal Geographical Society approached the government for funds but found that it would not provide more than the £1,000 already allotted, of which there was still a balance unexpended. So the society started a public appeal with a contribution of £500 and in a few weeks had raised over £4,000. The members of the expedition were quickly chosen: Lieutenant D. S. Dawson, R.N., in command, with Lieutenant W. Henn, R.N., and Livingstone's youngest son Oswell, aged twenty, as members. They sailed from Britain on 9 February 1872 and reached Zanzibar on 17 March, where they were joined by the Revd Charles New, a missionary who had worked for some years on the east coast. Having prepared his expedition, which included twenty *askari*, with the help of Kirk, Dawson moved across to Bagamoyo on 27 April intending to recruit porters there. The day after arrival, however, messengers sent ahead by Stanley reached Bagamoyo with the news that Livingstone was well. Dawson promptly returned to Zanzibar, in what appears to be a fit of pique, and resigned his command of the expedition. Henn and New stayed on to await Stanley's arrival on 6 May. They were uncertain what to do. Stanley made it plain that what Livingstone now wanted was porters whom he, Stanley, would provide without anyone else's help. In the end Henn and New resigned over a dispute as to who should be leader if they carried on. This left Oswell Livingstone, who had remained in Zanzibar but now crossed over to Bagamoyo, to take charge of the stores and men already recruited for the expedition. Then he, too, backed out for health reasons on Kirk's advice.[29] The members of the expedition undoubtedly resented the fact that an American citizen had already done what they as fellow-Britons were on their way to do for Livingstone.

While the members of the British search expedition were wrangling over what to do next Stanley had, with his customary drive and efficiency, followed up his successful American search expedition by recruiting fifty-seven men, most of whom had already been with him, and packing them off to Ujiji on 27 May, as an equally successful American relief expedition. They reached Livingstone at Unyanyembe on 14 August, and served him well until his death eight months later, many of them then taking part in the historic march of faithful Juma and Susi bearing their leader's body back to the coast.

Having sent Livingstone his porters, Stanley left Zanzibar at the end of May, reached London at the beginning of August, to be acclaimed a hero by almost the whole British public and press. There were a few dissenting voices: newspapers which took the line that Stanley was a fraud who had never been near Livingstone, and individual persons of influence who felt that they had been shown up as failing to take proper care of Livingstone in his lonely endeavours. A major point in Stanley's story, which aroused universal consternation, was his unwarranted attack on Kirk for failing, as the man on the spot, to send adequate succour to his former leader. Stanley soon sensed that in attacking Kirk he was alienating people from himself, and he let the matter drop. Kirk's reputation was sufficiently sound to withstand the attack but it was an unpleasant aspect of an otherwise outstanding piece of work on Stanley's part.

Before Stanley left Britain for the United States in November 1872, the Royal Geographical Society had taken steps to see that for the rest of his explorations Livingstone should be short of nothing. Although it was clear from his despatches that he now had all he needed to continue his work, the society did not intend to lay itself open to any further implications, or direct charges, of neglect. Two expeditions were organised, the first under Lieutenant W. J. Grandy, R.N., the second under Lieutenant V. L. Cameron, R.N. Both left Britain on 30 November. Grandy's expedition, financed by a grant of over £3,000 from Livingstone's old friend James Young, was to start from the west coast of Africa and follow the Congo to the interior in the hopes of meeting Livingstone should his explorations of the central African waterways lead him down that river. Grandy set off from the coast in January 1873. Over a year later he received news of Livingstone's death and of the recall of his expedition.

Cameron's expedition was financed from the surplus funds from Dawson's abortive effort of 1871. Along with three companions, Dr W. E. Dillon, a naval surgeon, Lieutenant C. Murphy, Indian Army, and Robert Moffat, grandson of the famous missionary, Cameron was to find Livingstone and then place the whole expedition at his disposal, in the furtherance of whatever exploration he might be engaged in. Cameron's expedition set off from Bagamoyo at the end of March 1873, but suffered greatly from defaulting porters and sickness (from which Moffat died in May). The survivors struggled on to reach Unyanyembe at the beginning of August, where they remained prostrated with illness until 20 October, when Cameron, on his sickbed, was astonished to receive a letter which announced the death of 'our father'.[31] He sent for the bearer of the letter and found it to be Juma who told him of Livingstone's death and that he and his companions were carrying the body to the coast. The letter had been written by Jacob Wainwright, one of the educated Africans among the party of fifty-seven sent by Stanley. A few days later the body arrived in the charge of Susi and the other faithful followers of Livingstone. Now that the primary object of Cameron's expedition was defeated by death, Murphy resigned, and, together with Dillon who was too ill to do anything else, returned with the body to Zanzibar. Cameron carried on alone to Ujiji, where he recovered a box of papers left there by Livingstone, and then made for the west coast, completing the crossing of the continent in November 1874 when he reached Benguela.

The first news of Livingstone's death at Chitambo on the southern shores of Lake Bangweulu on 1 May 1873 reached England in January 1874. Not surprisingly it was treated at first as another of the Livingstone scares to which the public was becoming accustomed. But confirmation in the form of letters from Cameron, Murphy and Kirk, who had seen the body, followed, and finally the last vestiges of hope, for those who remained hopeful to the end, were extinguished when the body reached Southampton, to be borne by special train to London, where it was buried on April 18 with full national honours in the nave of Westminster Abbey.

Notes

1 *Proceedings of the Royal Geographical Society*, vol. XIII, 1864, p. 44.
2 H. Waller (ed.), *The Last Journals of David Livingstone*, London, 1874, vol. I, p. 9.
3 *The Life and Explorations of David Livingstone, LL.D. Carefully Compiled from Reliable Sources*, London, 1887. (Consists mainly of long extracts from *Proceedings* and other contemporary sources.)
4 *Proceedings*, vol. XI, 1867, p. 135.
5 Ibid., p. 137.
6 Ibid., p. 142–3.
7 Ibid., p. 144–8.
8 Ibid., p. 154.
9 E. D. Young, *The Search after Livingstone*, London, 1868, pp. 46–52.
10 War Office Records, E.O. 76/10/F.270, and H. Faulkner, *Elephant Haunts*, London, 1868, p. 2.
11 F. M. Withers, 'A Sailor who did his Duty', *Nyasaland Journal*, vol. IV, no. 1, 1951.
12 Young, op. cit., p. 59.
13 Faulkner, op. cit., p. 18.

14 Young, op. cit., p. 103.
15 Faulkner, op. cit., p. 38.
16 Ibid., p. 148.
17 Young, op. cit., p. 48.
18 *Journal of the Royal Geographical Society*, vol. XXXVIII, pp. x and 111–18.
19 Faulkner, op. cit., p. 170.
20 Personal communication from Mrs J. Monechan, Co. Carlow, Eire, 13 March 1968.
21 Young, op. cit., pp. 194–5.
22 See 11 above.
23 R. Coupland, *Livingstone's Last Journey*, London, 1947, p. 261.
24 *Proceedings*, vol. XII, 1868, p. 280.
25 Coupland, op. cit., pp. 70–1.
26 Waller, *Last Journals*, vol. II, p. 156.
27 H. M. Stanley, *How I found Livingstone in Central Africa*, London, 1872, p. 693.
28 *Life and Explorations*, p. 436.
29 Coupland, op. cit., p. 190–5.
30 Ibid., p. 217.
31 V. L. Cameron, *Across Africa*, new edition, London, 1885, p. 121.

8 Livingstone's Contribution to Malawi: Some Aspects of the Medical Factor

Michael Gelfand

We can judge a man's contribution by his deeds, his words, the reaction of others and the events that follow his death. Thus we can assess the worth of David Livingstone. Of immediate concern to us is what brought him to the territory now known as Malawi and the influence he had on that country.

When Livingstone arrived in Africa, the two factors that were to have the greatest significance for his future and that of Malawi were already in evidence. The first was his deep Christian faith and background and the second the fact that he was a qualified medical man. Today one would talk of him as a medical missionary, that is, a person to whom medicine and religion are of almost equal concern. His master was God and through him he hoped to bring to the people amongst whom he worked the teaching of the gospel and at the same time alleviate the suffering of those afflicted with disease. In fact Livingstone was the first doctor to practise medicine as such in south central Africa and the second medical missionary to set foot in Africa, the first being the Revd Dr J. T. van der Kemp of the Cape.

Livingstone started in Africa at Kuruman Mission some 200 miles beyond the Orange River, working there for many years in close contact with the Bakwana and Bamangwato in what today is Botswana.[1] There he gained much experience in living and travelling in this environment. He also came into conflict with the Boers living close to the Botswana border.

Livingstone heard from ivory traders and others of the well-established dynasties of the African chiefs of tribes living in the far hinterland which malaria made it impossible to penetrate. He read deeply and thought hard. He was greatly interested in McWilliam's account of the deaths in the great Niger Expedition and came to the

175

conclusion that if quinine had been given right away in strong doses, accompanied by a strong purge to rid the liver of excess bile which had accumulated, the fever ought to have been controlled. So when he moved into the unhealthy regions to the north he tried out this method of treatment and was greatly encouraged by the results.[2] He started his travels with the idea of finding a suitable place to start his own mission station, a place where malaria could be controlled and from which he could teach the gospel to the great nations further north.

In April 1850 Livingstone, with his wife and their children, left Kolobeng in order to cross the Zouga River and so reach Sebitwane in the north. However, after reaching Lake Ngami and this river, his little boy and girl were seized with fever. He was able to try out his special malaria regime which was to play such a vital part in his ability to open up the routes of central Africa. Because of this illness he abandoned the attempt to reach Sebitwane but on 21 June 1851, again with his wife and family, he reached Sebitwane's country. Here he noted the prevalence of a very virulent form of fever amongst the Makololo, but the river people further north did not suffer greatly. The Makololo were newcomers, having migrated from the south from a country uninfected by malaria and so unlike the river people they were not immune to the disease. So concerned was Livingstone that he wrote, 'I offer myself as a forlorn hope, in order to ascertain whether there is a place fit to be a sanatorium for more unhealthy spots.'[3] He considered it unwise to settle in the swampy country of the Makololo and decided that when he came back he would go north to the territory of the Barotse. He left Linyanti in August 1851. At the Zouga river he met a party of Mambari slave traders; this prompted his idea of an English settlement in these regions to which manufacturers would come with their goods to trade and so put an end to the slave trade. While travelling along the Zouga River his child Thomas was smitten with fever three times. Livingstone moved Thomas to a higher locality, wrapped him in a wet sheet and gave him a large quantity of cold water to drink. This soon produced perspiration. After that he gave him quinine.[4] After taking his wife and children to Cape Town and sending them back to England so as not to risk their lives any further on his journeys, he set out again. From Kuruman he wrote, 'One of the chief objects of my present expedition is to investigate the character of that disease which is the main obstacle to Africa being opened to beneficial inter-course with the rest of the world. If I can only discover a healthy range of country and means to foil that terrible plague, I shall be content to let the unicorn sleep in everlasting oblivion.'[5] After a stay in Kuruman and Kolobeng he finally set out for the north on 14 December 1852.

He realised that if central Africa was to have a future it was necessary to control the fever. In 1853 he wrote in his journal, 'I would like to devote a portion of my life to the discovery of a remedy for that terrible disease, the African fever. I would go into the parts where it prevails most and try to discover if the natives have a remedy for it. I must make many enquiries of the River people in this quarter. What an unspeakable mercy it is to be permitted to engage in this most honourable and holy work.'[6] He noticed that the indigenous river folk were well built giants in comparison with the slender Makololo who were poorer in physique.[7]

Livingstone suffered his first attack of African fever on 30 May 1853 and, after trying out a remedy with quinine, he came to the conclusion that the most effective treatment was its combination with purgatives. He noticed that as soon as the slightest bowel movement took place the perspiration burst forth from the skin and the headache vanished. His recipe, which later became famous and known as 'Livingstone's Pill' or 'Zambesi Rouser' was three grains of calomel, three grains quinine, ten grains of rhubarb, four grains of essence of jalop mixed with a little opium. This was the secret of his survival in spite of attacks of fever. Although he suffered greatly from malaria he was confident of success and in October 1853 declared he would open a path into the interior of Africa or perish, so that the gospel might be preached.

Armed with quinine he set out to look for an outlet to the west coast in order that supplies to his mission might easily be sent. After a difficult journey he entered the port of Loanda on 31 May 1854. But he was dissatisfied with this route to the sea, so in September that year he set off again to find a better way to the east coast. As he travelled through central Africa he realised more than ever the importance to a missionary of being qualified medically:

> A most desirable missionary field is open here and I hope God may yet send His gracious message of mercy to desperately wicked inhabitants. A medical man has a better opportunity of ascertaining the state of the people than a mere missionary. As soon as they appreciate his real object they hide their feelings as much as possibly more people at home.[8]

When he eventually arrived at Quelimane, Livingstone decided to return to England and arrived there in December 1856. He had spent a long time travelling in Africa without doing much missionary work and although he still wished to return there in search of his healthy station he felt he could hardly expect the Directors of the London

Missionary Society to finance this venture, especially as he had already spent sixteen years in Africa and was still not settled.[9] Although a Christian missionary at heart he considered he needed an appointment which could give him the opportunity to trace the source of the Zambezi near the Batoka people in order to discover whether it was navigable and would thus afford a suitable entry to central Africa. Further he preferred to be his own master. With his obsessional make-up he was better off on his own without supervision and possible criticism. He was not an easy man to understand and not easy to get on with. He managed to enter into an arrangement with the British government whereby he would take an expedition on the Zambezi. In many ways he was well qualified for this task. He was determined to see it through and had the necessary drive and will power not to be put off by disappointments and failures. Most important of all he had a very good understanding of the African fever. He insisted on the members of the expedition taking prophylactic quinine and wrote to John Kirk, the medical officer and botanist to the expedition, about the virtues of his pill composed of resin of jalop, calomel and quinine. Livingstone was appointed Her Majesty's Consul in the district of Quelimane on the east coast of Africa, to study the methods of slavery in the interior of Africa from February 1858. The members of his expedition were to serve for two years.[10]

In March that year they set sail from Liverpool in the *Pearl* under the command of Norman Bedingfeld. Livingstone's first task was to sail up the Zambezi from the east coast to Tete from where he could inspect the Cabora Bassa rapids to discover whether they were navigable. Soon after they entered the river, bouts of fever broke out among the men, especially Thomas Baines and Charles Livingstone, and it was not surprising therefore that friction and quarrels followed. No matter what reasons are given for the differences between David Livingstone, Thomas Baines and others, there is no doubt that tempers were frayed because of the fever. Livingstone kept check and when Bedingfeld failed to take his daily quinine, relations between the two men became strained and Bedingfeld resigned and went back to Cape Town in July 1858.[11] Livingstone never underestimated the severity of malaria. He said, 'In endeavouring to open up the interior of Africa, the fever obviously required the greatest consideration. I shall therefore mention the precautions we have employed to escape its deadly power. We have with one exception continued the daily use of quinine ever since we entered the river.'

In November 1858 the expedition was ready to explore the Cabora Bassa rapids above Tete to ascertain whether they could be passed whilst

178

the river was low. When they entered the Cabora Bassa gorge Livingstone realised the river would have to be much higher and they would need a more powerful ship than the *Ma-Robert* to make it possible to navigate the river.[12] However, he returned a little later on 22 November and again he saw it was impossible to take a boat across the rapids. He still did not give up hope and decided to try again with a more powerful steamboat when the river was at its highest.

The realisation that the Cabora Bassa rapids were impossible to navigate must have been a great disappointment to Livingstone. His plans to use the Zambezi as a waterway to Barotseland had come to nothing, but he would not be defeated. He was sure there must be some other route or some other suitable place for his healthy mission. He had heard about a wide expanse of water related to the Upper Shire; perhaps this might be the alternative. So he decided to explore this possibility whilst waiting for the right time to go back to the Cabora Bassa rapids when they were full of water.[13] He had heard that the Shire River entered this great lake (Lake Nyasa) and so on 29 December he entered the river in order to find out if it would take him into the interior. He sailed for some days without meeting any obstacles until shortly after he passed the township of Chibisa when his way was barred by a cataract which he named the Murchison cataracts. He decided not to proceed further, returning to Tete on 2 February 1859. The rainy season was well established and fever prevailed. Charles Livingstone, Baines and Thornton all relapsed. David Livingstone was so determined to carry out his mission that he brushed aside all ideas of sickness lest it interfere with his project. His men became more irritable and relations between him and them became strained. More fever did not improve the situation. Livingstone with his obsessional personality became restless waiting for the end of the rainy season. By the middle of March he was able to set out again for the Shire; this time to attempt an overland expedition from the cataracts. The party reached Chibisa without incident. There Livingstone and Kirk left the ship and marched in a north-easterly direction across the Shire highlands in search of the lake of which they had heard. They were greatly impressed with the fertile country through which they passed. The weather was cold and they slept in the open for twenty nights without ill effects. They reached Mount Zomba on 16 April and two days later were on the shores of Lake Shirwa. They were only a short distance from Lake Nyasa but decided to leave their visit to the lake for another occasion as the main purpose of the expedition had been achieved.[14] Their discovery of the Shire Highlands was of greater significance than finding Lake Shirwa. These highlands afforded the healthy elevated fertile country, of easy access and suitable for European settlement – the land for which Livingstone had been searching for so long. He was delighted with his success. This region was 3,000–4,000 feet above sea level. Their return to the *Ma-Robert* was not too soon, for they found Walker delirious with fever. Livingstone was puzzled as he had taken his quinine regularly, whilst he and Kirk had ceased taking theirs in the Shire highlands and yet had escaped the fever.

On 23 June they were back at Tete where Charles Livingstone was ill with fever. Thornton was probably also afflicted and he was dismissed by Livingstone in July as being insufferably lazy. Baines was more severely affected and was often confused. He and Charles Livingstone were at loggerheads. Charles accused Baines of giving away expedition property to the Portuguese. A wiser man than Livingstone would have paid no attention to the accusations since both men were so badly affected by fever.

However, already irritated with Baines, Livingstone decided to part with him. He left Tete in the *Ma-Robert* on 11 July for another visit to the Shire, this time hoping to reach Lake Nyasa. After he had left he wrote to Baines dismissing him and saying that he could not accept ill health as an excuse for neglecting his duties.[15] Having spent the rainy season on the Zambezi, both Livingstone and Kirk felt that they had sufficient experience of the African fever to write a full report on it. They had also enjoyed the more salubrious climate of the Shire Highlands and noticed the effects of quinine on the crew; they considered that the Foreign Office should be informed of the suitability of central Africa for European settlers. They prepared a joint paper and sent it on 26 July 1859 to the Earl of Malmesbury, the Foreign Secretary, suggesting that it be published in one of the medical journals. The important point in their covering letter was the existence of two types of fever and they said, 'an advantage is probably gained by being attacked first by the milder type of disease in the highlands.' And to Sir James Clark they wrote, 'all Europeans should be sent on their arrival to the higher lands, so that if they contracted the fever, they might develop its milder form and carry that with them to the more unhealthy localities'. They mentioned, too, in this report that as a result of their experience they had decided to discontinue the use of prophylactic quinine. 'The limited experience we have had seems to indicate that the type once established had a constant tendency to recur.'[16]

Livingstone entered the Shire for the third time, leaving the *Ma-Robert* at Chibisa. On 28 August the main party set off on land striking northwards. Again they were delighted with the Shire Highlands and its streams, so obviously a country for European settlement. The
180

inhabitants were growing large quantities of cotton. Indeed such a land would be an asset to the commerce of Great Britain.[17] David Livingstone wrote to Murchison, 'We must have a small colony of our own Scottish poor in the eastern healthy highlands.' He also applied for a small steamer on Lake Nyasa. After passing a little lake known as Pamalombe, the party reached the shores of Lake Nyasa on 17 September 1859.[18] The following day they started on their return journey to the bitter disappointment of the weary men. When they reached the *Ma-Robert* they found Roe and Hutchins too ill to navigate the boat and they had to make their return journey to Tete on foot. Illness had broken out amongst the rest of the men resulting in great misery and frayed tempers. Dysentery was much in evidence. Livingstone himself was weak and weary. Now that the rainy season had started again little could be done. Each time the fever appeared it seemed to become worse and the malaria season of 1860 was one of the worst. Nevertheless, although most of his men succumbed to it, they generally responded to the Livingstone regime. The *Ma-Robert* was now no longer fit for the work required of her. The Foreign Office, still interested in the expedition, had begun negotiations to send out a more powerful vessel.[19] Livingstone also wanted a boat for use on Lake Nyasa as he considered this essential for transport and for stopping the slave trade. He therefore arranged to purchase one at his own expense.

Whilst waiting for the end of the rainy season to take his Makololo followers back to their own country to keep his promise to Sekelutu, David Livingstone was planning his next venture. He had written to the Foreign Secretary, Lord John Russell, advocating European settlement for central Africa. The Portuguese were becoming suspicious of his movements and they were not likely to favour British occupation of the interior. It seemed more likely that there would be difficulties over the use of the Zambezi route in order to reach Lake Nyasa. He was keen to find out whether the Ruvuma river was connected with the inland lakes, for if it was, there would be no need to go through Portuguese territory to reach the Shire Highlands. Therefore he sought permission from the Foreign Office to explore this river. This was granted on 17 April 1860.[20]

At this time Livingstone received a most important letter from Bishop Gray of Cape Town informing him of plans for the establishment of a mission to civilise and convert the people of central Africa to be led by the Revd Archdeacon of Zululand. This idea originated with a speech made by Livingstone at Cambridge on 4 December 1857. A society was then formed amongst the students of Cambridge, Oxford, Durham and Dublin to promote missionary work in central Africa.

Originally Bishop Gray had planned that the mission should follow closely David Livingstone's old route to the Makololo country. But Livingstone suggested that the healthy Shire Highlands would be easier to reach and also that it was the centre of the slave trade. Then, too, he was aware that missionary influence was already being extended to the Makololo by the London Missionary Society, so there was less need in this part for another station to be established.[21]

Whilst waiting for the arrival of a new ship David Livingstone, his brother Charles and Kirk set off for Sekelutu's country on 17 March 1860, reaching his village at Sesheke in August. There they heard about the sad fate of the party of missionaries from the London Missionary Society, who had nearly all perished. Livingstone was most upset as in many ways he felt responsible for their settling there. He had no doubt that they had died of fever and hastened to write to Lord John Russell to place at the disposal of the Foreign Office the remedy he had found so efficacious. He returned to Tete with sixteen Makololo on 3 November 1860, still distressed by the death of the Linyanti missionaries. He was determined to tell the world how malaria could be handled.[22] He wrote to General Charles Murray Hay telling him how he came upon his remedy. He had read that in the Niger expedition, at the autopsy in every fatal case, it was observed that the gall bladder was distended with black bile which was of the consistency of tar. With Livingstone's remedy the symptoms were relieved in five or six hours by causing the bile to be discharged. At the same time he wrote to the secretaries of the Oxford and Cambridge Mission, offering medical advice to the missionaries about to leave for the Zambezi.[23] He instructed them to ascend the Shire river between May and August, the healthiest time of the year. He was obviously concerned lest the same fate befall the new missionaries as those at Linyanti. He even went so far as to admit that it was better to rely on the indigenous Africans than those from elsewhere, since the indigenous people were able to stand up to the fever better than those who had not been exposed to the disease before. He advised them, too, with regard to the food they should take.

The next duty of the Livingstone expedition was to proceed to the coast to meet Bishop Frederick Mackenzie and his party and to take delivery of the new steamship – the *Pioneer*. The missionary party arrived in the H.M.S. *Sidon* with a new medical officer, Dr Charles Meller, to replace Kirk; he was well stocked with quinine.

While at the Kongone mouth David Livingstone decided that no time should be lost before exploring the Ruvuma. The Portuguese had already stationed six coloured soldiers at the mouth of that river and hoisted their flag. Instead of escorting the bishop and his party up the Zambezi to the Shire Highlands, Livingstone made up his mind to take them first with him to Ruvuma. He argued that it would be better not to enter the Zambezi in this unhealthy season and leave the missionaries without medical care (9 February 1861). Mackenzie was bitterly disappointed. He argued that a medical man would be joining him soon, but Livingstone had his way and the *Pioneer* proceeded straight to the Ruvuma mouth with both Livingstone and the bishop on board, arriving there on 25 February 1861. On 19 March, after they had travelled barely thirty miles up the river, they found the water falling rapidly. The steamboat could go no further. David Livingstone was most disappointed. Now he had no alternative but to return to the lower Shire.[24] When they reached the mouth of the Ruo fever broke out on board and within a few days everyone succumbed except the more seasoned members of the expedition.[25] They were forced to remain at anchor off the river mouth until the engineer was convalescent. They only reached the mouth of the Kongone in May and then entered the Zambezi. In such a laden ship it took six weeks to cross the fifty miles between the Elephant marshes and Chibisa. At Chibisa a small temporary station was started. Livingstone and the rest of the bishop's party set off for the highlands, the bishop leading the way with his pastoral staff in one hand and his gun in the other. At the top of the plateau they met a party of Tete slavers, whom they deprived of their guns, and released the slaves.[26] Further on they liberated another batch of over fifty slaves and on Zomba mountain still more were freed, and the missionaries continued in this way.

Magomero was chosen as the site for the mission by Livingstone but the missionaries disliked it from the beginning as it was in a hollow, in spite of the fact that it was over 3,000 feet high and therefore considered healthy by Livingstone.

By the end of August 1861 most of the missionaries were beginning to feel the effects of the climate and were suffering from fever. Then smallpox appeared amongst the Africans at the mission causing several deaths. In October, Bishop Mackenzie and six of his European missionaries joined the Nyanja in an expedition against the Yao, who fled. They left their slaves behind – fifty women and children – whom the bishop gathered to his flock even though the food supply at Magomero was already precarious. All their food had to be sought from the surrounding villages. Hearing that Livingstone was at Chibisa the bishop immediately left hoping to meet him there. In the meantime Livingstone and his party had carried a boat past the Murchison cataracts and then sailed in it up the Shire to Lake Nyasa. They skirted the western shores of the lake and named one of the small bays at its southern end Cape Maclear. Livingstone had failed in his main objective. He had hoped to find an outlet from the lake to the Ruvuma river and had not been able to cross to its eastern shore in such a small boat. The party returned to the *Pioneer* on the Shire river where Livingstone met the bishop. Livingstone was dismayed to hear that he had twice been involved in fights with the Yao. They made arrangements to meet again on 1 January 1862 at the junction of the Shire and Ruo, when Livingstone would take the bishop with him to the coast to meet his sister who was coming out to the mission.

Whilst the bishop was still there, on 19 November, the Revd Henry de Wint Burrup and Blair, a printer, arrived at Chibisa in a small boat to join the mission, and ten days later Dr Dickinson and Mr Clarke, a shoemaker, who were behind them in a smaller canoe, reached Magomero.

David Livingstone had left the bishop to sail to the coast and bring back supplies for the mission, which he could offload when he met the bishop on 1 January at the Ruo. Unfortunately, soon after his departure from Chibisa, the *Pioneer* ran aground on a mudbank and Livingstone had to remain there for six weeks. All hope of reaching the coast and returning with supplies in time for his appointment with the bishop was gone. As a result of this enforced sojourn in the marshes fever became rife on the *Pioneer*. Ferger, the captain, became ill suddenly on 16 December 1861 and died soon afterwards. An autopsy was performed; this was probably the first recorded case of blackwater fever in central Africa. As soon as they were able to leave the sandbank, Livingstone hastened down the Shire to the Ruo to keep his appointment with the bishop. In spite of the delay he arrived on the appointed day, but there was no bishop. Whilst the *Pioneer* had been stuck in the mud bank near Chibisa, Dr Dickinson and Mr Clarke had passed it on their way to the mission. Livingstone was certain that they would have told the bishop that his boat was still there, and the latter would realise that he could not possibly get down to the coast, pick up the supplies and return in time for their appointment. He was therefore not surprised that the bishop had not come to meet him.

Meanwhile Magomero mission was undergoing a critical period. Not only were supplies short but with the onset of the rains, sickness came as well. Fever and dysentery took their toll. The bishop was still embroiled in his neighbours' quarrels. He himself was suffering from diarrhoea but in spite of his illhealth, accompanied by the Revd Burrup, he left for Chibisa and Ruo on 3 January never doubting that Livingstone would wait for him. But Livingstone, who thought he would not come

I have heard nothing of Thornton except what you give. Am glad he has turned over a new leaf. I shall write and recommend him to try for Kilimanjaro but he is a curious being. I lent him a [?] me & white and chain. He sent back the the instrument without the chain & not a word of thanks or explanation!

The Portuguese have built a fort near the mouth of the Shire in order to collect cotton dues, while others are busily depopulating the country by slave hunting.

Kindest regards to Lady Murchison from yours ever affectionately
David Livingstone

Part of a letter from David Livingstone to Sir Roderick Murchison in which Livingstone refers to slave hunting in the region of the Shire River

Mr Joseph Bismarck

Some early products of Blantyre Mission. Standing, left to right: Lewis
Mataka Bandawe, Lawson Nyama, Richard Somanje; sitting, left to right:
Robertson Namate and Cedric Massangano.

The wedding at Blantyre Mission of Lewis and Grace Bandawe, 31 May 1913.
Revd Dr Alexander Hetherwick (in helmet) officiated.

any more, considered that it was time to leave for the coast, where he would be taking delivery of his new steamer for Lake Nyasa and meeting his wife and the bishop's sister. He did not want to lose time and continued his journey to the coast. At the Kongone mouth he met the H.M.S. *Gorgon* on 1 February 1862. On board were Mrs Mary Livingstone, the bishop's sister and the Revd James Stewart who had been sent out by the Foreign Mission Committee of the Free Church of Scotland to investigate the possibility of setting up a mission in the lands discovered by Livingstone.

When the bishop reached the Ruo he found that Livingstone had left four days before. He decided to wait on the island for him as the *Pioneer* was bound to return. Unfortunately their canoe overturned on the way and they lost not only their food but their medical supplies too, so they were without quinine when they both contracted fever. The bishop died on 31 January and Burrup decided to return to Magomero whilst his strength permitted. He arrived there but his condition deteriorated and he too succumbed on 21 February.[27] The loss of their bishop was a great blow to the missionaries and they were convinced they should abandon Magomero for a more healthy station – probably one nearer the Shire river, which was their main line of communication. Fifty women and children had died there since November and they decided to move to Chibisa. Rowley selected a site just above the river bank, hoping that it would be healthier than Magomero. By 6 May they were settled in their new station, little realising that it was far more unhealthy than Magomero. Again they had to deal with unsatisfactory neighbours. Instead of the hostile Yao they found themselves contending with unruly Makololo. The latter had behaved admirably in the employ of David Livingstone, but once they were left on their own settlement near Chibisa they used, to good purpose, the guns and ammunition Livingstone had given them for self defence. They plundered far and wide, waging wars against both Yao and Nyanja.

Livingstone was greatly upset by the bishop's death: 'His loss will be deplored by everyone who knew him and coming as this does on the back of the sad affair at Linyanti, I fear it will prove a sad blow to our hopes for Africa.' He wrote to Bishop Robert Gray of Cape Town urging him to send another head to the mission as soon as possible. He still believed that the highlands were healthy and he added in his letter, 'Please do impress on the new Bishop the importance of husbanding his strength and avoiding the lowlands in the wet season.'[28]

Bishop Tozer reached the coast in the *Orestes* in May 1863 with a party of reinforcements for the mission. He decided to leave the rest of the party behind while he went up to the mission to see it for himself.

So he and the Revd Charles Arlington travelled there and discussed the problem of a better site with the missionaries. The missionaries favoured moving back to the Shire Highlands if they could find a suitable spot, but Bishop Tozer set his heart on Morambala, a mountainous area in Portuguese territory. Before the matter was quite settled the bishop returned to the coast on 6 July to bring back the rest of his party. On 6 August, 1863 the mission was informed by a letter from Tozer that he had decided to move to Morambala. Livingstone was most anxious for the mission to return to the highlands, as he firmly believed that it could last only in a healthy region.

Just before Tozer reached the mission again, he sent a messenger with a dispatch from the Foreign Office to Livingstone, who was at the cataracts. This put an end to all Livingstone's dreams as he was told to abandon his expedition. The Foreign Office recognised the interesting geographical and scientific results of his exploration, but did not consider it of any great import to British commerce or humanity and did not believe that it could divert the energies of the local population from the slave trade. Livingstone was already disappointed as he had been unable to transport the *Lady Nyasa* to the upper Shire by land. Part of a waggon road was built but he was too debilitated by dysentery to continue that arduous task. The Foreign Office was probably influenced in their decision by a combination of factors, such as the deaths on the mission and on the Shire river, the continual sickness of the crew, the conflicts amongst the Africans and the suspicion with which the Portuguese viewed Livingstone's activities.[29] Although Livingstone favoured the Shire Highlands for the mission, he was satisfied that the Morambala mountains were healthy and that this attempt was being made to save the mission from being disbanded. He could not believe that central Africa was unfit for European habitation. The Portuguese were able to live in Tete, so surely the English should be able to survive in the highlands. He elaborated these views in his letter to Maclear and added, 'If they retire from other than lack of health, it will be I suppose, the first mission that ever turned tail.'[30]

The move to Morambala was soon completed but the life of the new station was short. It proved unsuitable and early in 1864 the bishop decided that central Africa was not favourable for missionary enterprise, which would be better furthered by moving to Zanzibar.

We can appreciate the value of the Livingstone regime for the treatment of the malaria when we compare the mortality figures of the U.M.C.A. mission in Nyasaland and that of the Livingstone Zambezi expeditions both in the *Ma-Robert* and the *Pioneer*. Although Livingstone's expedition had spent so many years in this very unhealthy part and so much in the rivers and low lying parts of the country, loss of life was very small. In the *Ma-Robert* 1858 to 1860 there were no deaths amongst the seven Europeans and on the *Pioneer* only three out of eighteen died (16.67 per cent).

Table I

Mortality figures for U.M.C.A. Mission to Nyasaland from 30 January 1861 to 6 August 1863

European	Number attached to mission (7 from 30 January 1861, 3 from 17 August 1861)..	12
	Number repatriated (the Revd Hawkins was repatriated but died later of fever in England)	2
	Number who died of malaria (Bishop Mackenzie, Scudamore, Burrup, Dickinson, Hawkins)..	5
Coloured	Number of Coloureds attached to mission..	4
	Number who were repatriated	3
	Number who died	0

Table II

Mortality from malaria in Livingstone's Zambezi expedition (May 1858 to January 1861) on the *Ma-Robert* – approximately twenty months

Number of Europeans on the expedition	10
Number who left the expedition (one because of malaria)	3
Number who died from malaria	0

Table III

Mortality figures on the Livingstone expedition to the Zambezi of people on board the *Pioneer* from February 1861 to October 1862

Number of Europeans (crew 18)	23
Number of deaths	2

(carpenter, Ferger, Mrs David Livingstone)

Table IV

Mortality figures on the Livingstone expedition to the Zambezi (and Shire) on board the *Pioneer* from 1 November 1862 to 30 June 1863

Number of European crew	18
Number who died from fever	2
Number invalided	1

Dr Charles Meller who succeeded John Kirk on the *Pioneer* felt that the prophylactic quinine worked on for so long by Livingstone helped tremendously. Even if a person had an attack of fever it was mitigated by the quinine. Both he and Livingstone noticed that the fever seemed to come when there were myriads of mosquitoes and Meller suggested using a net. He did not realise how near he was to knowing the cause of the transmission of the disease.[31]

Bishop Tozer moved the mission to Zanzibar as he considered Livingstone's scheme of settlement in the Shire Highlands both premature and unpractical. He intended using the new station as a base for further penetration into the African mainland and hoped to establish a mission in the Lake Nyasa region later. So he started work in the territory of Tanganyika under German rule in 1867 and it was not until 1879 that the U.M.C.A. returned to Nyasaland and not till 1885 that Bishop Smythes settled on the island of Likoma, when the work of the society in central Africa began in real earnest.

The services of a doctor were greatly needed at Likoma, which was not as fortunate as the Scottish mission at Blantyre. At least a start was made on the nursing side in 1886 when Miss Sophia Charlotte McLaughlin joined the U.M.C.A. But a doctor was only found in 1889 when John Edward Hine, D.D., M.D., came out to the mission. Despite the new dispensary he built, the patients were slow in coming to him and in 1893 he moved to Unangu in the hills, 2,000 feet high, among the Yao where he met a greater response.[32] Another nurse, Miss Whitbread, arrived in 1893 and the next doctor to join the mission was Frederick Augustine Robinson of Guy's Hospital, whose health could not stand up to the environment. The most outstanding medical officer of the mission was Robert Howard, M.A., D.M. (Oxon) who came out in February, 1899.[33] He advocated the use of mosquito nets, the fumigation of dwelling places and the destruction of mosquito larvae. By this time too, the better living conditions, started in 1896, had begun to bear fruit.[34] Howard was largely responsible for starting medical services at the other centres of the mission – Nkhota kota, Malindi, Mponda and Mtonya. As the work grew the missionaries found that they required a better steamer.[35] Money was collected in Britain to build one which was named *Chauncy Maples* in 1902. It was provided with a proper sick bay.[36]

Dr Howard was a pioneer in the training of African medical aides. In 1909 after some years of training, two senior aides, Edward Nemeleyani and Raphael Mkoma were regarded as satisfactory medical aides or 'dispensary boys'. That year Howard married Miss Edith Kathleen Minter,[37] a nurse at Mponda. Three years later Dr William C. Wigan arrived to serve the four medical stations of Likoma, Nkhota kota, Malindi and Mponda.[38] In 1914 the mission began training medical assistants with eight students.[39]

After the First World War the mission was faced with a financial crisis as monetary aid from Britain suddenly dropped. This affected all schools, hospitals and dispensaries in the diocese. But by that time western medicine had come to stay. Africans were keen to try the treatment of the missionaries and African medical assistants were working in all centres. The U.M.C.A. and its work in Nyasaland can therefore be said to have originated with Livingstone's scheme for establishing a mission in the Shire Highlands to teach the gospel and to cure the sick.[40]

Perhaps Livingstone's greatest influence on central Africa came mostly after his death through the missionaries who were swayed by his passionate desire to establish a station in the Shire Highlands, which he considered the healthiest part of this region. They saw their coming out to continue his work as a tribute to Livingstone's memory. All the Scottish mission bodies were imbued with Livingstone's ideal of preaching and healing at the same time, and so their efforts resulted in the establishment of hospitals and the training of medical assistants of a high standard. Their interest in health and education must have influenced thousands of Malawians throughout the territory. It was also a fine example to the authorities who eventually took over the main responsibilities from them, particularly after the First World War. Their work in these fields today is still of considerable importance in the lives of many Malawians who also look back on David Livingstone as the first white doctor to bring western methods to them.

Notes

1 David Livingstone, *Missionary Travels and Researches in South Africa*, London, 1857, p. 20.
2 J. P. R. Wallis (ed.), *The Zambezi Expedition of David Livingstone 1858–1863*, vol. I, London, 1956, p. 393.
3 Letter to the *Lancet*, London, 24 August 1861.
4 I. Schapera (ed.), *Livingstone's Private Journals 1851–1853*, London, 1960, p. 69.
5 M. Gelfand, *Livingstone the Doctor. His Life and Travels*, Oxford, 1957, p. 60. This quotation was taken from a letter from Livingstone to Thomas Maclear.
6 Schapera, *Private Journals*, p. 132.
7 I. Schapera (ed.), *Livingstone's African Journal 1853–1856*, London, 1963, vol. I, p. 311. Sebitwane complained that many of his children died from fever.
8 Ibid., vol. I, pp. 300 and 314.
9 Ibid., vol. II, pp. 287.
10 Wallis, *The Zambezi Expedition*, p. 420.
11 Ibid., p. 272.
12 Ibid., p. 292.
13 Ibid., p. 300.

14 Ibid., p. 319.
15 Ibid., p. 336.
16 Ibid., pp. 309 and 312.
17 Ibid., p. 407.
18 Ibid., p. 401.
19 Ibid., p. 341.
20 Ibid., p. 322.
21 Ibid., p. 351.
22 Ibid., p. 387
23 Ibid., p. 351.
24 M. Gelfand, op. cit., p. 166.
25 Ibid., p. 167.
26 Ibid., p. 170.
27 Wallis, *The Zambezi Expedition.*
28 M. Gelfand, op. cit., p. 193.
29 Wallis, *The Zambezi Expedition,* Dispatch from Lord Russell to David Living-stone, Foreign Office, 2 February 1863.
30 Ibid., pp. 368 and 385.
31 M. Gelfand, *Rivers of Death in Africa,* London, 1964, p. 84. All tables and quotations have been taken from this study.
32 R. M. Heanley (ed.), *Central Africa. A monthly record of the work of the Universities' Mission,* London, 1889, 7, p. 180.
33 A. E. M. Anderson-Morshead, *The History of the Universities' Mission to Central Africa,* vol. I 1859–1909, London, 1955, pp. 132 and 282. R. Howard, *A report to the Medical Board of the Universities' Mission on the Health of the European Missionaries in the Likoma Diocese,* London, 1904, p. 20.
34 Heanley, op. cit., 24, p. 189.
35 Ibid., 20, p. 204.
36 Howard, op. cit., p. 42.
37 Heanley, op. cit., 27, p. 40.
38 M. Gelfand, *Lakeside Pioneers,* Oxford, 1961, p. 22.
39 Heanley, op. cit., 32, p. 119.
40 Gelfand, *Lakeside Pioneers,* p. 25.

9 Livingstone and the Aftermath: The Origins and Development of the Blantyre Mission

Andrew C. Ross

Dr John Macrae of Hawick, on the news of the death of David Living-stone, persuaded his Presbytery, that of Jedburgh, to petition the General Assembly of the Church of Scotland to authorise the planning of a mission to the Lake Malawi region of Africa. This was explicitly to be a memorial to Livingstone. Thus in May 1874, only a month after Livingstone's funeral in Westminster Abbey, the Church of Scotland officially endorsed a plan to establish a mission 'among the natives of that part of Africa which has been hallowed by the last labours and death of Dr Livingstone'.[1] The petition was accepted by the Assembly, which went on to instruct the Foreign Mission Committee to undertake the preparation for and the carrying out of this mission. Dr A. J. Hanna, in his book on Nyasaland and north-eastern Rhodesia, comments about the Foreign Mission Committee and the new mission that: 'The subject was first mooted on the 2nd June, 1874, but the precise reason that brought it before the Committee has apparently been lost to history.'[2] The reason for this matter being on the agenda of the Committee is not lost; it was simply that the Committee was following the instructions given it by the Assembly held the month before. To carry out their remit, the F.M.C. set up a special sub-committee with Dr Macrae as Convener, to supervise both the setting up and the carrying out of the mission.

Dr Macrae started off in a most businesslike way by consulting all the people who might possibly have good advice to give, as a result of experience of work in the area of the projected mission. He travelled to the south of England and interviewed Sir Bartle Frere, John Kirk and Horace Waller, amongst others. In other respects however, things did not go well. Macrae approached Lieutenant E. D. Young to act as leader of the expedition to set up the mission. Young refused because

191

he had already been asked to do the same thing for the Free Church of Scotland party going to the same region. This party had already been recruited, while as yet Macrae had no recruits at all. The General Assembly had agreed to set up the mission at Macrae's request, but there was no movement at the grassroots of the Kirk.

From June 1874 onwards Macrae was writing in every edition of the *Missionary Record* and using all other means at his disposal to attract recruits to his new mission. In November a note of despair was beginning to appear in his article:

> Will no successors from Scotland be found to tread the path of her Christian Warrior? No volunteers of Scotland to go forth to endure hardness as becomes the soldiers of Christ . . . and shall the Church of Scotland be the only communion which has not planted her disciples on African soil?[3]

This tone continued in his monthly articles which reached a new level of hopelessness in March; he was driven to defend the need to send a mission to Africa at all, the needs of India and Scotland herself being suggested as being task enough. However, it was that same month that the first volunteer came forward.

This was Henry Henderson. He had lived for a number of years on the Queensland frontier and knew a great deal about pioneering in the bush. His offer to be a pioneer and pathfinder for the mission was quickly accepted and hurried arrangements were made for him to join Young and the Free Church party. His task was to find a suitable site for the new mission and then to await the arrival of the Church of Scotland party, for which there was yet not one recruit. He would then oversee the laying out and building of the first station.

Macrae's position was now desperate, and any sort of careful selection of candidates for service seems to have been dropped. Since no minister could be found willing to go it was decided to send a party consisting of laymen only. The group was headed by Dr T. Thornton Macklin, and a number of artisans, John Buchanan, George Fenwick, Jonathan Duncan, William Milne and John Walker. Of these men David Clement Scott later wrote, after his arrival in Blantyre in 1881:

> The character of the Mission's whole history has been uniformly consistent, and our whole church should learn the lesson. The key-note was sounded at the farewell meeting of the artisans in the hall behind St George's Church, at which I was most strangely present and which further is strangely impressed upon my mind. . . . Major

Malan said 'These men don't know for what they are going', and felt very dark in heart about it. . . . The men chosen for mission were most unaccountably fit [sic] – without profession of Christian life or missionary spirit, and not even good workmen.[4]

Meanwhile Henry Henderson had reached the Zambezi valley with the Free Church party. He travelled with them as far as Lake Malawi and played his full part in their arduous work which included the famous portage of their steamer, broken up into loads at Chikwawa and carried via Mbame and what was to be Blantyre on to the head-waters of the Shire, where it was reassembled. Henderson was on board when the little vessel made her voyage out of the Shire and on to the waters of the lake on 10 October 1875.

Henderson's task was to find a suitable site for the station of the Established Church in terms of the agreement between it and the Free Church about proximity and mutual aid between the two mission parties. He went with Laws and Young on the *Ilala* on their exploratory voyage which circumnavigated the lake, and made its full size known for the first time. However, he saw no suitable site on that journey. He decided that it would be better to seek a site somewhere further back on their very tenuous lines of communication. This made sense from the point of view of survival as well as of mission work. The Shire Highlands was densely populated, and was the area which Livingstone had always insisted was the most propitious for a mission, despite the withdrawal of the U.M.C.A. The Livingstonia Mission lent Henderson an interpreter, without whom Henderson would not have been a very effective agent. This man was Tom Bokwito, who had been freed from a Portuguese slave party by Dr Livingstone and Bishop Mackenzie. He had come with a number of other Africans, educated at the Lovedale Institution of Dr James Stewart in the Cape Colony, to be part of the Livingstonia staff.

According to both Hetherwick in his *Romance of Blantyre*,[5] and the Revd Harry Matecheta in *Blantyre Mission, Nkhani ya Ciyambi Cace*,[6] Henderson and Bokwito were still looking for a suitable spot when they reached the area of what is now the town of Blantyre/Limbe. From Cape Maclear they had come downstream on the Shire as far as Liwonde and then struck off into the highlands through the Kasupe pass. There they entered the area of the Yao chief, Malemia, where they stayed for a time with one of Malemia's headmen, Kalimbuka, in his village very near to where the present Malawi Parliament buildings now stand. The spot was well wooded and well watered; the people were friendly, and both Malemia and Kalimbuka wanted missionaries

193

to come and settle in their area. This was almost certainly with a view to gaining their aid or protection against Malemia's enemy, Kawinga, the most powerful and aggressive of the Yao chiefs south of the lake and one who was deeply involved in the Quelimane slave trade. Indeed, the main route for slaves to Quelimane skirted Malemia's land. For that very reason Henderson was not keen to fix a site in Malemia's chiefdom. Also, there on the slopes of Zomba mountain, beneath which Malemia's villages lay, he was still far from the furthest navigable point on the Shire.

Henderson and Bokwito went on, following a route which went roughly along the line of the present Zomba–Limbe road. They passed near to the old Magomero site of Bishop Mackenzie's mission, skirted Chiradzulu and then stayed for a time on Nguludi hill in the Yao village of Lopsa, where Bokwito knew some people. There a little boy named Kambwiri saw Henderson and heard for the first time the name of Jesus. This meant little or nothing to him then, but he grew up to be the Revd Harry Kambwiri Matecheta, the Yao evangelist of the Ngoni for many years.[7] Leaving Lopsa's, Henderson and Bokwito had only reached the nearby village of Chief Kapeni when Bokwito became seriously ill. This was a piece of good fortune for Henderson; he spent the three weeks of his comrade's illness in getting to know Chief Kapeni and the range of surrounding hills, Ndirande, Michiru, and Soche. This area was one that Livingstone had commended to Mackenzie as a site for a mission and Henderson soon came to see its advantages. It was about this time that the *Ilala* was sent down the Shire to try to get news of him. He went over to the river and gave the Free Church people the news that 'he was in great spirits regarding the country he had explored. It was the most attractive he had seen, very fertile and as healthy as Scotland, and *he had discovered an excellent site*.[8] Without any reference to his source for the story, W. P. Livingstone, Laws' biographer, says at another point in his book that the siting of Blantyre at Kapeni's was because the party of men under Macklin were so exhausted that they would go no further, and so there they stayed, though Henderson had actually chosen Magomero.[9] This is quoted by Dr Hanna in an authoritative way.[10] Yet, W. P. Livingstone elsewhere in his book, as we have seen, quotes Henderson as saying he had discovered a site, a strange phrase to use of Magomero, the famous site of Bishop Mackenzie's mission, where Bokwito had lived as a boy. Nowhere, except in W. P. Livingstone, and works quoting him, is there any reference to Henderson choosing Magomero. We know of Henderson's stays at Kalimbuka's, at Lopsa's and at Kapeni's, but nothing of a stay at or even a visit to Magomero. Also, Hetherwick says

that after the men with Macklin had been led by Henderson to Chikwawa, he hurried up to Kapeni's to confirm that the mission could
settle there before returning to the Shire to fetch them.[11] The Revd
Harry Matecheta knew of no other plan and insisted that Kapeni and
Henderson had come to a definite agreement before Henderson went
down river to meet the others. At times later in his life Henderson, in
turning aside praise for having found such a suitable spot for the mission,
often talked of it as being a matter of chance. This would seem to be a
reference to Bokwito's illness which had kept them at Kapeni's.

After descending to the Kongone mouth of the Zambezi and waiting
there for a fortnight, Henderson finally contacted the Blantyre party
at Mazaro on the Zambezi. By the time he got them to Kapeni's, they
were exhausted and ill, and in a state of depression, out of which he
seemed unable to rouse them. The first part of his official task was over,
but Henderson had to stay on for a while to try to initiate some sort of
organisation. After three months he despaired of achieving anything
himself. He decided that since the Free Church Mission had now
received reinforcements, he might be able to persuade Dr Laws, who
was after all on loan from the United Presbyterian Church to the Free
Church, to leave Livingstonia and come over to head his forlorn party
on the slopes of Nyambadwe hill. Dr James Stewart was at this time at
Livingstonia and was adamant that Laws could not be spared. However,
Laws and he met with Henderson and an agreement was made to supply
aid to the Church of Scotland Mission.[12]

In fact, the first man to take on this task at Blantyre, and one whose
character and approach were of crucial importance to the mission's
future, was not a regular missionary of the Free Church at all. He was
James Stewart, C.E., of the Public Works Department of the Indian
Government. He was a cousin of Dr Stewart, and Laws met him on the
Shire only a few days after he had received the appeal for help from
Blantyre. Stewart was on his way up to Livingstonia to offer his services
to the Free Church Mission during his furlough from India. It was
arranged that he should do a stint at Blantyre as head of station.
Hetherwick[13] and MacDonald[14] both testified in their writings to the
profound change he made in the situation at Blantyre. He shook
Macklin and the artisans out of their lethargy and got them working.
He got an especially good response from John Buchanan, who buckled
to with his gardening, as well as with language study, so that he was
later able to help the first minister to serve at Blantyre, Duff Mac-
Donald, with his CiYao translations.

In December 1877, Laws visited Blantyre and found the place
transformed.[15] What Stewart achieved was summed up by Hetherwick

in his *Romance of Blantyre*:

> He laid out the mission on the main lines of its present ground plan – an oblong – called the 'Square' – through which passed the main road from the Lower to the Upper River. On either side of the Square he built four bungalows in India fashion, which were used as dwelling houses, school, store and workshop. He laid out the mission garden, three terraces in a crescent, which remain to this day, and surveyed a channel over a mile long to bring into the mission water from a neighbouring stream.[16]

Perhaps his greatest feat was, with the cooperation of the staffs of both Blantyre and Livingstonia, the surveying and building of the road from Chikwawa to Matope. This road was vital for the connecting of the Lower and Upper Shire, and its Blantyre–Matope line was followed by the new M2 Highway in Malawi in the 1960s.

Yet this was a most extraordinary situation. Blantyre was now a viable entity, but it had been brought to that state by a man who was not an agent of the Foreign Mission Committee, nor in any formal sense a missionary. The mission still had no minister at all, and some of the staff were of a most unsuitable type. What was the mission there for and how did it intend to carry out its task?

The Free Church Mission had been most carefully planned and had been issued with most explicit instructions as to their aims and their conduct. No such clear planning had gone into the sending of the hurriedly assembled party under Macklin, nor had they been issued with clear and explicit instructions. Henderson had been left to make the best arrangements he could, and with the help of the Free Church mission he had just managed to avoid total disaster. The ineptness of Macrae and his committee continued to threaten the development of the mission.

Just how disorganised things were in Scotland, can be seen from a letter written to Macrae by MacLagan, the treasurer of the F.M.C. in February 1877. Only at that time, with Henderson more than a year out in the field and the pioneer party in desperate need of leadership, was the committee preparing an advertisement for the post of mission superintendent. At that late date MacLagan still needed to ask:

> What salary is to be given? What is to be the exact position with reference to Macklin? What is to be the length of engagement? Would we now take a married man, allowing his wife to go with him, and if so would we pay the wife's passage? Would the terms for

a clergyman or layman be the same?[17]

Poor organisation in Scotland combined with a staff of doubtful quality in the Shire Highlands was a bad start for the new enterprise. However, the appointment of Duff MacDonald to be the head of the mission and its first clergyman, and the increasingly effective role being played by Dr Macklin and John Buchanan, might have been enough to set the mission on its feet. This was not to be because Macrae's leadership of the project contributed more than simple inefficiency. He had a vision of Blantyre as a Christian colony that inevitably involved the mission in serious difficulties. Macrae's intentions were never spelt out in any clear report to the General Assembly. Because of the later close similarities between the Livingstonia and Blantyre Missions, and because the report of the Commission of Enquiry of 1881 placed the blame for the troubles on the staff in the field, the crisis which led to the enquiry has been seen as the result of the personalities of the men involved in a difficult situation.[18] It would seem however that the fundamental cause of the crisis was the policy of the Africa sub-committee, particularly as formulated and carried out by its Convener, Dr Macrae. As MacDonald asserted, Macrae and his committee had been committed to the creation of some kind of colony from the beginning.[19] It is also clear that active intervention in the slave trade was part of Macrae's policy from the beginning. In the difficult situation of the Shire Highlands in the late 1870s this policy was bound to spell disaster whatever the quality of the staff.

In southern Malawi at that time the Ngoni, the Kololo and a large number of Yao chiefs were vying for political power, and Portuguese and Swahili slave traders were taking advantage of the unstable situation for their profit. There was no Moshweshwe or Kabaka, from whom the missionaries could seek protection and through whom they could gain position and status in African society. After the mistakes of the U.M.C.A. mission of Bishop Mackenzie, the Livingstonia Mission consciously tried to avoid falling into the same traps, and carefully instructed the staff to stay out of local quarrels and to make no direct attempt to interfere with slavery and the slave trade. In addition Laws soon decided that expulsion from the mission village was the only suitable punishment for anyone who came to live as part of the mission and then behaved criminally. This would often mean his being sold into slavery and this was a bitter pill for many of the staff to swallow because of their vision of following Livingstone the pioneer in healing the running sore which he had revealed. One half-hearted attempt at a flogging however, was enough to convince Laws that there was no alternative.[20]

Despite all that had happened at Magomero, Macrae seemed to have fixed from the beginning on a vision of a colony, which would actively combat the slave trade. Although this was never debated in the F.M.C., there can be no excuse for churchmen of the day pleading that it was a private or secret policy because Macrae made his ideas clear enough. In this connection it is not without significance that two of the men he consulted while planning the mission were Sir Bartle Frere and Dr Kirk. Both were associated with the setting up by the Church Missionary Society and the Methodist Missionary Society of mission colonies on what is now the Kenya coast at Frere Town and Ribe in 1875. These were communities of freed slaves under the civil jurisdiction of a missionary superintendent. They acted as havens for runaways, and as a Christian and free presence in a slave area.[21] Sir Bartle Frere was particularly keen on this type of station being the basis for the Christian mission in East Africa. While Livingstonia rejected such ideas, Dr Macrae seems to have become an advocate of them. As early as February 1875 he was responsible for placing in the *Missionary Record* a policy statement about the new mission which is very revealing: 'The Committee are advised that the Mission should be of an industrial as well as an evangelistic nature. In forming a Christian settlement, it would be necessary to teach the natives some of our industries, as gardening, ploughing, and joinery work.' After a long passage about the horrors of the slave trade and the urgent need to check it, the article goes on:

That this great sore of the world may be healed is certain. The commencement will be made as soon as a mission is planted at Lake Nyassa. No Arab gang will come near an Englishman, if they can help it. With them the English name is synonymous with destroyer of slavery. ... We are assured that a mission once established, the Africans will settle around it, receive our instruction and our help, place themselves under our authority, and rise by order and Christian observance into the state of civilised communities.[22]

It must be noted that this article was signed by Lord Polwarth, Dr J. L. Herdman and Mr Alex Pringle, as well as by Dr Macrae. It was fully in keeping with this article that Macrae wrote to James Stewart C.E. instructing him to act as magisterial head of Blantyre. This whole approach owes little to David Livingstone, it owes something to Bartle Frere but perhaps even more to that veteran missionary in East Africa, Dr J. L. Krapf who in May 1875 wrote a long letter to Macrae which the
198

latter published in the *Record*. It was so long that it had to appear in two parts, which confirms the importance Macrae attached to it. Krapf insisted in the letter that freed slaves should be the basis of the work. He goes on: 'What a glorious event it would be, if the people residing around Lake Nyassa, and between the Lake and the coast should be christianised and civilised through their own people, under the instruction and superintendence of Christian Europeans.'[23] He goes on to refer to the work in the dangerous image of being greater than the Crusades of the Middle Ages.

Dr Macklin, who under the guidance of Stewart and Laws had gained enough confidence to take over the leadership when Stewart returned to India, certainly saw the mission as a Christian colony crusading against both slavery and the slave-trade. He reported in these terms to Macrae and the committee in March 1878.

The Mission in its civil and social aspects is making reasonable and satisfactory progress. As an asylum for the poor and persecuted slave, Blantyre is becoming known and prized. We have now six fellow creatures rescued from the lash of the slave-driver, and miseries worse than death. This in turn prepares them for giving a ready reception to the free offers of the greater emancipation, salvation by grace through Christ our Lord. My present circumstances give a new emphasis to the old law of the city of refuge. Just think of the poor, fainting woman bearing her child, fleeing for her life, but sustained by the hope that if only she can reach the British flag, which already she sees fluttering in the evening breeze, her child shall live and herself be free.[24]

Macklin was continuing the headship of a Christian colony along the lines that Stewart had laid down. This was as a result of Macrae's prompting, and the whole sequence of events was regularly reported to Macrae. The first floggings took place under Stewart.[25] Instructed by Macrae to be a magistrate, faced with the problem of the disturbed state south of the lake at this time, Stewart determined to act firmly. As head of a small group of missionaries, freed slaves and 'foreign' Africans at the end of a long, very vulnerable line of communications, he felt there was no alternative. As his cousin Dr Stewart wrote to Laws 'This thieving must be brought to an end or it will end us.'[26]

In continuing this policy Macklin reported his doings to Scotland. In one particular instance we have the story in detail because he was so gratified that one of the most persistent thieves had been caught. Kapeni's people were particularly pleased when it turned out to be a

Mang'anja from the river and not a Yao. This was in February 1878 and Macklin reported on the courage and enterprise of the Livingstonia teacher, Mapas Ntinthili in catching the thief, also that the thief had been given nine dozen lashes in two instalments. He went on:

We kept him in all about a month, and then the people being all assembled, we made proclamation that if after two days the prisoner should be found on the Yao territory, or on this side of the Kabula river, the people were at liberty to kill him. Of course this proclamation was made by the Yao headman. After this proclamation was made, the prisoner was escorted out of the Yao country by armed men.[27]

Here indeed was a colony with magistrate, police and prisons, as well as client chiefs.

When Duff MacDonald was appointed, he refused to accept any responsibility for this whole side of the mission.[28] He was determined to be a missionary in the simplest sense of the term and that he was.

On arrival at Blantyre with his wife in July 1878, Duff MacDonald immediately plunged into the work he felt he was sent out to do; learning the language, getting to know the people and working at developing the school. Up till then the school had been conducted by William Koyi and other Africans sent by Laws from Livingstonia. MacDonald worked hard at the language and in the school and soon became a fluent speaker of CiYao. As a result he was able to wander in the nearby villages and make the kind of contact with the people that none of the other white staff had even attempted till then. He did the first serious preaching and teaching that had been done except by African staff lent by Livingstonia. MacDonald soon began to plan the expansion of the work by the planting of a new station elsewhere in the Shire Highlands. The earlier friendliness of Malemia and Kalimbuka was recalled and MacDonald made a journey through to Zomba to meet with them. They agreed to accept a missionary and John Buchanan was sent to open the new work. When MacDonald, early in 1880, returned to Zomba with his wife, he was pleased to find that a small school was flourishing and that very friendly relations with Kalimbuka had been established, but that Buchanan was not preaching in CiYao regularly to a large congregation of interested villagers. This was in distinct contrast with the beginnings of Blantyre itself, where months passed before any attempt at effective communication with the local people was even attempted. On November 28 1880 MacDonald preached in CiYao to a congregation of three hundred at Kalimbuka's.

In many ways MacDonald was an ideal missionary. In a brief time he got to know CiYao, translated two of the Gospels and *Pilgrim's Progress* into it, and later in Volume I of his *Africana* he made a worthwhile beginning to a serious study of Yao culture. Of it Professor Shepperson has said:

> By his evident skill in observation and his sympathy with much, if not all of the African viewpoint, he produced an invaluable account of African society, particularly Yao society, in the Shire Highlands when it was still relatively untouched by the white man's way of life.[29]

Unfortunately MacDonald was not of the stuff needed to deal with the mission staff and the policy they had been operating before his arrival. He would not be a magistrate, and he took no active steps to change the mission from its role of organising a politically independent Christian colony. Macrae and his committee were no help, since their response to his refusal was to instruct Henderson, who was returning at the end of 1878 to Blantyre, to take over the role of magistrate and civil governor. Henderson also refused,[30] but this did not deter the committee which continued to hold to its original policy. It is not clear how this was carried out after Dr Macklin left Blantyre on furlough. From MacDonald's *Africana* and what little correspondence has survived, a committee of artisans seemed to have run the civil side of the mission.

The stubbornness of the committee and the aggressiveness of men like Walker and Fenwick, make MacDonald's attitude understandable, though hardly justifying it. However, at the end of 1878 an incident took place which did force him to try to change things. A girl from one of the mission villages was raped and shot and the miscreant was captured. What was to be done? He was tried by a committee of missionaries and village elders, found guilty, condemned to death and executed.[31] After the execution, which took place in February 1879, MacDonald began to persuade the staff that a new policy must be developed and the sub-committee in Edinburgh were sufficiently shocked by this and a serious skirmish between mission carriers and men from Mittoche's village near Chiradzulu, to begin to question at least their policy and to seek possible changes. Perhaps they were forced to change because they had at last found out that British statute law forbade British subjects to exercise civil authority beyond the Queen's dominion. They now recommended what MacDonald had already begun to carry out. That is, in the cases of minor offences to let African elders deal with them in their own way, while serious offenders were to be expelled from the mission. In addition, MacDonald who knew very well the distinction, important at least in African eyes, between domestic slavery and the slave trade, also got agreement at Blantyre that no more runaways should be received. This greatly helped relations with local people since most of these fugitives were not escaping from slave-traders but from domestic bondage.[32]

It was just possible that at that late stage, MacDonald might have succeeded in at least getting the Blantyre Mission on to a more effectively missionary footing, but fate intervened in the shape of a Scottish traveller, Andrew Chirnside. He learned of the floggings, one of which had ended in death, of the execution, and to top it all he witnessed despairing fugitives being turned away, which he also felt to be a savage and unmissionary act. He is perhaps not to be too severely blamed for being unable to see that one action was an attempt to remove the need for the other actions he deprecated. On his return to the United Kingdom he published a severe attack on Blantyre Mission.[33] Chirnside's pamphlet caused enough fuss for the Foreign Office to be concerned, let alone church circles in Scotland. However Lord Salisbury decided to let the Kirk try to put its own house in order before considering any government action. In his self-defence in *Africana* MacDonald used letters which are no longer anywhere available to researchers, to confirm that all that had taken place had been reported to the Africa sub-committee and had been in accordance with the policy of the Convener, Dr Macrae, and that he had continuously opposed that policy. All of Dr Macrae's correspondence has disappeared, though the vast majority of all other Foreign Mission records have been preserved. However, when MacDonald's book was published in 1882 no one challenged the authenticity of his quotations. In addition, one of the very few letters remaining pertaining to the period is most revealing, it is from the treasurer MacLagan to MacDonald:

> Be particular as to dates, for in regard to the murder of the woman and the execution of the murderer he is evidently all wrong – placing the whole of these events subsequent to March 1879 – whereas the woman was shot in December 1878, and the execution took place in February 1879.[34]

Surely clear confirmation of MacDonald's assertion that the committee had been kept in full touch with events.

Dr Rankin of Muthil and Mr Pringle, an Edinburgh lawyer, were sent out as the General Assembly's Commissioners to investigate the situation. The result of their report to the General Assembly was that MacDonald, Buchanan and Fenwick were dismissed. Macklin who was held to be blameworthy for several of the floggings had already left the service of the Foreign Mission Committee as had Walker.[35]

At the Commission of the General Assembly on March 2 1881, their report had been heard and several resolutions adopted including this:

III. That while regretting that the Church did not, through the Foreign Mission Committee, distinctly instruct their agents when the Blantyre Mission was originally established, that they must not in any circumstances attempt to exercise civil jurisdiction there the Commission condemn in the strongest terms, and bitterly deplore, the conduct which certain of these agents – assuming this jurisdiction – were on various occasions guilty in the earlier days of the Blantyre Mission.[36]

The phrase 'earlier days' was an acceptance that MacDonald, as we have seen, had by the end of 1879 begun to modify the whole conduct of the mission. However, to regret that civil jurisdiction had not been forbidden in a clear enough fashion, when in fact the subcommittee had touted the post of magistrate around the senior members of staff, shows either dishonesty on the part of the Commissioners or on the part of those giving evidence. The General Assembly of 1882 partly redeemed this story of what amounted to a betrayal of MacDonald. During the actual sittings of the Assembly in May of that year, a special committee was set up to go over MacDonald's appeal. This evidence was drawn from the Africa sub-committee's files, and MacDonald reproduced it in Volume II of his *Africana* later that year. Their report went a long way to clear MacDonald, yet they still flinched from admitting the clear colonial approach of Macrae, instead they refer to 'perplexing instructions' from the committee.[37] None of the evidence was published in Assembly papers which would have enabled the church in general to judge for itself. Worse than this, although MacDonald had been allowed access to the sub-committee's files, it was reported to the Assembly that these files were now in Dr Macrae's personal possession. It was resolved that they should be returned.[38] The matter does not re-appear in any church records, but when the Foreign Mission archives were sent to the National Library of Scotland, the Blantyre Mission Correspondence for that period was missing, apart from a few letters of MacLagan. Nor could the missing material be traced in the church offices. One can only assume that in 1882 Dr Macrae quietly ignored the General Assembly's instruction and that, with a desire to put an end to scandal, no one subsequently challenged him.

Although the March 1881 Commission of Assembly agreed that the mission at Blantyre should be continued, it was left with only two of its staff, Jonathan Duncan and Henry Henderson, and the previous almost total inability to recruit suitable staff gave little ground for optimism. However, the future of Blantyre was assured by the young minister who had commented so severely on the original party under Macklin, while attending their dedication. This was David Clement Scott.

Scott saw the task of the missionary in Africa as being both a bearer of the gospel and of modern culture. This was how he interpreted Livingstone's dictum about the need for 'Christianity and Commerce'. The culture brought by the missionaries was not, he believed, simply European culture, something belonging to the white race as the then fashionable social Darwinism maintained, but simply modern culture with a world-wide relevance and significance. He insisted that Africans were as much its inheritors as were Europeans. He denied the claims of those who thought it both possible and obligatory to attempt to transmit the gospel without transmitting their culture. He fully realised that culture would be imparted even if the missionary tried to suppress such exchange. Scott held that since Africans were the co-inheritors of world culture it should be imparted consciously in the educational process, always hoping that as with the gospel it would ground itself in African forms.

The Assembly Commissioners, Pringle and Rankine had recommended new courses for the mission that were contrary to the spirit and the letter of this approach. They both insisted that the mission should concentrate on being an evangelistic mission in the most normal sense. Even the simple cultural impact of literacy and technical education was to be kept to an absolute minimum: being able to read the Bible in the vernacular was the height of their educational aims.[39] In endorsing their report, the General Assembly of the Church of Scotland turned away from any understanding of mission that could possibly be said to owe anything to David Livingstone. He had appealed for commerce and Christianity to transform the old societies of Zambesia which were being torn apart by the turmoil created by the slave-trade and the aftermath of the Ngoni migrations. Pringle insisted that Malawi society was best left alone.[40] Perhaps the most important symbolic break with the Livingstone tradition was the assertion in the Assembly report that artisans were simply not a suitable class from which to recruit missionaries.[41] In fact the overwhelming majority of British missionaries in the first seventy years of the nineteenth century were drawn from exactly the same class as Livingstone himself.[42]

However, this feeling that Livingstone had been wrong and that the business of mission was simply religious was widespread at that time.

It was expressed most clearly by Bishop Steere of the U.M.C.A. in an article quoted by Mr H. A. C. Cairns in his book *Prelude to Imperialism.*[43] Cairns also quotes from *Africana* in this context where MacDonald shares some of Steere's views.[44] Cairns asserts that these two men represent an attitude which respected African culture as opposed to the very prevalent missionary attitude of aversion to things African. Cairns goes on to say about this attitude:

> Kerr, Jephson and Bruce-Knight, tended to express comparatively favourable attitudes to African culture. Yet, as Jephson indicated, this could be coupled with the assumption that Africans were incapable of being Europeanised, and with a distaste which existed even at this early date, for the Africans who 'aped' the European in such matters as clothing.
>
> An apparent respect for African culture may veil a disrespect for African capacity, or a distaste for the breaking down of cultural distinctions. The Scottish Missions with their emphasis on civilisation displayed less respect for tribalism, but their approach was possibly indicative of a greater optimism as to the capacity of the African to assimilate a range of western values and traits which would, eventually, place him on a level of equality with Europeans in more than spiritual matters. This, however, is dangerous ground for which explicit evidence is sparse.[45]

Quite apart from what evidence there is about Blantyre or any other Scottish mission, it is significant that modern African nationalists in the pre-independence period of their struggles have always been most suspicious of those who would insist on the preservation of the integrity of African culture, with some justification since the whole structure of the apartheid system is built on just such an insistence.

However, had Cairns been able to consult the extant letters of D. C. Scott and his columns in *Life and Work in British Central Africa*, he would have seen that at Blantyre there was someone who still maintained the old traditions of Wilberforce, Philip and Venn, the tradition that Philip Curtin has dubbed 'conversionist'. It was an attitude which certainly did not always place much weight on traditional culture but it did always emphasise the equality of all who were educated and Christian.

Joseph Bismarck, a man who became Scott's leading assistant, having begun his stay at Blantyre under MacDonald, used often to tell of Scott's insistence that the group of young Africans he gathered around him were the equal of the staff recruited in Scotland. One of Bismarck's favourite stories was that one day he was standing outside the carpenter's office waiting for the carpenter, John MacIlwain. He was standing, hat in hand when Scott approached. Scott came up to him and said, 'No, no, Bismarck, when MacIlwain comes you simply raise your hat that's all, you and he are brothers. You both keep your hats off while speaking to me, because I am your father, but you two, you are brothers.'

Such oral tradition is confirmation that Scott acted as he wrote, for in the columns of L.W.B.C.A. he makes his views quite explicit. In May 1894, he had read an article in a British journal which he unfortunately does not name, attacking the Livingstonian concept of Christian missions and insisting on a transmission of the gospel detached from the transmission of culture. He wrote in reply:

> When one comes, however, here in Africa into practical touch with the everyday life of the native, and has to live in their midst, one cannot help imparting the civilisation one has received to *those whose co-inheritance it is,* and who certainly desire it . . . unless then he (the missionary) cut himself off from all that is human and declare himself an ascetic, or unless he fall beneath the appreciation of culture he must perforce take interest in and develop the people round him to the best of his ability.
>
> He does not produce a non-native product, he only brings a civilisation before the native spirit not merely to develop a native Christianity, but to become a conscious member of the Catholic Church of Christ.
>
> At Blantyre we have striven accordingly to the impress with which the Mission started and in answer to Livingstone's appeal and prayer, to supply an ideal of Christian industry; to tangibly aid the colony; to give the native the place in the development of this land to which he is called; to prove he is fit for it; and to see him through.[46]

For David Scott it was fundamental that Africans were part of the same humanity as Scotsmen or Portuguese, that they could contribute to the Christian Church as well as receive from it, that the civilising and christianising task of the mission must result in a civilisation and Church that was African as well as Christian. If his *Cyclopaedic Dictionary of the Mang'anja Language* were the only thing of his left to us, it would be enough to convince us of his fundamental respect and affection for African culture, despite his being a 'civiliser'.

So we have the situation in 1881 that the General Assembly had endorsed the report of two commissioners, who recommended a complete turning away from any kind of Livingstonia in approach to the task. At the same time they appointed to head the mission, Scott, an explicit and firm believer in the civilising aspect of mission. He wrote a letter to his close friend, James Robertson, in which he outlined what he believed were his main difficulties.[47] These were four.

First, the aftermath of bad relations created with a number of neighbouring chiefs, and the continued presence in the district of troublemakers like Fenwick.

Second, the antagonism of the Portuguese who controlled the mission's only lines of communication was a constant threat to the continued existence of the work.

Third, the existence of three large villages of freed slaves on the land of the mission, was an immediate administrative problem, the one that above all had caused the downfall of MacDonald. On grounds of humanity they could not be simply dispersed. Scott's realism which so often came in to balance the imaginative and poetic side of his personality, made him add that it would take enormous force to disperse them in any case.

The fourth problem was one which he thought most difficult and not peculiar to Blantyre, though it was scarcely seen so clearly by other missionaries at that time. This problem was the contrast between his situation and that of St Paul. The latter was of a poor nation going to rule the rich, in contrast to himself who was, as Scott said, of a rich conquering nation going to the conquered.[48]

In Blantyre Scott found waiting to help him a group of assistants whose ready help, wisdom and integrity left a lasting mark on his attitudes and the success of the mission. These were a small group of Africans who had been attracted to the mission by MacDonald and had stayed on at his request. The three leading men of this group were Joseph Bismarck, Rondau Kaferanjila and Donald Malota.

The mission proper was physically in a bad way. It still consisted of the eight wattle and daub houses built round the square by James Stewart. The stone house built by Buchanan for MacDonald had fallen into an uninhabitable condition and was abandoned. There was no church building, which he thought was of some significance after four years of missionary activity, so the building of a small wattle and daub church was the first task undertaken and completed under his regime.

The four key problems he outlined to Robertson had to be dealt with. The fourth was one which was always present for him in everything he attempted. It had no specific solution, though his consciousness of it was at least part explanation of his role as critic of the British Administration of Malawi from its inception till his departure from Malawi in 1898. The other three had specific solutions and he set about dealing with them immediately. The second problem he listed, that of the Portuguese, he tried to deal with by campaigning to persuade the British government to proclaim some sort of sphere of influence so as to minimise or even eliminate any threat from the Portuguese to the development of Malawi along the lines he believed to be right.

The first and third problems were closely related and also amenable to a more rapid resolution than the threat of the Portuguese. The freed slave villages created a problem of law and order, but their existence was also a living memento of the bad relations which had existed until then with many of the local Yao chiefs. Scott decided that law and order had to be maintained along with the building of good relations with the mission's neighbours, yet without breaking faith with the ex-slaves.

He made it known in the neighbourhood that all who had any claim on any of the runaways should come to see him. If they could substantiate the claim, then they were paid compensation. This effected the freeing of the slaves by traditional law. Scott was here basing his actions on the distinction that MacDonald had pointed out, between traditional domestic slavery and the slave-trade.[50] In these discussions he used Joseph Bismarck and his other African assistants in the way a village chief would use his village elders. He followed the Malawi way of *mlandu*, that is of all cases being discussed freely by the parties concerned and the local elders, the chief at the end trying to articulate what he considered to be the consensus of the meeting. Through this process Scott began to learn both the language and the customs of the people.

These moves succeeded in creating good relations with all the neighbouring chiefs except two. These were Mittoche of Chiradzulu, whose men had fought a skirmish with mission carriers, and Chikhumbu of Nsoni. With the help of Chiefs Mpama and Kapeni as intermediaries, Scott went with his wife to visit Mittoche and initiated a friendship which lasted throughout Scott's life in Malawi. One of his first major collisions with Commissioner Johnston in 1892, was over the latter's treatment of Mittoche,[51] whom Johnston classed as a brigand along with most other Yao chiefs.[52] However, none of Scott's attempts got anywhere with Chikhumbu, who was a very aggressive man, closely involved with the slave-trade to Quelimane. At last Chikhumbu's aggressiveness was his undoing and solved Scott's problem for him. As the Revd Harry Matecheta recorded, 'Chikhumbu anali ndi anthu akudziwa cifwamba, ndipo anthu ambili anasauka.'[52] (Chikhumbu had people who were expert man-stealers and caused many people to suffer.) As a result of these activities, the Yao chiefs Nkhanda and Kapeni got together with the aid of the Kololo paramount, Kasisi and drove

Chikhumbu from the district. He settled in the area, later called the Fort Lister Gap, to the north of Mulanje mountain, astride the slave route to Quelimane.

At the same time, Scott had to deal with the problem of the mission villages. Since any form of European colony was out of the question both legally and from his own convictions, Scott found the solution in much the same way as with his relations with the chiefs; by following African traditional practice. Each village appointed its own headman and elders who heard all cases. If no decision could be agreed on, and in the case of an inter-village dispute, the headmen and elders formed a court with Scott acting as principal headman and, following traditional custom, decisions were reached.

An example of this practice at work was recorded by Hetherwick in his diary and later published.[54] In it he described how on his first day in Blantyre in 1884 a fierce controversy had arisen between the Chipeta of one of the mission villages and the followers of one of the Yao chiefs, Kuntaja, over the killing of a Chipeta man. Scott intervened to prevent fighting from breaking out and, after a long and exhausting *mlandu*, achieved agreement over compensation to be paid to the relatives of the dead man. Nothing could be further from the atmosphere of the previous era of Stewart and Macklin with their European law, their floggings and execution.

The *mlandu* was, and is, a long and time consuming process. It demanded of Scott great patience as well as sympathy with and understanding of African tradition. It meant that he became a chief among chiefs, and Blantyre Mission became a small state among the many small African states in the Shire Highlands, but now it was in many ways an African state. Tragically, like so much else that Scott did, this work was not appreciated or understood in Scotland, where his whole involvement in *mlandu* both on mission land and among the neighbouring chiefs, was seen as a waste of time and a distraction from his real work.[55]

As the place of the mission in local society became more secure, Scott was able to turn his attention to evangelistic and educational work. He completely ignored the recommendations of the 1881 Commission of Enquiry, who had wished the mission to be narrowly evangelistic, and proceeded along avowedly Livingstonian lines. The gospel was to be proclaimed, but culture was also to be transmitted.

Scott inherited from MacDonald a school which had been primarily a boarding establishment. It had not simply been a place for producing readers of the vernacular scripture, but a vehicle for the best education MacDonald could provide. The school soon provided Scott with some surprising confirmation of the efficacy of its teaching. During the crisis in the relations between the Kololo and the African Lakes Company, after Fenwick had killed Chipatula and had then been killed by the chief's enraged followers, the Kololo sent to Mandala their terms for the reopening of the Shire to A.L.C. boats, in a letter written in Cinyanja by one of MacDonald's old boys.[56] The school's effective training was put to even more dramatically effective use in this same conflict. A letter was sent by the Kololo on A.L.C. notepaper, written in English and purporting to come from the A.L.C. manager, to Gowk,[57] the captain of an A.L.C. vessel waiting for permission to come up river. Gowk obeyed the instructions in the letter and his vessel fell into Kololo hands.[58] Clearly the Blantyre school had by 1884 added a new dimension to the espionage and diplomacy of southern Malawi.

Despite this interesting proof of the initiative of the old boys of the school, and their ability to adapt their education to the exigencies of African life, Scott did alter school life from the pattern which had existed in MacDonald's day. Previously the majority of the boys had been Kololo aristocrats with their personal slaves in attendance. The boarding house had been a rowdy boys' village with at least one fight that had led to a death.[89] The new school under Scott was a more traditional type of boarding establishment and no personal slaves were allowed. Day boys were also encouraged from the mission villages and others nearby. A planned day of school work, manual work, recreation and rest was laid on for all the boys. It was this establishment that Scott hoped would produce the young men who would build an African Christianity as well as a new Africa. These boys were Scott's central concern and Hetherwick tells how on the day of the Chipeta-Yao conflict, despite the long exhausting *mlandu*, Scott still found time for his regular evening chat with his 'laddies' in the boarding house.[60]

A steady stream of young men, as they finished their time at school, were added to the nucleus of able Africans that Scott had inherited from MacDonald. The group's unofficial but firmly acknowledged head was Joseph Bismarck. It was from this group that the first baptised Christians and the first teacher-evangelists were drawn.

After he had persuaded John MacIlwain to leave the service of the A.L.C. and join the mission staff in 1884, Scott was able to add building and carpentry to the agricultural and literary skills taught at the school. The next year, he himself began work as a technical missionary when a printing press arrived from Scotland. With the aid of the accompanying instruction manual, Scott and a bright Yao lad named Chisuse (later baptised Mungo),[61] assembled the machine and the two taught themselves to print. By the end of 1887 there was a group of young appren-
210

tice printers working the press and cutting and stitching together books in English, Cinyanja and CiYao.

Scott also used this new tool to create the first regular newspaper north of the Limpopo; in January 1888, he began the monthly magazine, *Life and Work*, which in 1892 became *Life and Work in British Central Africa*. This was not simply a vehicle for mission news but was a regular bearer of political news and comment. It was through the columns of this magazine that Scott explained his aims for the new church, his hopes for its future and for the future of Africa. Through *Life and Work* he tried to influence the growing European population into a better relationship with African people. He campaigned for a British Protectorate to forestall the Portuguese and in the 1890s he campaigned against Rhodes' designs to take over the Protectorate. The magazine also served as a vehicle for criticism of the Protectorate's administration.[62]

There was another more fortuituous area of mission influence. This was provided by the large need for labour to carry on the mission's various activities. This was mainly of a casual nature – labourers to help the skilled men with building, men to work in the fields of maize and beans and porters to carry the goods from Mandala, brought upstream by the A.L.C. In the period 1888 to 1891, when Scott was building his famous Blantyre church, about 2,000 people a year were being employed on the task, directly and indirectly.[63]

Some men and women became more or less permanently attached to the mission, but the vast majority came only for a time, attracted by the opportunity of earning cloth. These people were brought into contact with the Christian gospel by attending morning and evening prayers. Very few at that time became Christians, but on going back to their villages, which covered a large area of the southern region and the Ncheu district of the central, they helped prepare the way for the spread of Christian teaching when more formal missionaries arrived. They also spread news of the mission and its achievements which attracted enterprising young men to Blantyre to learn what they could of the new ways at the school.

Although daily life on the mission at Blantyre was not very different in its outward routine from what one reads about many other missions at that time in the contemporary missionary press, Scott had certain ideas which were different and of critical importance. One of these was moonlight dances. On nights when the moon was full, Scott had the boarders gather on the *bwalo* to dance, sing and play games as they would have done in their villages on such a night. He supervised the session to see that no unseemly songs or dances were performed. This performance was in stark contrast with the usual Protestant horror of traditional dancing and music. Another feature was Scott's Saturday tea-parties. Every Saturday afternoon that he was free, senior boys and girls were invited to the manse for tea. These gatherings were intended as friendly relaxed occasions which Scott used in a twofold way. First, he taught the boys and girls how to behave easily in a European milieu; secondly he took the opportunity to learn from them about traditional customs, as well as their reactions to what was going on around them. Later in the 1890s this meeting became one for his senior African staff and their wives, Scott's 'deacons', whom he hoped would be the leaders of his new African church. At that period the tea-party was one of his main sources of information about the African reaction to the new massive European impact on Malawi, which he then attempted to express in *Life and Work*.[64]

The Blantyre Mission station under Scott was soon a thriving and well-organised community, but it would have to expand if it was to evangelise the Shire Highlands. It could expand in two ways: first, by using new staff to start stations along lines similar to Blantyre in new areas; secondly by the creation of schools and then worshipping communities in the area around the station. The methods were not exclusive but complementary, though with his constant difficulty in obtaining either staff or money from Scotland, Scott sometimes had to make a difficult choice between the two.

In 1884 Scott sent Hetherwick and Henderson on a tour to look for a site suitable for a new station. After a long journey via Mulanje and Lake Chirwa, they arrived in the territory of Henderson's old friend, Male-mia, who welcomed them and agreed to a station being opened in his lands at Domasi. Later that year, Hetherwick began the building of the station. In 1885, when Scott had to go to Scotland on sick leave, Hetherwick took his place at Blantyre and left Domasi in the competent hands of Joseph Bismarck, aided by other African teachers, notably Rondau Kaferanjila. This reliance on African teachers was to characterise the whole of Scott's leadership of the Blantyre Mission. The overt trust in African ability must go a long way to explain the fact that Blantyre never suffered, as did Livingstonia and many other missions in southern Africa, from the breaking away of senior African leaders to form independent churches.

Major opportunities for expansion came with David Scott's return in June 1887 along with a group of new missionaries, his brother-in-law, Dr John Bowie, the Revd Robert Cleland and a teacher, Miss Janet Beck. He also brought back Naco Mtimawanzako whom he had taken to Scotland at his own expense in order to widen Naco's education so that he might help with the final stages of producing Scott's monumental *Cyclopaedic Dictionary of the Mang'anja Language.* Scott believed in sending Malawi youths abroad for further education and such a scheme had been begun by Duff MacDonald. He sent Kagaso Sazuze, Joseph Bismarck, Rondau Kaferanjila, Evangel Sawelayera and Cinkolimbo to Lovedale for higher education. In addition, Dr Rankine had returned to Scotland after his visit with the Commission of Enquiry with Henry Cowan Kapito and Donald Malota whom he educated in Scotland. They returned to serve the mission in 1884. Scott, apart from sending Mungo Chisuse to Nelson's in Edinburgh for further training as a printer in 1890s, was not able to continue the programme because the F.M.C. would not provide funds for it.[65]

Now in 1887, Scott had a good staff of Scots and Africans, two well-run stations, and many friendly contacts with chiefs. Perhaps the most important was the contact which he had established in 1885 with Nkhosi Chikusi Kaphatikiza, the Paramount of the Maseko Ngoni.[66]

Hetherwick and his African teachers began to build up Domasi to Blantyre-like proportions, with its village out-schools at Katungulu and Mlungusi to parallel Blantyre's satellites at Mandala, Chilimoni and Ndirande. Robert Cleland was sent to open a new station at Chiradzulu near Mittoche's. From there he began to make journeys into the Mulanje district, and, with great tact and patience, gained the friendship of the mission's old enemy, Chikhumbu. In 1889 came a triumph in Scott's eyes, when his old adversary gave permission for the starting of a mission station in his lands.[67]

By the end of 1890 the work of the mission had expanded to cover most of the Shire Highlands. This was paralleled by a real growth in church membership, which was not a 'mass movement' but one of individuals. They were, at first, mainly the young men who gathered round Scott as teachers and helpers, but they were followed by a significant number of teenage pupils from the schools. Slowly older people also came forward in the villages close to the stations seeking permission to enter the class leading to baptism.

To understand the whole growth of Christianity in the area affected by the Blantyre Mission under David Scott, it is important to note that no one was ever asked or told to join the class. Of course the atmosphere in school and on the stations encouraged an interest in Christianity, but there was no pressure or coercion. R. I. Rotberg has listed[68] what he rightly calls forms of pressure amounting to coercion, used in missions in Zambia and Malawi. He focuses especially on two forms this took, when the missionaries 'reserved the educational experience to nominal Christians. More significantly they provided employment only for those who professed some seemingly sincere interest in the Christian message.' At Blantyre, apart from attendance at morning and evening prayers, nothing else was demanded of scholars or employees. A man could become an employee of the mission at any level from labourer to teacher, without having to be baptised, or even entering the class. Scott, deliberately, and quite explicitly, avoided the situation where a professed interest in Christianity became a gateway to employment or education.[69] Two notable examples of his policy are the cases of John Chipuliko and Mungo Chisuse, who were not baptised until November 1889, when they had already been responsible members of Scott's staff for five years. Chisuse was already in charge of the printing works which produced the magazine in which the notice of his baptism appeared.

This policy of Scott's slowed down the rate of formal church growth, but it guaranteed real sincerity and commitment on the part of those who did join.

By 1888 an African Christian Church was emerging in the Shire Highlands. In order to deal with vastly increased numbers attending worship and to create a symbol of his vision for African Christianity, Scott decided to build the present Blantyre Church. This building, designed by Scott and built by African craftsmen and labourers, was dedicated in May 1891. Its catholic cruciform shape surmounted by Byzantine dome and towers, were meant by Scott to symbolise his hopes for an African Christianity free from the petty quarrels of Europe.[70]

With the completion of the new building and the coming of the British administration, a new era opened for the mission and for Malawi. It was an era in which David Scott and the mission played a prominent part, but it is another story. By 1891 the Blantyre Mission was truly launched. Many played their part in its growth, but David Clement Scott and his close circle of African helpers were the key group. Their influence has had a permanent effect on the growth of Christianity in southern Malawi. Although in the 1890s Scott failed for a great many reasons to institutionalise in actual church structures his belief in the vital importance of African leadership and authority in the Church, yet through these same African leaders he left a permanent mark which remains imprinted on the Blantyre Synod of the Church of Central Africa Presbyterian. Scott did not bandy about Livingstone's name as so many have done, but he built a mission along lines that related to his great forerunner's attitudes to African people, to culture and to the gospel. Scott, however, added a flavour of his own, his unique poetic imagination that made him loved by so many Africans, yet distrusted
214

and misunderstood by most Europeans and most significantly by the church authorities in Scotland. His imagination and daring are best summed up by something he wrote near the end of his time in Malawi, when he was deeply distressed by the actions of the British South Africa Company in Rhodesia. He wrote

But in order to put down the slave trade you must have a proper doctrine of humanity, a true appreciation of the slave. Just as Christ took upon Him the form of a slave long ago, so He takes upon Him the form of Africa today. Africa bears the sins of the world's rulers. How long are we as a nation going to lay our selfishness, our meanness, our falsehood, our lusts, yea, and the whole burden of our sins upon this Lamb of God?[71]

This vision of the African as a Christ figure brought him a stern rebuke from Scotland. But, although it was never formally worked out, it was this vision that inspired his whole service in Malawi, a service which did much to advance the Christian cause for which Dr David Livingstone had laboured.

Notes

1 A. Hetherwick, *The Romance of Blantyre*, London, n.d., p.14.
2 A. J. Hanna, *The Beginnings of Nyasaland and North Eastern Rhodesia, 1859–1895*, Oxford, 1956, p. 12.
3 *Home and Foreign Missionary Record*, vol. IX, November 1874.
4 D. C. Scott to James Robertson, December 1881. Edinburgh University Library, Ms. 717/10.
5 Hetherwick, op. cit., pp. 17–19.
6 H. M. Matecheta, *Blantyre Mission: Nkhani ya Ciyambi Cace*, Blantyre, 1951, p. 1.
7 Ibid. This information was also gathered from interviews with the late Revd H. K. Matecheta during 1960.
8 W. P. Livingstone, *Laws of Livingstonia*, London, 1921, p. 90.
9 Ibid., p. 106.
10 Hanna, op. cit., p. 24.
11 Hetherwick, op. cit., p. 21.
12 W. P. Livingstone, op. cit., p. 107.
13 Hetherwick, op. cit., pp. 28–9.
14 Duff MacDonald, *Africana*, vol. I, Edinburgh, 1881, p. 21.
15 W. P. Livingstone, op. cit., p. 131.
16 Hetherwick, op. cit., p. 131.
17 McLagan to Macrae, 15 February 1877, National Library of Scotland, Ms. 7541.
18 C. P. Groves, *The Planting of Christianity in Africa*, III, London,1948–55, p. 87; and Hanna, op. cit., pp. 26–7.

19 MacDonald, op. cit., vol. I, pp. 111 and 167.
20 W. P. Livingstone, op. cit., p. 138.
21 R. Oliver, *The Missionary Factor in East Africa*, London, 1952, p. 56.
22 *Home and Foreign Missionary Record*, February 1875, p. 271.
23 Ibid., August 1875, p. 441.
24 MacDonald, op. cit., vol. II, p. 32.
25 Ibid., pp. 31–5.
26 W. P. Livingstone, op. cit., p. 134.
27 Macklin to Martae, March 1878, reproduced in MacDonald, op. cit., vol. II, pp. 31–7.
28 Ibid., pp. 252, 111 and 167.
29 G. Shepperson, Introduction to new edition of MacDonald, *Africana*, London, 1969, p. x.
30 MacDonald, op. cit., vol. II, p. 167.
31 Ibid., p. 109.
32 Ibid., p. 168.
33 A. Chirnside, *The Blantyre Missionaries: Discreditable Disclosures*.
34 McLagan to MacDonald, May 1880, N.L.S., Ms. 7545.
35 *Reports to the General Assembly of the Church of Scotland, 1881*, F.M.C. Report, East Africa Section, p. 78.
36 *Assembly reports, 1881*, F.M.C. Report, East Africa Section, p. 79.
37 *Assembly reports, 1882*, Special Report to the Assembly on Duff Macdonald's Petition, pp. 147–9.
38 Ibid., pp. 51–3.
39 *Assembly Reports, 1881*, F.M.C. Report, Appendix A, pp. 86–90 and 90–7.
40 Ibid., p. 92.
41 Ibid., p. 97.
42 Max Warren, *Social History and Christian Mission*, London, 1967, p. 43.
43 H. A. C. Cairns, *Prelude to Imperialism*, London, 1965, p. 219.
44 MacDonald, op. cit., p. 248.
45 Cairns. op. cit., p. 221.
46 *Life and Work in British Central Africa*, May 1894.
47 Scott to James Robertson, 20 December 1880, E.U. Library, Ms. 717/10.
48 This part of the letter is most significant at the beginning of an era when European power was seen too often as a positive factor contributing to the effectiveness of the missionary task, cf. T. O. Ranger, *Revolt in Southern Rhodesia, 1896–7*, London, 1967, pp. 36–40.
49 Hetherwick, op. cit., p. 39.
50 MacDonald, op. cit., vol. II, p. 168.
51 *Life and Work in British Central Africa*, May 1893.
52 H. H. Johnston to F.O., 29 December 1891, F.O. 84/2114.
53 Matecheta, op. cit., p. 2.
54 *Central Africa News and Views*, vol. 2, no. 1. July 1896.
55 McMurtrie to D. C. Scott, 27 October 1887, N.L.S. Foreign Mission Committee Letter-book, M.1.
56 Journal of F. J. Morrison, E.U. Library, Ms. Room. Entry for March 7, 1884.
57 'Gowk' in Scots means a fool, singularly appropriate in this instance.
58 Morrison's journal, May 24, 1884.
59 Macdonald, op. cit., vol. II, p. 181.
60 *Central Africa News and Views*, vol. 2, no. 1, July 1896.

61 A member of a chiefly clan of the Amangoche Yao; head of a family that produced many leaders in Malawi life in the 1950s and 1960s, including Dr Harry Bwanausi, the late Mr Augustine Bwanausi, a member of the first Malawi Cabinet, and Mrs Chechiwa Khonje, Malawi's first B.B.C.-trained broadcaster.

62 I have dealt with this conflict in 'The African: Child or Man' in E. Stokes and R. Brown (eds.), *The Zambesian Past*, Manch...er, 1965.

63 *Life and Work in British Central Africa*, June 1891.

64 This paragraph is based on conversations with the Revd Harry Matecheta, Mr Lewis Bandawe, M.B.E. and Mr Lester Chopi.

65 *Assembly Reports, 1882*, F.M.C. Report, p. 84.

66 Matecheta, op. cit., pp. 2–3.

67 *Life and Work in British Central Africa*, December 1890.

68 R. I. Rotberg, *The Rise of Nationalism in Central Africa*, p. 9.

69 *Life and Work in British Central Africa*, October 1892.

70 Ibid., May 1894.

71 Ibid., December 1897.

10 Livingstone and the Aftermath: the Origins and Development of Livingstonia Mission

John McCracken

Among the group of missions founded in the aftermath of David Livingstone's death, none can claim such a close yet ambiguous relationship with the explorer as the Livingstonia mission of the Free Church of Scotland. Launched within fourteen months of Livingstone's funeral in Westminster Abbey, Livingstonia was presented to the Scottish public as the national memorial to the missionary hero. Its first site at Cape Maclear at the south end of Lake Malawi was one to which Livingstone had pointed as early as 1861 as a suitable harbour for expeditionary operations.[1] He had recommended the use of a small prefabricated steamer on the Upper Shire and lake;[2] he had advised the recruitment of trained artisans for a pioneer party.[3] James Stewart's desire to create in central Africa 'an institution at once industrial and educational to teach the truths of the Gospel and the arts of civilised life to the natives'[4] was an accurate reflection of Livingstone's aims.

But while it is clear that Livingstone influenced the character of Livingstonia, the precise nature and extent of that influence is difficult to determine. At a simple level it is possible to argue that the founding of the mission owed much less to the explorer than has often been imagined. More fundamentally, Livingstonia provided not the justification of Livingstone's theories but rather a practical demonstration of their unrealistic nature. Few missions have had as great an influence on the people among whom they have worked as had Livingstonia, but her success came with the abandonment of Livingstone's theories, or rather with their adaption to African realities.

At 6.30 a.m. on 12 October 1875 a small battered steamer pushed its way out of the Shire river into the open waters of Lake Malawi and thus brought to a climax a process set underway over sixteen years

218

earlier by David Livingstone.[5] To Livingstone, as to his companion John Kirk, the exploration of the Upper Shire and Lake Malawi regions in 1859 and 1861 was only the prelude to the establishment of Christian and commercial settlements. Finding what Livingstone described as a 'prodigious' population living near the lake and excited by the evidence of cotton growing and of other agricultural skills, the explorers were quick to devise an ambitious scheme by which British merchants would purchase cotton and ivory from the local inhabitants and thus 'cut off the slave trade of a large district at its source'.[6] The U.M.C.A. were already committed to the Shire Highlands but the claim of the lake regions was strongly put to James Stewart on his pioneer visit in 1862. If freedom of access could be guaranteed by the Portuguese the Shire-Zambezi waterway would serve as the best communications route into the interior. For a man such as Stewart appeared to be, wrote Livingstone, 'I would say there are no very serious obstacles in the way'.[7]

Elsewhere in this volume Mrs Brock gives a sensitive description of Stewart's growing disillusionment with Livingstone and the failure of his tour of reconnaissance.[8] When the young Scotsman set off to Africa in 1861 he shared with Livingstone his belief in the beneficial effects that would result from the increased production of raw materials in the new continents for the use of industrialists in the old. 'If the mission comes to be established,' he noted in his diary, 'one of the most important things – in fact the most valuable of all things would be to take a steam-engine of two four or six horse power with abundance of belts and mills to fit.'[9] Flour mills, coffee mills, saw mills and planing machines would serve in the vanguard of the missionary movement.

By the time he turned away from the Zambezi over eighteen months later such plans were scattered to the winds. The failure of the Universities' Mission, the lack of success of Livingstone's Zambezi expedition, the slender amounts of cotton discovered and the primitive methods of spinning in use all told against the founding of a new missionary settlement. The report presented by Stewart to the committee that had financed his visit is a catalogue of obstacles overlooked in Livingstone's earlier despatches. The Zambezi-Shire route, he noted, was shallower and more difficult to navigate than any earlier account had suggested. Portuguese hostility could result in the levying of prohibitive duties. The climate of the river valley was unfavourable to the health of white men. In only one passage did the river route appear in a favourable light. The Zambezi alone would be of little value for transport purposes, Stewart noted, 'yet as the inlet to the river Shire . . . communicates with Lake Nyassa and as the latter is separated, though by some considerable distance from the still larger lake of Tanganyika it may in time after all prove to be the real high way into the lake regions.'[10]

How far the events of the 1860s are connected with the establishment of mission stations in the mid-1870s is difficult to determine. The failure of the Zambezi expedition not only alienated Livingstone from British government opinion; it also created in missionary circles a much more wary approach to his appeals.[11] During the next decade the explorer publicly and in private correspondence deplored the withdrawal of the Universities' Mission, called for the establishment of a British steamer on the lake and wrote enthusiastically of the opportunities awaiting Scottish agents in the area. But after the failure of earlier years the response was not encouraging. James Stewart, despite the chill that had crept into his relationship with Livingstone, did stay firmly convinced of the need for missionary operations that were 'very much more extended than what is usually embodied in the phrase *a mission station*'.[12] But even Stewart, as he revealed in a letter of October 1864, differed from his former hero in the type of settlement that he wished to see established. While Livingstone hoped for the emigration of working-class farmers and traders from Britain, Stewart argued that the introduction of commerce could not be attempted for some time to come and that black not white labour should be the basis of any colonial settlement.[13] It was hardly surprising that no role could be found for him on Livingstone's last expedition. In the light of his earlier criticisms it was equally unsurprising that the Free Church authorities gave no encouragement to his 1867 scheme to open a station in the region of the lake to be supervised from his new base at Lovedale, South Africa.[14]

What changed the situation has not yet been adequately demonstrated by modern historians. Most writers have tended to give Livingstone almost a monopoly of credit for the sudden expansion of missions to central Africa that took place in the 1870s and 1880s.[15] Undoubtedly the exploits of his last expedition – the false report of his murder, the meeting with Stanley and the picturesque death at Ilala – all contributed to a massive resurgence of interest in his work. In October 1869 Horace Waller was able to inform the explorer 'that the interest in this country about you is as intense as ever I could wish it to be. . . . The report of your murder, Sir Roderick's vehement denial, Young's most successful clear-up of Moosa's lie have all tended so to surround you with a halo of romance such as you can't imagine.'[16]

Yet even when these events are taken into account one may still question whether they had more effect in outweighing Stewart's earlier objections than did the increased economic involvement of Europeans in East Africa from the 1870s. The decisive step was probably the opening of the Suez Canal in 1869 and the consequent improvement of communications up the east coast through the creation in 1872 of a monthly mail service between Aden and Durban via Zanzibar run by the British India Steam Navigation Company, a Scottish firm owned by William Mackinnon.[17]

For ten years the Free Church, with other societies, had ignored Livingstone's appeals. But with the establishment of a monthly line of steamers up the coast the Foreign Missions Committee under the leadership of Dr Alexander Duff, formerly a notable missionary in India, turned its attention in that direction.[18] In January 1874 Duff met Sir Bartle Frere at a dinner following a lecture the latter had given in Edinburgh. Frere had recently returned from a visit to Zanzibar and the east coast which had impressed him as a suitable field for missionary labour.[19] He suggested that the Free Church should take up work among the Somalis, a people he had admired in Aden as labourers and out-of-door servants. Duff got Murray Mitchell, the secretary of the Committee, to write to Dr John Wilson, the head of the Free Church College, Bombay, asking his opinion of the proposed mission, and requesting that he 'send some natives of India without delay to see and report upon the field'.[20] Wilson approved heartily of the proposal and promised, according to Murray Mitchell, to send not Indians but 'two if not three Natives of East Africa – connected apparently with a Galla tribe – whom he considers well fitted to go out and act as pioneers'.[21]

This was the situation when early in 1874 James Stewart, now the head of the Lovedale Institution, returned to Scotland to raise money for the daughter college of Blythswood. In April he attended Livingstone's funeral in Westminster Abbey. A month later he drew up a memorandum on 'Livingstonia, Central Africa', the gist of which was presented to the General Assembly of the Free Church in a speech Stewart delivered on 19 May. 'Somali land,' Stewart commented, 'is in every way unsuitable' for a Free Church mission; 'It can never be a place of entrance into the continent, or of exit from it. Its productions must be comparatively limited and its soil is not remarkably fertile.' The southern end of Lake Malawi, on the other hand, could be reached from the coast by water with only a single interruption. With Lovedale as 'the base of operations' for the new mission, its success would not be in doubt.[22] Such a station 'placed on a carefully selected and commanding spot in central Africa' would 'grow into a town, and afterwards into a city and become a great centre of commerce, civilisation, and Christianity'.[23]

Stewart's proposal came at a timely juncture for the Free Church authorities. Their own plan for Somaliland had failed to create much interest in Scotland,[24] and even its architects were quickly won over.

Bartle Frere was reported to be much taken with the new scheme, though he did not want the Somali country to be entirely given up, while Wilson wrote from Bombay giving the information – new apparently to Murray Mitchell, and he thought to Duff as well – that Livingstone himself had suggested the borders of Lake Malawi as the locale for a Free Church mission.[25] Not only was the Free Church's decision to found a mission in East Africa unconnected with Livingstone's appeals; its authorities were ignorant of the area he had selected for evangelisation. Only the fortuitous appearance of Stewart and his suggestion of a title and location for the new mission connected Livingstone with its foundation at all.

Yet if Livingstone's ideas were of little importance to the authorities of the Church, their influence on those who were to finance and administer the mission cannot easily be questioned. Stewart, though he recognised the need to obtain the approval of the Foreign Missions Committee for his scheme, looked for financial support to a group of businessmen from the Clyde Valley whose assumptions were similar to his own. A meeting held in the Queen's Hall, Glasgow, on 3 November, was of great importance for the future of the mission. Anxious to commemorate in Livingstone a man who had celebrated the virtues of Victorian industry, the Glasgow businessmen present demonstrated their acceptance of Stewart's assessment of the economic potential of the Lake Malawi area by unanimously agreeing to 'the desirableness and practicability of the enterprise and of planting an industrial and educational settlement at the region indicated'.[26] A gift of £1,000 from James Stevenson, a chemical manufacturer and an ardent enthusiast for African development, marked the starting point in the financial campaign. By March 1876 over £10,500 had been raised, largely through individual contributions from Scottish entrepreneurs of similar persuasion, and by the same date several of these had banded together to take on the management of the mission's affairs.[27] Not till 1914 was Livingstonia to be placed on the same administrative footing as other missions, and by that time the dreams of economic expansion in the Malawi regions had been proved to be without foundation.[28]

Meanwhile the composition of Livingstone's expeditionary party clearly demonstrated the expectations of those responsible for its selection. Led by a naval officer, E. D. Young – commander of the search party to Lake Malawi in 1867 – it contained only one ordained missionary, the young United Presbyterian Robert Laws, but five artisans skilled as engineers, gardeners, blacksmiths and carpenters. The character of the artisans is a key to the nature of the mission. As dourly devout and as restlessly ambitious as Livingstone, they saw in central Africa a gateway to personal achievement. To Stewart and his business friends their role was clear. After establishing a settlement they would attract Africans to live there, teach them technical skills and provide demonstrations of European industry. For the artisans themselves, however, their appointment was to be a prelude to greater advancement. Of the five who sailed from London on 21 May 1875 two were later to become doctors, one a clergyman and one a respected trader.[29] Livingstone could have reasonably faulted the first Universities' Mission expedition on the grounds that the devotion of its members was not matched by their knowledge of practical skills. The Livingstonia party, on the other hand, had attracted the talents he particularly admired. For the first time the theory of the 'industrial mission' was to be put to the test by men well qualified to do so.

The seven years following the arrival of the pioneer party in Africa can be seen as a period of experiment during which the disadvantages of the 'Christian colony' strategy were made increasingly clear. In the first few weeks Livingstone's suggestions were followed with considerable success. Bearing in mind the advice he had given to the Convenor of the Foreign Missions Committee, Dr Tweedie, nearly fourteen years earlier,[30] the missionaries brought with them a small prefabricated steamer so constituted that it could be taken to pieces at the foot of the Murchison cataracts and rebuilt when the journey round the rapids had been completed. On 23 July 1875 they arrived aboard a German schooner off the Kongone mouth of the Zambezi and quickly set to work recruiting gangs of local Africans for the arduous task of bolting together the steel plates of their vessel. On 3 August the *Ilala* was launched and a week later the journey upstream began. A temporary setback came with the capsizing of an accompanying sailing-boat, the death of two of its crew and the loss of most of the missionaries' personal possessions. But by 6 September the foot of the rapids had been reached and contacts with Makololo chiefs successfully established.[31]

The close alliance forged by Livingstone with the Makololo played an important part in the missionaries' plans. When Stewart first travelled up the Shire in 1862 they were still living together in one village as Livingstone had left them.[32] In the next thirteen years they spread out through the Lower Shire Valley, establishing their dominance over many of the local Mang'anja and creating a loose political federation headed by Kasisi (or Ramakukan) but with Chipitula, Masea, Malima and others virtually independent beneath him.[33] Aliens in a hostile land and lacking the contacts with the lake possessed

223

by the Yao, the Kololo, as Laws pointed out, were 'placed between two markets', and hence 'would welcome any communication with the English'.[34] When visited by the missionaries in early September they responded by bringing firewood and provisions for sale, and by sending their villagers to work. Within a month up to a thousand porters were recruited, the steamer was dismantled (with the exception of the boiler) into 50 lb loads, the sixty-mile trek past the rapids was accomplished and the steamer was rebuilt and relaunched.[35] On 11 October the *Ilala* sailed through Lake Malombe and anchored opposite the Yao chief Mponda's village at the river crossing south of the larger lake. The next day, having received from Mponda permission to settle where he wanted at Cape Maclear, Young called for the Old Hundredth to be sung as the first steamer to enter Lake Malawi sailed onto its waters.[36] Just under a week later, on 17 October, after a first short tour of reconnaissance, the landing at Cape Maclear was finally effected. 'Livingstonia is begun,' wrote Laws, 'though at present a piece of canvas stretched between two trees is all that stands for the future city of that name.'[37]

The years spent by the missionaries at Cape Maclear were essentially a period of adjustment in personnel and policies alike to the realities of the African situation. In common with all pioneer missions much time was spent combating the physical challenge of the new environment. In the first year a row of houses was built facing the lake and a wooden fort was constructed against possible invaders; the ground was drained, gardens cultivated and a start made at building a timber slipway for the *Ilala*.[38] E. D. Young, however, though a skilful sailor, had few of the talents that make for effective missionary leadership. To James Stewart, who replaced him at the head of a party of reinforcements, including three Africans from Lovedale, in October 1876, his work had about it 'a commonness and absence of all comfort inside and out that is to me very unsatisfactory'.[39] But Stewart was no more successful than Young in creating a harmonious missionary community. Aged over forty when he arrived at Cape Maclear, he believed himself to be too old to respond to the challenge of his own creation. Impatient to get back to Lovedale, he was consumed by 'a slow burning anger . . . that I should be kept toiling away at rough work which suited me 20 years ago but does not suit me at all now'.[40] Under the strain imposed upon him by malaria he became so despotic and irritable that at least one observer thought he was going out of his mind.[41] It was only after his departure in December 1877 and the elevation of Robert Laws to the headship that Livingstonia as an effective community got fully underway.

How can one assess the impact of a story-book hero? Originally regarded as a temporary member of the expeditionary party, Laws spent fifty-two years in the service of the mission and became a legend in Malawi during his lifetime. By abolishing the gulf established between artisans and ordained missionaries – formerly they had even taken their meals at separate tables – he forged a sense of common identity between all agents, African as well as European, that was to survive the strains of racial tension that entered the mission in the mid-1880s.[42] Always austere, sometimes obstinate, he possessed an appetite for work that was almost unbelievable. In the pioneer years he looked after the health of the mission party and gave simple medical assistance to thousands of Africans, mostly with the aid of Epsom salts and rhubarb pills.[43] He kept meteorological observations, collected linguistic material and taught the first pupils to come to the station from May 1876. Through his initiative the Scottish agents read the Greek New Testament, conducted Sunday services in neighbouring Yao and Mang'anja villages and demonstrated through picture-book and magic-lantern displays the spherical form of the earth, its revolutions round the sun, the cause of day and night, God's purposes with men.[44] Hardly a major exploratory or diplomatic expedition was undertaken without Laws in the first decade, and hardly a decision of major substance was not referred to him. Up to the appointment of Donald Fraser and James Henderson[45] in the mid-1890s he possessed no intellectual peer among the missionaries, and even after their arrival his ideas, though regarded as old-fashioned by the new generation of agents were arguably more far-sighted than any that replaced them. If Livingstonia did not succeed in its primary purpose of establishing a residential settlement which could act as the nucleus for the introduction of 'legitimate' trade in opposition to the slave trade the cause lay not in a failure of missionary leadership but rather in a miscalculation of what was involved.

In retrospect it is possible to argue that most of the difficulties confronting Livingstonia at Cape Maclear stemmed from the attempt to undertake temporal responsibilities independent of any political authority. One such problem concerned the relation of the mission to external African forces. By the mid-1870s Yao migrations into the Malawi regions had resulted in the creation of a string of territorial chieftancies round the south end of the lake, those most frequently visited by the missionaries being Makanjira's on the eastern shore and Mponda's on the river-crossing to the south. Of diverse origin these chieftaincies were led by rulers (among whom Mponda was a typical example)[46] who owed their power less to conventional hereditary rights than to their success as traders and raiders. Monopolising the ownership of guns and ammunition in their states, these caravan chiefs actively involved themselves in the east coast trade in ivory, malachite and slaves, and turned their central villages into entrepots where caravans from as far west as Mwase Kasungu's could be provisioned and where Arab middlemen could operate in profitable security.[47]

At a superficial level such men were rarely averse to the establishment of alliances with the mission. Products of a competitive and unstable environment, they envied Livingstonia's material wealth and looked to exploit her wider technological connections. Mponda, for example – a drunken braggart in the eyes of the Scots, but also a much-travelled trader with an adventurous political past – encouraged the missionaries to settle in his territory and asked them for information on the manufacture of guns and mass-produced cloth.[48] For three years from 1875 he used them as technicians and medical advisers, gave them a musical box to be mended and requested military assistance against his enemies.[49]

What prevented this tactical alliance from being transformed into a more lasting relationship was the incompatible aims of the parties involved. To Mponda the maintenance of political power was dependent if not on the continuance of the slave trade at least on its substitution by a trade as profitable and as easy to control.[50] To the missionaries on the other hand the slave trade was an abomination to be checked by the moral presence of a British steamer on the lake, and to be superseded by the introduction of legitimate commerce. Forbidden by their home committee to use force in the furtherance of this campaign[51] they resorted under the belligerent E. D. Young to a mixture of moral exhortation and threat which may have temporarily startled the dhow captains of Nkhota kota in 1875, but which certainly had no long-term effects on the patterns of east coast trade.[52]

More practical was the attempt to assist independent trading concerns through missionary endeavour. Begun at the end of 1876 following the arrival of the quixotic H. B. Cotterill, along with a steel boat donated by the boys of Harrow,[53] the policy was put into practical effect only with the foundation of the African Lakes Company in July 1878 and the arrival of its managers John and Fred Moir at Quelimane two months later.[54] In many ways the company was a logical extension of Livingstonia. Financed by the same Glasgow businessmen – James Stevenson prominent among them – as had started the mission, it utilised the services of Livingstonia's artisans in the first few years and took over the running of the mission's steamer.[55]

But just as Yao chiefs were unaffected by the exhortations of the missionaries so they ignored the economic blandishments of the company. Restricted by the modest capital resources available to them and by the high cost of transport to the coast, the Moir brothers shelved schemes for agricultural expansion during the 1880s and concentrated instead on the export of ivory.[56] Hugh Macmillan's recent study of the A.L.C. provides a scholarly survey of the melancholy results.[57] Hindered as much by the limited carrying capacity of their steamers as by their ban on the sale of guns and gunpowder, the two managers found it almost impossible to break the Yao and Arab monopoly. The prices they offered were frequently rejected by Yao traders who could make greater profits by selling their ivory at the coastal ports. In consequence, up to 1883, the company was forced to rely on white hunters to shoot most of the ivory it exported. In the next three years extensive purchases were made from Arab entrepreneurs at Karonga, but the trade in slaves was not thereby affected, and Yao economic patterns continued as before. Frequent caravans still passed through Mponda's at the end of the 1870s and beginning of the 1880s, and the number of armed Arabs resident at the entrepot appears to have increased. Some forty coastmen were noted in the town in 1884, and the chief boasted of the number of Enfield rifles he now possessed.[58]

The failure to create a viable new economic structure on the lake was accompanied by a growth in tension between Livingstonia and the neighbouring Yao chieftaincy. Founded as an enclave to which African settlers could be attracted, the mission gradually took on some of the characteristics of an expanding colony. In the first year Africans resident at the station were limited to half a dozen personal servants and interpreters, four of them Yao and Nyanja disciples of Bishop Mackenzie, recruited at Cape Town where they had been taken after the Universities' Mission's collapse.[59] Stewart's arrival in 1876, however, was followed by a rapid expansion in the size of the settlement. Begun towards the end of the year with the temporary appearance of a band of Makololo scholars[60] the increase in numbers was accelerated by the arrival of the first refugees, most of them local Yao and Mang'anja, who established villages under mission protection early in 1877.

Some fifteen strong in February, the number of dissident villagers rose to over 300 in August 1878 and to perhaps 550 in mid-1880, by which time their defiance of the authority of local chiefs was provoking angry reactions.[61] The case of Sogoli, a sub-chief of Mponda's, whose village disintegrated in the face of competition from Livingstonia, has been documented in considerable detail. Started innocuously in March 1876, when a handful of villagers went to work for a few days at the neighbouring station, the process of disintegration got under way in January 1877 with the first defections and reached a climax in March 1878 following the missionaries' rejection of Sogoli's plea for the return of his dependents.[62] What followed was the virtual breakdown of relations between the mission and its neighbour. Faced with a severe loss of power and prestige, Sogoli, even before his last dramatic appeal, began to kidnap those villagers who could not be induced to return through persuasion. The missionaries in reply sent out an armed posse under the artisan Thomas Crooks to rescue its settlers. And the consequence was an indecisive brawl in Sogoli's village, bitterly contested, though virtually bloodless.[63]

In 1879 further kidnapping incidents were being followed by the seizure of those Yao thought to be responsible, their imprisonment and in one case, the flogging of a ring-leader; African agents of the mission were being struck and insulted in neighbouring villages; local authorities were shunning the station for fear of instant arrest.[64] Some headmen still continued to request the aid of the mission in dealing with such natural hazards as man-eating leopards and marauding elephants. But by and large, Livingstonia's relationship to her neighbours had become alarmingly isolated. Faced by a shortage of fertile land near the station and by a high incidence of sickness, the prospects of the mission appeared increasingly bleak. Laws had initially opposed Stewart's proposal to move the site, but by 1880 his resistance was stilled. In October 1881, six years almost to the day since the arrival of the missionaries, the *Ilala* sailed north to Bandawe half-way up the west coast taking with her the last Europeans from the station.[65]

The history of Cape Maclear in the 1880s reveals all too clearly the failure of Livingstonia to make a significant impact on the lakeside Yao. Although most of the scholars and servants attached to the mission moved up to Bandawe, the village settlements remained. These Laws placed under the headmanship of the first refugee to settle, one Chimlolo, whom he made responsible for civil jurisdiction. A Mang'anja scholar, Andrew Mwana Njobru, was put in charge of Sunday services and of the school at the settlement, while another, Harry Zamatgona, was given the care of the store and ordered to buy salt to be bartered for provisions at the other stations.[66] A year later, an evangelist Charles Konde, supported by the Bandawe congregation at the rate of three shillings per month, was sent to replace Njobru. And he in turn was replaced in 1884 by the mission's first convert, Albert Namalambe, formerly a Mang'anja follower of the Makololo,

228

who remained there till his death in 1908.[67]

The immediate consequence of the missionaries' departure was the collapse of the educational system they had constructed. In the absence of Europeans, followers of Mponda began 'committing thefts in the neighbourhood and giving great annoyance to the people in the mission village'.[68] Under such harassments the numbers attending school dropped from an average of forty to about eight or nine in June 1882, and to nothing at all three months later.[69] The foundation of a new station of Livlezi, near enough for Europeans to make regular visits, in 1887, caused a temporary increase in activity; but the schools opened were all in the immediate vicinity of the settlement. In contrast to men like Chimlolo, who threw in his lot with the Europeans and provided assistance to the Lakes Company following the disruption of trade by the Makololo in 1884, most of the Yao became increasingly wary as the European presence began to loom large.[70] The expansion of Islam is one indication of the continued independence of Yao institutions. Accepted as a religion of the court by only a handful of chieftaincies in the mid-1870s,[71] Islam was firmly established at Mponda's by 1886 when the chief and also several of his young men were said to be believers.[72] Five years later the town possessed a dozen Koranic schools run by their own *Mwalimus*,[73] and by 1895 conversions were still taking place.[74] The comment of a Dutch Reformed Church missionary in 1910 dramatically illustrates the extent of its growth; 'Among the Yao on the lake shore,' wrote A. L. Hofmeyr, 'it is becoming the natural thing to be a Mohammedan – they look on it as their natural religion. The Yao who does not accept it will soon find himself a stranger among his own people.'[75]

Although the decision to evacuate Livingstonia to Bandawe in 1881 is usually ascribed to the unhealthiness of the Cape Maclear site, it is not too fanciful to argue that it resulted at least as much from the failure of Livingstone's policy. Looking in perspective at the results of the first six years' effort one is struck time and again by the inability of the missionaries to carry into effect the strategies he had favoured. The presence of a mission steamer on the lake in no way checked Arab activity. The introduction of 'legitimate' commerce was not by itself an answer to the slave trade, nor could it be achieved with the resources available. The creation of a residential settlement, far from adding to the influence of the missionaries, only increased their isolation from the political leaders they wished to impress. If indeed the missionary presence had any effect on Yao economies it was paradoxically in increasing domestic demand at slave-trading centres. Faced by the need to provide food-supplies for a settlement incapable of feeding itself the missionaries met their requirements through regular visits to such entrepots as Makanjira's where the surpluses of maize and mapira for sale had probably been generated through earlier demands from slave caravans.[76] But though Livingstonia's early strategy was at fault, it would be unfair to close the story of the mission on a note of failure. Operating among the mixed Tonga, Tumbuka and Ngoni communities of northern Malawi in the years after 1881, the influence of Livingstonia was striking and effective. There is no space in this chapter to describe the major events of the next two decades – the creation of a Christian revolution among the lakeside Tonga, the emergence of new elites related to the old in northern Ngoniland, the appearance of a generation of Malawi evangelists anxious to carry their beliefs into neighbouring territories.[77] What one can say, however, is that the profound changes of the 1880s and 1890s were brought about by a mission whose 'residential' policies had been modified by its earlier experiences, and took place in a political environment where the challenges of the east coast trade were no longer of major concern. If Livingstonia succeeded it did so by leaving the area where Livingstone had wanted a Scottish mission to work. If some later missions among the Yao (notably the U.M.C.A.) were to achieve a modicum of influence they were to do so after abandoning Livingstone's policy of economic revolution. That David Livingstone was an inspiration to later missionaries it would be impossible to deny; that his ideas were largely ineffectual it is also necessary to conclude.

Notes

Much of the material in this chapter is drawn from two unpublished theses: K. J. McCracken, 'Livingstonia Mission and the evolution of Malawi 1875–1939', Cambridge Ph.D., 1967, and H. W. Macmillan, 'The Origins and Development of the African Lakes Company, 1878–1908', Edinburgh Ph.D., 1970.

 1 David and Charles Livingstone, *Narrative of an Expedition to the Zambezi and its tributaries, and the discovery of Lakes Shirwa and Nyassa, 1858–1864*, London, 1865, pp. 371–2.
 2 David Livingstone to Dr Tweedie, 2 November 1861, National Library of Scotland 7792.
 3 David Livingstone to Lord John Russell, 20 November 1859, and to Roderick Murchison 14 December 1862, printed in J. P. R. Wallis (ed.) *The Zambezi Expedition of David Livingstone 1858–1863*, London, 1956, vol. II, pp. 343 and 377–8.
 4 Quoted in James Wells, *Stewart of Lovedale*, London 1908, p. 125.
 5 The arrival of the *Ilala* is described in the Livingstonia Mission Journal entry for 12 October 1875, N.L.S. 7908.

6 Livingstone to Dr Tweedie, 2 November 1861, N.L.S. 7792; Livingstone to the Earl of Malmesbury, 15 October 1859, printed in Wallis, *Zambezi Expedition*, vol. II, p. 332. See also John Kirk to Alexander Kirk, 29 November 1859, printed in R. Foskett (ed.) *The Zambesi Journal and Letters of Dr John Kirk*, Edinburgh 1965, vol. II, pp. 535–7.

7 Ibid. Livingstone to Tweedie, postscript of 1 March 1862.

8 See pp. 86–110.

9 James Stewart Journal entry for 12 July 1861, Stewart Papers ST/1/2/1, National Archives of Rhodesia, Salisbury.

10 James Stewart, 'Report on the Practicability of the establishment of a Mission on the river Zambezi', November 1863, Stewart Papers, ST 1/1/1.

11 G. Shepperson (ed.), *David Livingstone and the Rovuma*, Edinburgh, 1965, pp. 34–8.

12 James Stewart to David Livingstone, 4 October 1864, Stewart Papers ST 1/1/1.

13 Ibid.

14 This episode is discussed in greater detail in chapter 4 of this volume.

15 See, for example, R. Oliver, *The Missionary Factor in East Africa*, London, 1952, pp. 7–9, 34–5.

16 H. Waller to D. Livingstone, 25 October 1869, Waller Papers I, Rhodes House, Oxford.

17 R. Coupland, *The Exploitation of East Africa, 1856–90*, London, 1939, pp. 82–5; George Blake, *B.I. Centenary 1856–1956*, London, 1956, pp. 143–7.

18 Alexander Duff, *The Proposed Mission to Lake Nyassa*, Edinburgh, 1875, p. 8.

19 Henry Bartle Edward Frere (1815–84) had a distinguished career as a civil servant in India, which culminated in his appointment in 1862 as Governor of Bombay. In 1872 he was sent to Zanzibar to negotiate an anti-slavery treaty with the Sultan. In 1876 he became Governor of Cape Colony, a post he held to 1880. His views on mission work are contained in the study he wrote following his visit to Zanzibar and the east coast: Sir Bartle Frere, *Eastern Africa as a Field for Missionary Labour*, London, 1874.

20 J. Murray Mitchell to Dr J. Wilson, 8 January 1874, N.L.S. 7770.

21 J. Murray Mitchell to Sir Bartle Frere, 20 March 1874, N.L.S. 7770.

22 James Stewart, 'Memorandum on "Livingstonia" Central Africa', May 1874, Stewart Papers ST 1/1/1, Salisbury.

23 Stewart in his speech to the General Assembly of the Free Church of Scotland, May 1875, quoted in J. W. Jack, *Daybreak in Livingstonia*, Edinburgh, 1901, p. 26.

24 Minutes of the acting Foreign Missions Committee of the Free Church of Scotland, entry for 21 July 1874, Church of Scotland Offices, Edinburgh.

25 J. Murray Mitchell to Dr Wilson, 30 July 1874, N.L.S. 7770.

26 Minutes of a meeting in the Queen's Hall, Glasgow, 3 November 1874, N.L.S. 7913.

27 A more detailed discussion of the administrative and financial background of Livingstonia, containing full documentary references, can be found in K. J. McCracken, 'Livingstonia as an industrial mission, 1875–1900: a study of commerce and Christianity in Nyasaland', *Religion in Africa*, Centre of African Studies, Edinburgh, 1964.

28 K. J. McCracken, 'Livingstonia Mission and the evolution of Malawi, 1875–1939', Cambridge Ph.D., 1967, pp. 346–7.

29 George Johnson and John McFadyen were the two artisans who later became

doctors; the clergyman was Alexander Riddel and the trader (for a time an employee of the African Lakes Company) Alan Simpson. Significantly the only artisan who failed to improve his position was the one outside appointment, the Royal Naval seaman William Baker.

30 'A mission, to be effective must have a steamer of its own, and made capable of being unscrewed at the bottom of the cataracts and carried past them in Scotch carts.' Livingstone to Tweedie, 2 November 1861, N.L.S. 7792.

31 Livingstonia Mission Journal entries for 23 July to 6 September 1875, N.L.S. 7908.

32 J. P. R. Wallis (ed.), *The Zambesi Journal of James Stewart 1862–1863*, London, 1952, p. 90.

33 W. H. J. Rangeley, 'The Makololo of Dr Livingstone', *Nyasaland Journal* XII, 1, 1959, pp. 84–91; Stewart to his wife 9 August 1876, Stewart Papers ST 1/1/1.

34 R. Laws to A. Duff (?) 21 February 1876, N.L.S. 7876.

35 Livingstonia Mission Journal entries for 3 September to 6 October 1875, N.L.S. 7908.

36 Ibid., entries for 11 and 12 October 1875.

37 R. Laws to 'a friend at home', 19 October 1875, printed in a pamphlet *East Central Africa Livingstonia; the Mission of the Free Church of Scotland to Lake Nyassa*, Edinburgh, 1876.

38 E. D. Young, *Nyassa: A Journal of Adventures*, London, 2nd edition, 1877, pp. 86–8.

39 James Stewart to his wife, 22 November 1876, Stewart Papers ST 1/1/1.

40 James Stewart to his wife, 1 June 1877, Stewart Papers ST 1/1/1.

41 This was the pioneer trader, H. B. Cotterill who communicated his fears to Horace Waller. See Waller to Secretary of the Free Church, Foreign Missions Committee, 28 May 1877, N.L.S. 7872.

42 I have discussed this episode at greater length in the mission's history: McCracken, 'Livingstonia Mission and the evolution of Malawi 1875–1939', pp. 319–25.

43 Medical Report for 1876 and 1877, Livingstonia Mission Journal N.L.S. 7908.

44 Livingstonia Mission Journal entries for 14 November 1875, 16 and 30 January 1876.

45 The careers of Fraser, one of the most influential writers on mission affairs in Africa in the post First World War period, and of Henderson, from 1905 to 1930 Principal of the Lovedale Institution, are summarised in Agnes R. Fraser, *Donald Fraser of Livingstonia*, London 1934, and in M. M. S. Ballantyne and R. W. Shepherd (eds), *Forerunners of Modern Malawi*, Lovedale, 1968.

46 According to W. H. J. Rangeley, Mponda, a son of the chief in a matrilineal society, used his power as war leader to seize control of the chieftainship following the death of his father about 1866. W. H. J. Rangeley, 'The Amacinga Ayao', *Nyasaland Journal*, XVI, 2, pp. 51–3.

47 The best modern discussion of the Yao in the nineteenth century is Edward Alpers, 'Trade, State and Society among the Yao in the Nineteenth Century', *Journal of African History*, X, 3, 1969.

48 Rangeley, 'Amacinga Ayao'; Livingstonia Mission Journal, 3 and 14 April 1867, N.L.S. 7908.

49 Livingstonia Mission Journal, 20 January, 1 and 2 March, 14 April 1876.

50 Mponda's position was summarised by Consul J. F. Elton who interviewed him on 21 August 1876; 'His argument was, "If slave-trade is unlawful, you

must find some one to buy my ivory," and he produced some very large tusks.'
J. F. Elton, *Travels and Researches among the Lakes and Mountains of Eastern and Central Africa*, London, 1879, p. 276.

51 'Instructions to Lake Nyassa Party given by the Foreign Missions Committee of the Free Church', *Eastern Central Africa*.

52 Livingstonia Mission Journal entries for 14 October and 10 December 1875.

53 Jack, op. cit., pp. 85–6.

54 H. W. Macmillan, 'The Origins and Development of the African Lakes Company 1878–1908', Edinburgh Ph.D., 1970, pp. 94–9. Originally known as the Livingstonia Central Africa Company, the A.L.C. only changed its name in 1881.

55 Minutes of the Livingstonia sub-committee, 18 March 1878 and 9 March 1880, N.L.S.

56 Macmillan, op. cit., pp. 161–3.

57 Ibid., pp. 211–17.

58 R. Laws to J. Stewart 20 May 1878, Stewart Papers ST 1/1/1; Frederick Morrison's Diary entry for 2 March 1884, quoted in A. C. Ross, 'The Origins and Development of the Church of Scotland Mission, Blantyre, Nyasaland, 1875–1926', Edinburgh Ph.D., 1968, p. 124.

59 Livingstonia Mission Journal prefatory note, N.L.S. 7908.

60 The first Makololo pupils were sent by their fathers to join Stewart in October 1876. By May 1878 all had returned home or had been sent to the school at Blantyre. McCracken, 'Livingstonia Mission', pp. 80–3.

61 Cape Mclear Journal entries for 2 January 1877, August 1877, appendix N.L.S. 7909; Diary of John Gunn entry for 5 April 1877 and 14 December 1878, N.L.S. 7906; J. Stewart to his wife 10 February 1877, Stewart Papers ST 1/1/1; W. P. Livingstone, *Laws of Livingstonia*, London, 1921, pp. 194–5.

62 Livingstonia Mission Journal 19 March 1876; Cape Maclear Journal 29 January, 11, 15–16, 21 February, 9 October 1877, 24 August 1878. Sogoli's statement, as recorded by the missionaries, is worth quoting: 'Three years ago the English came into the country with a steamer. They called on Mponda asking him to stay in his country and saying that they wished to live at peace with all men. Mponda gave them ground to settle on and he never since stirred up strife or war. What had he done? Nothing! His people were leaving him and finding shelter with the English. A large number of his own [Sogoli's] people had run to the English ... so that his village was now completely shattered. He had sent after these people but each one was allowed to plead his own cause and the result was that none of them were restored to him.'

63 Cape Maclear Journal, 1–5 June 1878.

64 Ibid., 23 September 1878, 2, 20–1 November, 12–17 April 1879.

65 R. Laws, 28 October 1881, quoted in *Free Church of Scotland Monthly Record*, March 1882, p. 83.

66 W. P. Livingstone, op. cit., p. 207; F.C. of S. Monthly Record, December 1883, p. 357.

67 W. Scott to R. Laws, 30 October 1884, in the collection of Professor Shepperson, Edinburgh University. I wish to acknowledge the generosity of Professor Shepperson in allowing me to examine the papers in his possession.

68 A. G. Hawes to R. Laws, 3 April 1887, Shepperson Collection.

69 W. Harkness to R. Laws, 21 June and 11 September 1882, Shepperson Collection.

70 W. Harkness to R. Laws, 12 January 1885, Shepperson Collection.
71 Alpers, 'Trade, State and Society among the Yao' mentioned in note 47 above provides a useful summary of its extent at that time.
72 A. G. Hawes to Foreign Office, 3 June 1886, F.O. 84/1751, Public Record Office.
73 This information is taken from an as yet unpublished study of Roman Catholic missions in Malawi by Ian and Jane Linden.
74 Livingstonia Mission Report, January–July 1895, p. 1.
75 *Proceedings of the Third General Missionary Conference of Nyasaland*, Mvera, 1910, p. 39.
76 Cape Maclear Journal 25 January, 1 and 13 March 1877. The restructuring of domestic economies that took place, at least partly, as a consequence of long-distance trading pressures is a subject of major importance in the history of late nineteenth-century Malawi, though it has not yet been studied in any detail.
77 I have discussed some of these issues in greater detail elsewhere: John McCracken, 'Religion and Politics in Northern Ngoniland, 1881–1904', in B. Pachai (ed.), *The Early History of Malawi*, London, 1972.

Bibliography

Alpers, Edward A., 'The Mutapa and Malawi Political Systems to the Time of the Ngoni Invasions', in T. O. Ranger (ed.), *Aspects of Central African History*, London, 1968; 'Trade, State and Society among the Yao in the Nineteenth Century', *Journal of African History*, X, 3, 1969.

Anderson-Morshead, A. E. M., *The History of the Universities' Mission to Central Africa*, London, 1897.

Ballantyne, M. M. S. and Shepherd, R. W. (eds), *Forerunners of Modern Malawi*, Lovedale, 1968.

Bennett, Norman Robert, 'The East African Slave Trade', in T. O. Ranger (ed.), *Emerging Themes of African History*, Nairobi, 1968; 'David Livingstone: Exploration for Christianity', in R. I. Rotberg (ed.), *Africa and its Explorers*, Cambridge, Mass., 1970; (ed.), *Stanley's Dispatches to the New York Herald, 1871–1872, 1874–1877*, Boston, 1970.

Bennett, Norman Robert and Ylvisaker, Marguerite (eds), *The Central African Journal of Lovell J. Procter 1860–1864*, Boston, 1971.

Berlioux, E. F., *The Slave Trade in Africa in 1872*, London, 1872, reprinted 1971.

Biddis, Michael D., *Father of Racist Ideology: The Social and Political Thought of Count Gobineau*, London, 1971.

Blaikie, William Garden, *The Personal Life of David Livingstone*, London, 1880.

Blake, George, *B.I. Centenary, 1856–1956*, London, 1956.

Brown, G., see Stokes, E. and Brown, G.

Cairns, H. A. C., *Prelude to Imperialism*, London, 1965.

Cameron, V. L., *Across Africa*, London, new edition 1885.

Chadwick, Owen, *Mackenzie's Grave*, London, 1959.

Chamberlin, D. (ed.), *Some Letters from Livingstone 1840–1872*, London, 1940.

Chirnside, A., *The Blantyre Missionaries: Discreditable Disclosures*, London, 1880.

Cope Devereux, W., *A Cruise on the Gorgon*.

Coupland, Ronald, *Kirk on the Zambesi. A Chapter of African History*, Oxford, 1928; *The Exploitation of East Africa 1856–90*, London, 1939; *Livingstone's Last Journey*, London, 1945.

Duff, Alexander, *The Proposed Mission to Lake Nyassa*, Edinburgh, 1875.

Elton, J. F., *Travels and Researches Among the Lakes and Mountains of Eastern and Central Africa*, London, 1879.

Faulkner, H., *Elephant Haunts*, London, 1868.

Foskett, R. (ed.), *The Zambesi Doctors. David Livingstone's Letters to John Kirk 1858–1872*, Edinburgh, 1964; *The Zambesi Journal and Letters of Dr John Kirk, 1858–1863*, Vol. 1, Edinburgh, 1965.

Fraser, Agnes R., *Donald Fraser of Livingstonia*, London, 1934.

Frere, Sir Bartle, *Eastern Africa as a Field for Missionary Labour*, London, 1874; *Correspondence*, see Martineau, John.

Gelfand, M., *Livingstone the Doctor, His Life and Travels*, Oxford, 1957; *Lakeside Pioneers*, Oxford, 1964; *Rivers of Death in Africa*, London, 1964.

Gregory, Robert, *India and East Africa*, Oxford, 1971.

Groves, C. P., *The Planting of Christianity in Africa*, London, 1948–55.

Hanna, A. J., *The Beginnings of Nyasaland and North Eastern Rhodesia 1859–1895*, Oxford, 1956.

Heanley, R. M. (ed.), *Central Africa. A Monthly Record of the Work of the Universities' Mission*, London, 1889.

Hetherwick, A., *The Romance of Blantyre*, London, n.d.

Howard, R., *A Report to the Medical Board of the Universities' Mission on the Health of the European Missionaries in the Likoma Diocese*, London, 1904.

Jack, J. W., *Daybreak in Livingstonia*, Edinburgh, 1901.

Kirk, Dr John, *The Zambesi Journal and Letters*, see Foskett, R.

Langworthy, H. W., 'Chewa or Malawi Political Organisation in the Pre-Colonial Era', in Pachai, B. (ed.), *The Early History of Malawi*, London, 1972.

Lary, Peter, see Wright, Marcia and Lary, Peter.

Laws, Robert, *Reminiscences of Livingstonia*, Edinburgh, 1934.

Lewis, Grassic Gibbon, *Niger. The Life of Mungo Park*, Edinburgh, 1934.

Livingstone, David, *Cambridge Lectures*, see Monk, W. (ed.); *Family Letters 1841–1856*, *Missionary Correspondence 1841–1856*; *Private Journals 1851–1853*, see Schapera (ed.); *Last Journals*, see Waller (ed.); *Letters to John Kirk 1858–1872*, see Foskett, R. (ed.); *Some Letters from Livingstone 1840–1872*, see Chamberlin, D. (ed.); *The Life and Explorations of David Livingstone, LL.D. Carefully Compiled from Reliable Sources*, London, 1887 (consists mainly of long extracts from the *Proceedings of the Royal Geographical Society* and other contemporary sources); *Missionary Travels and Researches in South Africa*, London, 1857.

Livingstone, David and Charles, *Narrative of an Expedition to the Zambesi and its tributaries: and of the discovery of Lakes Shirwa and Nyassa, 1858–1864*, London, 1865.

Livingstone, W. P., *Laws of Livingstonia*, London, 1921.

Lloyd, B. W., *Men of Livingstone*.

McCracken, K. J., 'Religion and Politics in Northern Ngoniland 1881–1904', in Pachai, B. (ed.), *The Early History of Malawi*, London, 1972; 'Livingstonia as an Industrial Mission, 1875–1900', in *Religion in Africa*, Centre of African Studies, Edinburgh, 1964.

Macdonald, Duff, *Africana*, Edinburgh, 1881, new edition London, 1969.

Macnair, James J., *'Livingstone the Liberator'*, London, 1940, reprinted 1958.

Martelli, George, *Livingstone's River: A History of the Zambesi Expedition 1858–1864*, London, 1970.

Martineau, John, *The Life and Correspondence of the Right Hon. Sir Bartle Frere*, London, 1895.

Matecheta, H. M., *Blantyre Mission: NKhani ya Ciyambi Cace*, Blantyre, 1951.

Monk, William (ed.), *Dr Livingstone's Cambridge Lectures*, Cambridge, 1858.

Newitt, M.D.D. 'The Massingire Rising of 1884', *Journal of African History*, XI, I, 1970.

Oliver, Roland, *The Missionary Factor in East Africa*, London, 1952.

Oswell, W. E., *William Cotton Oswell, Hunter and Explorer*, London, 1900.

Pachai, Bridglal, *Malawi: The History of the Nation*, London, 1972; 'Christianity and Commerce in Malawi: Some Pre-Colonial Aspects', in *Malawi Past and Present*; (ed.), *The Early History of Malawi*, London, 1972.

Pachai, B., Smith, G. W. and Tangri, R. K. (eds), *Malawi Past and Present*, Blantyre, 1971.

Procter, Lovell J., *The Central African Journal 1860–1864*, see Bennett, N. R. and Ylvisaker, M.

Rangeley, W. H. J., 'The Makololo of Dr Livingstone', *Nyasaland Journal*, XII, 1, 1959; 'The Amacinga Ayao', *Nyasaland Journal*, XVI, 2, 1963.

Ranger, T. O. (ed.), *Emerging Themes of African History*, Nairobi, 1968; *Aspects of Central African History*, London, 1968; *Revolt in Southern Rhodesia*, London, 1967.

Ransford, Brian, *Livingstone's Lake*, London, 1966.

Robertson, Olive H., 'Trade and the Suppression of Slavery in British Central Africa', *Nyasaland Journal*, XII, 2, 1960.

Ross, Andrew C., 'The African: Child or Man', in E. Stokes and C. Brown (eds), *The Zambesian Past*, Manchester, 1965.

Rotberg, R. I., *The Rise of Nationalism in Central Africa*, Cambridge, Mass., 1966; (ed.), *Africa and its Explorers*, Cambridge, Mass., 1970.

Rowley, The Revd Henry, *The Story of the Universities' Mission to Central Africa*, London, 1867.

Russell, C. E. B., *General Rigby, Zanzibar and the Slave Trade*, London, 1935.

Schapera, I. (ed.), *David Livingstone. Family Letters 1841–1856*, London, 1959; *Livingstone's Missionary Correspondence 1841–1856*, London, 1961; *Livingstone's Private Journals 1851–1853*, London, 1960; *Livingstone's African Journal 1853–1856*, London, 1963.

Seaver, George, *David Livingstone: His Life and Letters*, London, 1957.

Shepherd, R. W., see Ballantyne, M. M. S. and Shepherd, R. W.

Shepperson, George, (Ed.) *David Livingstone and the Rovuma*, Edinburgh, 1965; 'David Livingstone the Scot', *The Scottish Historical Review*, XXXIX, 2, 1960; 'The Intellectual Background of Charles Darwin's Student Years at Edinburgh', in M. Barton (ed.), *Darwinism and the Study of Society*, London, 1961; 'The African Abroad or the African Diaspora', in T. O. Ranger (ed.), *Emerging Themes of African History*, Nairobi, 1968.

Simmons, Jack, *Livingstone and Africa*, London, 1955.

Stanley, H. M., *Dispatches to the New York Herald, 1871–1872, 1874–1877*, see Bennett, N. R.; *How I found Livingstone in Central Africa*, London, 1872.

Stewart, James, *Livingstonia: Its Origin*, Edinburgh, 1894; *The Zambesi Journal*, see Wallis, J. R. R.; *Dawn in the Dark Continent*, Edinburgh, 1903.

Stokes, E. Brown, and G. (eds), *The Zambesian Past*, Manchester, 1965.

Tabler, E. C. (ed.), *The Zambesi Papers of Richard Thornton*, London, 1963.

Thornton, Richard, see Tabler, E. C.

Tozer, Bishop, *Letters*, see Ward, G.

Waller, Horace, (ed.), *Last Journals of David Livingstone*, London, 1874; see also Young, E. D., *The Search after Livingstone*.

Wallis, J. P. R. (ed.), *The Zambesi Journal of James Stewart, 1862–1863*, London, 1952; *The Zambesi Expedition of David Livingstone 1858–1863*, London, 1956.

Ward, Gertrude (ed.), *Letters of Bishop Tozer*, London, 1902.

Warren, Max, *Social History and Christian Mission*, London, 1967.

Warhurst, P. R., 'Portugal's Bid for Southern Malawi', in Pachai, B. et al. (eds), *Malawi Past and Present*, Blantyre, 1971.

238

Wells, J., *Stewart of Lovedale*, London, 1908.

Whiteley, W. H. (translator), *Maisha ya Hamed bin Muhammed el Murjebi Yaani Tippu Tip Kwa Maneno Yake*, Nairobi, 1966.

Withers, F. M., 'A Sailor who did his Duty', *Nyasaland Journal*, IV, 1, 1951.

Wolf, J. B. (ed.), *Missionary to Tanganyika, 1877–1888*, London, 1971.

Wright, Marcia and Lary, Peter, 'Swahili Settlements in Northern Zambia and Malawi', *African Historical Studies*, 4, 1971.

Ylvisaker, M., see Bennett, Norman Robert and Ylvisaker, M.

Young, E. D., *The Search after Livingstone*, revised by H. Waller, London, 1868; *Nyassa: A Journal of Adventures*, London, 2nd edition, 1877.

Index